ouff —
whew

French
verb handbook

Kate Dobson

D0061894

**Berlitz Publishing /
APA Publications GmbH & Co. Verlag KG,
Singapore Branch, Singapore**

French Verb Handbook

CONTACTING THE EDITORS
Every effort has been made to provide accurate information in this publication, but changes are inevitable. The publisher cannot be responsible for any resulting loss, inconvenience, or injury. We would appreciate it if readers would call our attention to any errors or outdated information by contacting Berlitz Publishing, 95 Progress Street, Union, NJ 07083, USA. Fax: 1-908-206-1103. email: comments@berlitzbooks.com

Published by Berlitz Publishing/Apa Publications GmbH & Co. Verlag KG, Singapore Branch, Singapore

Berlitz Trademark Reg. U.S. Patent Office and other countries. Marca Registrada. Used under license from Berlitz Investment Corporation.

Cover Photo © Andy Sitt/Alamy; inset photo © Photo Alto

Printed in Singapore by Insight Print Services (Pte) Ltd., February 2005

The Author:

Written by **Kate Dobson**, an experienced teacher at the primary school, high school, and adult level.

The Series Editor:

Christopher Wightwick is a former UK representative on the Council of Europe Modern Languages Project and principal Inspector of Modern Languages for England.

CONTENTS

iv

How to use this handbook

This Handbook aims to provide a full description of the French verb system for all learners and users of the French language. It provides the following information:

• a chapter on the verb system;
• the conjugation in full of sixty-one common verbs, grouped to show the common patterns underlying the system;
• a full subject index;
• a verb index containing over 2,200 verbs with their English meanings.

An important feature of the Handbook is that examples, showing many of the verbs in use, are given in the model verb pages.

Verbs in French: their functions and uses

This section describes the functions of verbs in general. Information is given on word order, the use of tenses, the way verbs govern different cases and prepositions, and the way they are formed.

Model French verbs

This section gives the conjugation in full of every tense of a verb. The reflexive verb form is also illustrated. Fifty-six common verbs are then set out as models.

A selection of verbs that follow the same pattern as each individual verb is listed underneath. Examples are then provided of these verbs in use, to illustrate different tenses and a wide range of different meanings and idiomatic constructions.

The subject index

The subject index gives paragraph references for all the main grammatical terms used.

The verb index

For each verb, information is given on whether it is transitive or intransitive, the auxiliary it takes in the past tenses, the prepositions that it governs, and its English meaning. Common secondary meanings are illustrated in a brief phrase. The most important and up-to-date forms of verbs are listed.

USE OF HANDBOOK

How to find the information you want

If you want to check on the form, meaning, or use of a verb, first look it up in the index. This gives a range of information:

• Any preposition that normally follows the verb.
• Whether the verb is transitive, intransitive, reflexive, or impersonal, and whether it takes the auxiliary **être** in the compound past tenses. If no auxiliary is shown, the verb takes **avoir**.
• The English meaning of the verb. Only the basic meaning is shown for most verbs.
• A number indicating on which model verb page or pages you will find further information about the verb or others like it.
• A short phrase or sentence following some verbs, giving important subsidiary meanings.

If you want further information on the form or use of the verb, turn to the model verb reference given. On these pages you will find:

• the full conjugation of the present, perfect, imperfect, and simple past of each model verb;
• the first person singular form of other tenses;
• a list of other verbs following the same pattern;
• notes indicating any exceptions to this pattern;
• short dialogues and sentences illustrating some of the different tenses and usages of these verbs.

If you want to know the full form of other tenses you should note that they are always regular. They can easily be checked by looking up the full tense of the relevant verb:

• **marcher** [➤1] a regular **-er** verb taking **avoir**;
• **tomber** [➤2] a regular **-er** verb taking **être**;
• **se laver** [➤3] a regular reflexive **-er** verb;
• **finir** [➤16] a regular **-ir** verb;
• **vendre** [➤28] a regular **-re** verb.

For further information on how the verb system works, refer to PART A, "Verbs in French: their functions and uses."

A
VERBS IN FRENCH: THEIR FUNCTIONS AND USES

---

1 *What do verbs do?*

2 *What verbs govern*

3 *Attitudes to action: modal verbs*

4 *Verb forms not related to time*

5 *What else do French verbs do?*

For a full treatment of this topic, see Berlitz *French Grammar Handbook*.

What do verbs do?

1a Full verbs

"Full" verbs in French do the same job as in English: that is, they communicate the action or feeling state or changing state of the subject. Their position in the sentence is similar to English word order:

Subject (noun or pronoun) – verb – rest of sentence

Mon frère a bu tout le champagne.	My brother has drunk all the champagne.
Il aime le vin rouge aussi.	He likes red wine too.
Maintenant il a la gueule de bois.	Now he has a hangover.

1b Auxiliary verbs

Some verbs have a use as "auxiliary" verbs. In French, **avoir** (to have) and **être** (to be) are the auxiliary verbs; this means they are used in their various simple tenses, with the past participle of other verbs, in the formation of all the compound tenses. (Compare the use of the verb *to have* in English.)

- avoir:

j'ai mangé	I have eaten
j'avais mangé	I had eaten
j'aurais mangé	I would have eaten

- être:

je suis tombé	I have fallen over
j'étais tombé	I had fallen
je serais tombé	I would have fallen

What verbs govern

All sentences consist of a subject and a predicate. The predicate may be just a verb, or a verb plus more information.

2a Subject + verb + complement

Some verbs just link the subject to the rest of the information, which is known as the "complement." The verb **être** (to be) is frequently used in this way.

Il est pharmacien.	He is a pharmacist.
Elle a été actrice.	She was an actress.

2b Verbs that need no further completion

Le facteur arrive.	The mailman is coming.

In this sentence the verb is complete in itself. Other information could be added, such as **maintenant** (now), or **à vélo** (by bike). The verb would nevertheless be complete. This type of verb is called "intransitive." Verbs which are only intransitive in use are marked "intr" in the Index of this handbook.

2c Verbs that have an object

Il regarde les adresses sur les lettres.	He's looking at the addresses on the letters.

Here, the verb requires a noun phrase (addresses) to complete the sense. The direct object of the verb is the item(s) or person(s) directly affected by the action. **Regarder** is a verb that needs a direct object. Such verbs are called "transitive" and marked "tr" in the Index.

A considerable number of verbs can be either transitive or intransitive. These are marked "tr/intr" (e.g., **changer**).

3

2d Verb + preposition + object

French verbs do not always have the same relationship with the rest of the sentence as their English counterparts. Verbs that are transitive in English may need a preposition before the object in French; and the converse is true.

Je me suis emparé *de* **la bouteille, et j'ai téléphone** *au* **docteur.**	I grabbed the bottle and phoned the doctor.
J'ai attendu le docteur une demi-heure.	I waited half an hour *for* the doctor

A list of verbs like **attendre** would include:

chercher	to look for	**habiter**	to live in/at
demander	to ask for	**regarder**	to look at
écouter	to listen to		

Here it is the English that adds the preposition. When a verb requires a preposition in either language, the preposition is given in the Index. For a full list of these verbs ➤Berlitz *French Grammar Handbook*, 8e.

2e Verbs that have two objects

(i) Direct and indirect objects

Le facteur a donné deux lettres à mon patron.	The postman gave two letters to my boss.

Here the direct object of the verb consists of the two letters, given to the indirect object, the boss.

(ii) Sometimes in English we omit the word "to" in such sentences. In French sentences involving both direct and indirect objects, the indirect object always follows **à**.

Il donne les lettres au patron.	He gives the boss the letters.

When pronouns are involved the word order makes the meaning clear.

4

| Il m'a offert des fleurs. | He gave me some flowers. |
| Il me les a offertes pour mon anniversaire. | He gave them to me for my birthday. |

| – Où est ton stylo? | – Where's your pen? |
| – Je le lui ai donné. | – I gave it to her. |

2f Reflexive verbs

(i) Some verbs express an action that is turned back on the subject: the object is the same person as the subject.

| Je me pèse une fois par semaine. | I weigh myself once a week. |

(ii) Sometimes people are doing the action not to themselves but to each other, in which case the subject is invariably plural.

| Ils s'aiment à la folie. | They love each other madly. |

(iii) In many cases the French reference to self or each other is not expressed in English.

| Je m'habille dans ma chambre. | I get dressed in my room. |
| Il se fatigue vite. | He gets tired quickly. |

(iv) With some verbs the reflexive idea has largely disappeared, but the grammatical form still applies.

| Je me suis aperçu de son indifference. | I noticed his indifference. |

2g Verbs governing verbs

(i) *Combining verbs*

More complex sentences are made in both French and English combining two verbs. The combinations are not always parallel.

J'aime aller en France.	I like to go to France *or* I like going to France.
Je dois partir demain.	I must leave tomorrow.

Je t'invite à m'accompagner.	I invite you to come with me.
J'ai oublié d'acheter des chèques de voyage.	I've forgotten to buy travelers' checks.

Each of these complex sentences in French follows one of two possible patterns:

- verb + infinitive;
- verb + preposition + infinitive.

The infinitive is the part of the verb that has the meaning "to do," "to play" etc. [➤4a].

The commonest prepositions used in the structure are **à** and **de**, and the student needs to check which verb follows which pattern. The Index and larger dictionaries give this information. (➤Berlitz *French Grammar Handbook*, 8f.)

(ii) It should be noted that the French present participle (**jouant**, **cherchant**) cannot be used here, even though in English the form ending in *-ing* may be possible.

J'aime chanter.	I like singing/I like to sing.
Je préfère nager.	I prefer swimming/I prefer to swim.

(A) Some of the verbs followed immediately by an infinitive are the modal verbs [➤3] and:

souhaiter	to wish to
espérer	to hope to
monter	to go up
aller	to go/to be going to
entendre	to hear (someone doing something)
voir	to see (someone doing something)
faire	to have/get something done

Je souhaite vraiment faire sa connaissance.	I really hope to meet him.
On espère vous voir au concert.	We hope to see you at the concert.
Nous allons partir en vacances.	We're going to go on vacation.
On les entend crier.	You can hear them shouting.
Je l'ai vu venir.	I saw him coming.
Je fais réparer la télé.	I'm getting the TV repaired.
Je fais construire une maison.	I'm having a house built.

(B) Verbs requiring **à** before an infinitive include:

apprendre à	to learn to
commencer à	to begin to
demander à	to ask to
hésiter à	to hesitate to
réussir à	to succeed in (doing)
renoncer à	to give up (doing)

J'apprends à faire de la planche à voile.	I'm learning windsurfing.
Il a hésité à parler au patron.	He hesitated to speak to the boss.
On a réussi à réparer le voiture.	We managed to repair the car.

(C) Verbs requiring **de** before an infinitive include:

accuser de	to accuse (*someone of doing*)
demander à (quelqu'un de faire quelque chose)	to ask (*someone to do something*)
essayer de	to try to
oublier de	to forget to
permettre de	to allow to

J'ai oublié d'aller chercher mon appareil.	I forgot to fetch my camera.
Elle m'a accusé de tricher.	She accused me of cheating.
On va essayer de finir avant cinq heures.	We're going to try and finish before five o'clock.

This is a much bigger group than the other two, and most verbs fall into this category.

Attitudes to action: modal verbs

3a Action of modal verbs

Modal verbs are not usually complete in meaning in themselves: they create a mood for, or an attitude toward, the verb that follows. The following verb must be in the infinitive in French.

Je dois partir.	I must leave.
Pouvez-vous appeler un taxi?	Can you call a taxi?
Je voudrais arriver chez moi avant minuit.	I'd like to get home by midnight.

3b French modal verbs

devoir	to have to
falloir	to be necessary (only exists in the third-person singular form as an impersonal verb)
pouvoir	to be able to
savoir	to know how to
vouloir	to want to

More examples of their use are given on the corresponding verb pages.

 Devoir, **savoir**, and **vouloir** also have independent uses, as well as modal function. They mean "to owe," "to know" and "to want" respectively.

4 Verb forms not related to time

4a The infinitive

(i) This is the name part of the verb, determining its entry in the dictionary and its use as a noun, as a verb in the various structures outlined above, and after certain prepositions.

Infinitives in French can be identified by the endings **-er**, **-ir**, **-re**, and **-oir**. *All infinitives have one of these endings, but the endings are not exclusive to verbs.*

(ii) Infinitives as nouns

le rire	laughter	**le devoir**	duty
le déjeuner	lunch	**le souvenir**	memory, souvenir

Some infinitives appear as nouns, but not all can be used this way; it is advisable to check in a dictionary.

 Sometimes an infinitive may appear as the subject of the verb:

Travailler ici me rend malade!   *Working* here makes me ill!

(iii) Useful expressions that can be used for any person, in combination with any tense:

pour arriver	in order to arrive	**avant de partir**	before leaving
afin d'arriver	in order to arrive	**sans attendre**	without waiting

4b Present participle

(i) The present participle can be formed from the **nous** form of the present tense, by replacing the **-ons** with **-ant**.

(ii) The present participle is used as an adjective and, occasionally, as a noun. It is also used with **en**, meaning "by," "while," "in," "on" doing something; the form does not change, regardless of the associated noun's gender or verb's tense. For example:

9

Elle est passée nous voir *en rentrant* chez elle.	She popped in to see us on the way home. (*Literally, "while going home"*)

[➤also 4c(iv) below.]

In French "before doing" and "without doing" both require the *infinitive*, not the present participle: **avant de faire, sans faire.**

No progressive or continuous present tense can be constructed using this participle.

Je travaille.	I am working.

4c *Past participle*

(i)   Past participles of regular verbs are formed by adding **-é** (**-er** erbs, **-i** (**-ir** verbs), or **-u** (**-re** verbs) to the stem of the infinitive. The stem is formed by removing **-er**, **-ir**, or **-re**. Irregular verbs may not follow this pattern, and many past participles need to be learnt individually: e.g., **boire – bu**; **écrire – écrit**; **faire – fait**; **lire – lu**.

(ii)   The past participle is used:

• as the second item in all the compound past tenses.
• with any tense of **être** to create the passive form: e.g., **Il a été cassé** (It has been broken);
• as in English as an adjective, when it follows the noun: e.g., **la voiture volée** (the stolen car).

(iii)   Note also the French for "after doing something," which uses a past infinitive made with **avoir** or **être** + the past participle.

***Après avoir acheté* les timbres, il est parti.**	*After buying* the stamps, he left.
***Après être arrivés*, ils ont loué une voiture.**	*After arriving*, they hired a car.

(iv)   The equivalent of English "having done something," is formed by combining both participles:

Ayant acheté les timbres . . .	Having bought the stamps . . .

(v)   In literary contexts the past participle of certain verbs – those conjugated with **être** in compound tenses – may be used alone in an absolute construction:

Une fois arrivé à Paris, il a cherché un hôtel.	Having arrived in Paris, he looked for a hotel.

For rules governing the agreements of the past participle in compound tenses ➤Berlitz *French Grammar Handbook*.

11

What else do French verbs do?

The various tenses in common use given in the verb tables are listed below, with their characteristic endings and meanings.

For a full study of French tenses ►Berlitz *French Grammar Handbook*, 11.

5a Pronouns

The verb tables are presented with the personal subject pronouns, which are used in French very much as in English.

- **je** – "I"; (**j'** before vowel or mute **h**).
- **tu** – "you" (singular). This is the form of address for family members, close friends, small children, and pets.
- **il** – "he"; also "it," when the name of a thing is masculine.
- **elle** – "she"; also "it," when the name of a thing is feminine.
- **on** – This is presented in this book as a separate entry because of its great importance in the French language, particularly the spoken language. It is commonly used for "we" (colloquially, alongside **nous**, because the shorter verb forms are quicker), "you" (generally), "they," "everyone," "people," "someone," and occasionally "one."
- **nous** – "we."
- **vous** – "you." Used as the normal form of address to a single individual who is not a close friend or relative and as the plural "you" when talking to a group of people.
- **ils** – "they," Refers to people and things that are either all masculine or a mixture of masculine and feminine.
- **elles** – "they," Refers to people and things that are all feminine.

5b Pronunciation

These few pointers may prove useful when studying verbs.

(i) Pronounciation of pronouns

The **-s**, which is normally silent at the end of pronouns **nous**, **vous**, **ils**, and **elles** must always be pronounced as **z** if the verb begins with a vowel or mute **h**. This is called "*liaison.*"

Ils aiment les films italiens.	They like Italian films.
Nous arrivons à midi.	We are arriving at midday.
Ils habitent à Milan.	They live in Milan.

Note that words beginning with aspirate **h**, marked with an asterisk in the index and in dictionaries, require no liaison.

(ii)   *Pronounciation of verb endings*

- **-er**, the ending of very many infinitives, is pronounced like **é**.
- **-ant**, the ending of the present participle, is pronounced without the **-t**, as the single nasal vowel of the word **en**.
- **-e**, **-es**, **-s**, **-x**, **-t** endings on all verbs are silent.
- **-ons**, the ending for **nous** (first-person plural), is pronounced like the end of **bon**, the **-s** being silent.
- **-ez**, the ending for **vous** (second-person plural), is pronounced like **é**.
- **-ent**, the ending for third-person plural verbs, is always silent.
- **-ont** has the same pronunciation as **-ons**.
- **-ais**, **-ait**, **-aient** endings of the imperfect tense are pronounced like "e" in the English word "let."

5c   *French verb forms given in this book*

(i)   *Infinitive* ⎫ ➤*4a*
         Present participle ⎬ ➤*4b*
         Past participle ⎭ ➤*4c*

(ii)   *Imperative*

(A) Imperatives are given in the verb tables. They are the expressions used for requests and commands. They are normally the **tu**, **nous**, and **vous** present-tense forms *without the subject pronoun*; **-er** verbs drop the final **-s** of the **tu** form except before **y** and **en**.

va-à la maison	go home!	*but:*
vas-y	go to it!	

(B) As the imperative form can sound rather abrupt, it is common to find requests phrased:

Veux-tu/Voulez-vous ouvrir la porte?	Will you open the door?

Or

Tu pourrais/vous pourriez ouvrir la porte?	Could you open the door?

(C) When instructions are given for a process, as in recipes, it is also common to find the infinitive used as the imperative:

Délayer le beurre et le sucre.	Cream the butter and sugar.
Ajouter 500 grammes de farine.	Add 500 grams of flour.

(iii)   Tenses of the indicative

The indicative tenses are the ordinary verbs that make statements about what is happening, has happened, or will happen. However, they do not only communicate the timing of the action; they may also give the speaker's or writer's perspective on the event.

Use of tenses in French is not directly equivalent to English. The following examples, taken from the verb **parler** (to speak), make this clear.

(A) Simple tenses (where the verb is a single word)

• Present tense: **je parle**
There are three "regular" patterns for the present tense of verbs whose infinitives end in **-er**, **-ir**, and **-re**. All these and the variants and exceptions are set out in the model verb pages.

The French present tense covers the usages of all three English versions: "I speak," "I am speaking," "I do speak." In journalistic accounts it is also very common to find the present tense used to recount the action of the story more vividly than if a past tense were used. This is called the historic present.

• Imperfect tense: **je parlais**
This tense refers to incomplete or continuing action in the past. It can mean: "I spoke," "I was speaking," "I used to speak" or "I would speak" (often).

With the exception of **être (j'étais)**, all verbs form the imperfect tense using the **nous** form stem from the present tense. Simply remove the **-ons** ending of the present and add the endings:

(je) -ais	**(il/elle/on) -ait**	**(vous) -iez**
(tu) -ais	**(nous) -ions**	**(ils) -aient**

14

• Simple past: **je parlai**
This tense, used mainly in written narrative to tell the events of the story, means "spoke." In regular verbs the stem is that of the infinitive minus **-er/-ir/-re**. The endings are:

-ai, -as, -a, -âmes, -âtes, -èrent (**-er** verbs)
-is, -is, -it, -îmes, -îtes, -irent (**-ir** and **-re** verbs)

There are a number of irregular verbs, with the endings:

-us, -us, -ut, -ûmes, -ûtes, -urent

(➤ Model French Verb)

• Future: **je parlerai**
The simple future is the equivalent of English "shall speak/will speak." The endings for the future are derived from the present tense of **avoir**:

-ai, -as, -a, -ons, -ez, -ont

These are added to a stem which in most verbs is the whole infinitive (**-er** or **-ir** verbs) or the infinitive minus the final **-e** (**-re** verbs). There are a number of exceptions to this simple rule; these need to be learned individually.

• Conditional: **je parlerais**
This tense means "would speak." The stem is that of the future tense, and the endings are those of the imperfect tense:

-ais, -ais, -ait, -ions, -iez, -aient

(B) Compound tenses (verb consists of two words or more)

• Perfect tense: **j'ai parlé**
This is the tense for completed action in the past, in speech and in writing, meaning "I spoke," "I did speak" or "I have spoken." It is formed from the present tense of **avoir** or **être** and the past participle of the verb. Most verbs use **avoir** as the auxiliary. A small number of very common verbs and *all* reflexive verbs use **être**.

• Past perfect or pluperfect: **j'avais parlé**
This tense means "had spoken." It is formed from the imperfect of **avoir** or **être** and the past participle.

• Past anterior: **j'eus parlé**
This tense is found in written narrative where the main action is conveyed in the simple past. It has the meaning "had spoken." It occurs after conjunctions of time (**quand**, **dès que**, **aussitôt que**) and is formed with the simple past of **avoir** or **être** and the past participle.

- Future perfect: **j'aurai parlé**
This tense means "will have spoken." It is formed from the future tense of **avoir** or **être** and the past participle. It expresses probability and must also be used after conjunctions of time (**quand, dès que, aussitôt que**) referring to the future.

- Conditional perfect: **j'aurais parlé**
The meaning of this tense is "would have spoken." It is formed from the conditional tense of **avoir** or **être** and the past participle.

(iv) *Tenses of the subjunctive*

The subjunctive is used in French in subordinate clauses after conjunctions such as **quoique** (although), **pourvu que** (provided that), **afin que** (in order to), and after verbs of wishing, fearing, doubting, and other emotions. It also occurs occasionally as a main verb to express a formalized wish: **Vive la France!**

The present and perfect tenses are the ones most frequently used, and are in practice the main tenses in colloquial use. The imperfect subjunctive may occur occasionally in speech in its shorter forms; this and the pluperfect subjunctive are more likely to be found in literary texts. Giving an English equivalent of each tense is not practical, as often structures do not correspond in the two languages.

- Present tense: **que je parle**
Apart from a few irregular verbs, the present subjunctive is formed from the third-person plural of the present indicative. For the singular and the third person plural, simply delete the **-ent** ending and add the endings:

-e, -es, -e, -ent

The **nous** and **vous** forms are the same as in the imperfect indicative:

-ions, -iez

These endings also apply to irregular verbs, but the stem changes. The verbs that are irregular in the present subjective are:

avoir – que j'aie	que nous *ayons*
être – que je sois	que nous *soyons*
aller – que j'aille	que nous allions
faire – que je fasse	que nous *fassions*
falloir – qu'il faille	
pouvoir – que je puisse	que nous *puissions*
savoir – que je sache	que nous *sachions*
valoir – que je vaille	que nous valions
vouloir – que je veuille	que nous voulions

(The *italics* show **nous** and **vous** forms that are also irregular.)

Je veux que tu *ailles* chez Michel.	I want you to go to Michel's.
Je veux bien lui parler pourvu	I don't mind talking to him
qu'il *vienne* avant dix heures.	provided he comes before ten.

• Perfect tense: **que j'aie parlé**
This is formed from the present subjunctive of **avoir** or **être** plus the past participle.

C'est dommage que tu *aies*	It's a pity *you've lost* your purse.
***perdu* ton porte-monnaie.**	

• Imperfect tense: **que je parlasse**
This tense is not often found except in the third-person singular (**parlât**). It is replaced in conversation by the present subjunctive.

J'ignorais qu'il *possédât* un	I didn't know *he had* a gun . . .
fusil . . .	

• Pluperfect tense: **que j'eusse parlé**
This is formed from the imperfect subjunctive of **avoir** or **être** and the past participle. It is not often found in speech.

. . . et je fus indigné qu'il *eût*	. . . and I was annoyed that *he had*
gardé* un si beau secret.	*kept* such a fine secret to himself.

* (Marcel Pagnol: *La Gloire de mon père*)

(v) *The passive*

When the action is done *to* the subject of the sentence, the passive form may be needed. This is composed of the appropriate tense of **être** (to be) followed by the past participle.

L'enfant a été blessé.	The child was hurt.

The passive is as widely used in French as it is in English, but sometimes the passive in English is replaced by **on**:

Ici on parle anglais	English is spoken here

17

Or by a reflexive verb:

Ce vin se trouve facilement en Bourgogne.　　That wine is easily found in Burgundy.

5d　Asking questions

In French there are three possible ways of asking a question. To ask, "Do you like shellfish," one can say:

• **Aimes-tu les fruits de mer?** (*Verb and subject change places.*)

• **Est-ce que tu aimes les fruits de mer?** (*The formula* **est-ce que** *precedes the statement and makes it into a question.*)

• **Tu aimes les fruits de mer?** (*Same word order as a statement, but the voice tone rises at the end of the sentence, creating the question.*)

The same variations are possible when a question word, such as **quand?** (when?) or **où?** (where?) is involved.

• **Où habitez-vous?**

• **Où est-ce que vous habitez?**

• **Vous habitez où?**

Note that when the subject is a noun phrase, it is only possible to use the first variation by adding a pronoun:

Les Borgia ont-*ils* empoisonné tous leurs ennemis?　　Did the Borgias poison all their enemies?

As this is fairly formal, in conversation the second and third forms are more usual for such longer, more complex questions.

5e　Not, never, no more

(i)　Making statements and questions negative in French involves using one of the following expressions:

ne . . . pas	not
ne . . . plus	no more, no longer
ne . . . rien	nothing, not anything

ne . . . jamais	never, not ever
ne . . . personne	nobody, not anybody
ne . . . que	only, nothing but
ne . . . aucun (+ noun)	no, not any

Je *n'*aime *pas* les fruits de mer.	I don't like seafood.
Vous *n'*avez *pas* d'allumettes?	Haven't you any matches?
Il *ne* fume *plus*.	He doesn't smoke any more.
Il *ne* boit *rien*.	He doesn't drink anything.
Elle *ne* m'écoute *jamais*.	She never listens to me.
Il *n'*y a *personne*.	There's no one (there).

(ii) These negative expressions are positioned around the verb. In compound tenses the negative expression is usually around the auxiliary verb.

Je *n'*ai *pas* trouvé mon sac.	I haven't found my bag.
Elle *n'*a *rien* bu.	She didn't drink anything.
Nous *n'*y sommes *jamais* allés.	We've never been there.

Except:

On *n'*a vu *personne*.	We didn't see anyone.
Il *n'*a apporté *que* trois bouteilles de vin.	He only bought three bottles of wine.
La police *n'*a trouvé *aucune* trace des voleurs.	The police found no trace of the thieves.

For a more comprehensive treatment ➤Berlitz *French Grammar Handbook*.

B

MODEL FRENCH VERBS

Index of model verbs

Verb tables are set out on the following pages. Some verbs are given in full; others show the full forms of the present, perfect, imperfect, and simple past tenses only, giving the first-person singular of the other tenses. These tenses then follow the patterns laid out in the full conjugation pages.

The following verbs are discussed in detail in Chapters 6 to 10. Notes on similar verbs, usage, and exceptions are appended where appropriate.

6 *Full conjugations*

6a	**marcher**	to walk
6b	**tomber**	to fall
6c	**se laver**	to wash, get washed
6d	**avoir**	to have
6e	**être**	to be
6f	**être blessé**	to be hurt, wounded

7 -er *verbs:*

7a	**parler**	to speak
7b	**aller**	to go
7c	**appeler**	to call
7d	**acheter**	to buy
7e	**céder**	to give way
7f	**employer**	to employ
7g	**manger**	to eat
7h	**placer**	to place
7i	**payer**	to pay

8 -ir *verbs:*

8a	**finir**	to finish
8b	**acquérir**	to acquire
8c	**cueillir**	to pick
8d	**courir**	to run
8e	**dormir**	to sleep
8f	**faillir**	to almost do
8g	**fuir**	to flee
8h	**mourir**	to die

8i	**ouvrir**	to open
8j	**sentir**	to feel
8k	tenir	to hold
8l	**vêtir**	to dress

9   -re *verbs:*

9a	**vendre**	to sell
9b	**boire**	to drink
9c	**conclure**	to conclude
9d	**conduire**	to lead, drive
9e	**connaître**	to know
9f	**coudre**	to sew
9g	**croire**	to believe
9h	**dire**	to say
9i	**écrire**	to write
9j	**faire**	to do
9k	**lire**	to read
9l	**mettre**	to put
9m	**moudre**	to grind
9n	**naître**	to be born
9o	**peindre**	to paint
9p	**plaire**	to please
9q	**prendre**	to take
9r	**résoudre**	to resolve
9s	**rire**	to laugh
9t	**soustraire**	to subtract
9u	**suivre**	to follow
9v	**vaincre**	to defeat
9w	**vivre**	to live

10   -oir *verbs:*

10a	**s'asseoir**	to sit down
10b	**devoir**	to have to
10c	**falloir**	to have to
10d	**pleuvoir**	to rain
10e	**pouvoir**	to be able to
10f	**promouvoir**	to promote
10g	**recevoir**	to receive
10h	**savoir**	to know
10i	**valoir**	to be worth
10j	**voir**	to see
10k	**vouloir**	to wish, want

Full conjugations

6a   Marcher, *to walk*
*Example of verb using **avoir** in compound tenses*

Imperative
marche! (tu)   marchez! (vous)   marchons! (nous)

Present
je marche
tu marches
il/elle marche
on marche
nous marchons
vous marchez
ils/elles marchent

Perfect
j'ai marché
tu as marché
il/elle a marché
on a marché
nous avons marché
vous avez marché
ils/elles ont marché

Imperfect
je marchais
tu marchais
il/elle marchait
on marchait
nous marchions
vous marchiez
ils/elles marchaient

Simple past
je marchai
tu marchas
il/elle marcha
on marcha
nous marchâmes
vous marchâtes
ils/elles marchèrent

Past perfect
j'avais marché
tu avais marché
il/elle avait marché
on avait marché
nous avions marché
vous aviez marché
ils/elles avaient marché

Past anterior
j'eus marché
tu eus marché
il/elle eut marché
on eut marché
nous eûmes marché
vous eûtes marché
ils/elles eurent marché

Present participle	**Past participle**
marchant	marché

Future
je marcherai
tu marcheras
il/elle marchera
on marchera
nous marcherons
vous marcherez
ils/elles marcheront

Future perfect
j'aurai marché
tu auras marché
il/elle aura marché
on aura marché
nous aurons marché
vous aurez marché
ils/elles auront marché

Conditional
je marcherais
tu marcherais
il/elle marcherait
on marcherait
nous marcherions
vous marcheriez
ils/elles marcheraient

Conditional perfect
j'aurais marché
tu aurais marché
il/elle aurait marché
on aurait marché
nous aurions marché
vous auriez marché
ils/elles auraient marché

Present subjunctive
que je marche
que tu marches
qu'il/elle marche
qu'on marche
que nous marchions
que vous marchiez
qu'ils/elles marchent

Perfect subjunctive
que j'aie marché
que tu aies marché
qu'il/elle ait marché
qu'on ait marché
que nous ayons marché
que vous ayez marché
qu'ils/elles aient marché

Imperfect subjunctive
que je marchasse
que tu marchasses
qu'il/elle marchât
qu'on marchât
que nous marchassions
que vous marchassiez
qu'ils/elles marchassent

Pluperfect subjunctive
que j'eusse marché
que tu eusses marché
qu'il/elle eût marché
qu'on eût marché
que nous eussions marché
que vous eussiez marché
qu'ils/elles eussent marché

Notes

1. This example of a verb conjugated with **avoir** in compound tenses is given in full for reference.
2. **Marcher** is a regular **-er** verb; the majority of regular and irregular verbs use **avoir** as the auxiliary verb to form the compound tenses.

J'*ai* bien *travaillé* ce matin.	I*'ve worked* well this morning.
J'*ai gagné* le gros lot!	I*'ve won* the jackpot!
Les copains *ont proposé* d'aller à la plage.	The friends *suggested* going to the beach.
Nous *avons manqué* le train.	We *missed* the train.
Vous *avez retrouvé* votre portefeuille?	*Did* you *find* your wallet?
On *avait fini* de travailler avant midi.	We *had finished* working before midday.
Je *suppose* que tu n'*auras* pas *eu* le temps de lire les documents?	I *suppose* you won't *have had* time to read the documents?
Je suis désolé que vous n'ayez pas pu *assister* à notre mariage.	I'm so sorry you weren't able *to come* to our wedding.
J'*aurais invité* mes parents, mais ils sont en Australie.	I *would have invited* my parents, but they're in Australia.
On *aurait pris* un pot si on *avait eu* le temps.	We *would have had* a drink if we'*d had* time.

6b Tomber, *to fall*

*Example of verb using **être** in compound tenses*

Present participle	*Past participle*
tombant	tombé

Imperative

tombe! (tu) tombez! (vous) tombons! (nous)

Present
je tombe
tu tombes
il/elle tombe
on tombe
nous tombons
vous tombez
ils/elles tombent

Perfect
je suis tombé/tombée
tu es tombé/tombée
il est tombé
elle est tombée
on est tombé
nous sommes tombés/tombées
vous êtes tombé/tombée/
  tombés/tombées
ils sont tombés
elles sont tombées

Imperfect
je tombais
tu tombais
il/elle tombait
on tombait
nous tombions
vous tombiez
ils/elles tombaient

Simple past
je tombai
tu tombas
il/elle tomba
on tomba
nous tombâmes
vous tombâtes
ils/elles tombèrent

Past perfect
j'étais tombé(-e)
tu étais tombé(-e)
il était tombé
elle était tombée
nous étions tombés(-es)
vous étiez tombé(-e/-s/-es)
ils étaient tombés
elles étaient tombées

Past anterior
je fus tombé(-e)
tu fus tombé(-e)
il fut tombé
elle fut tombée
nous fûmes tombés(-es)
vous fûtes tombé(-e/-s/-es)
ils furent tombés
elles furent tombées

Future
je tomberai
tu tomberas
il/elle tombera
on tombera
nous tomberons
vous tomberez
ils/elles tomberont

Conditional
je tomberais
tu tomberais
il/elle tomberait
on tomberait
nous tomberions
vous tomberiez
ils/elles tomberaient

Present subjunctive
que je tombe
que tu tombes
qu'il/elle tombe
qu'on tombe
que nous tombions
que vous tombiez
qu'ils/elles tombent

Imperfect subjunctive
que je tombasse
que tu tombasses
qu'il/elle tombât
qu'on tombât
que nous tombassions
que vous tombassiez
qu'ils/elles tombassent

Future perfect
je serai tombé(-e)
tu seras tombé(-e)
il sera tombé on sera tombé
elle sera tombée
nous serons tombés(-es)
vous serez tombé(-e/-s/-es)
ils seront tombés
elles seront tombées

Conditional perfect
je serais tombé(-e)
tu serais tombé(-e)
il serait tombé
elle serait tombée
on serait tombé
nous serions tombés(-es)
vous seriez tombé(-e/-s/-es)
ils seraient tombés
elles seraient tombées

Perfect subjunctive
que je sois tombé(-e)
que tu sois tombé(-e)
qu'il soit tombé
qu'elle soit tombée
qu'on soit tombé
que nous soyons tombés(-es)
que vous soyez tombé(-e/-s/-es)
qu'ils soient tombés
qu'elles soient tombées

Pluperfect subjunctive
que je fusse tombé(-e)
que tu fusses tombé(-e)
qu'il fût tombé
qu'elle fût tombé
qu'on fût tombé
que nous fussions tombés(-es)
que vous fussiez tombé(-e/-s/-es)
qu'ils fussent tombés
qu'elles fussent tombées

Notes

1. The verbs that are conjugated with **être** in compound tenses are listed under the auxiliary verb itself (➤**être** *5*).

2. All compound tenses using auxiliary **être** require gender agreements on the past participle. The agreement is with the subject of the verb, and may be feminine singular (add an **-e**), masculine plural (add an **-s**), or feminine plural (add **-es**). All possible variations are given in these verb tables. The full list of possible alternatives is given here for the perfect tense; abbreviated forms are given in subsequent compound tenses.

3. A plural agreement is possible for **on est tombés**, where meaning clearly requires it.

4. **Tomber** is a regular **-er** verb.

Je *suis tombé* dans la rue.	I *fell over* in the street.
Sans la ceinture de sécurité, il *serait tombé* à l'eau.	Without the safety belt, *he would have fallen* in the water.
Elle *est tombée* amoureuse.	She's *fallen* in love.
On m'a dit qu'il *était tombé* d'une fenêtre.	They told me he'*d fallen* out of a window.
On *est allés* à Versailles.	We *went* to Versailles.
Les enfant *sont sortis* à cinq heures.	The children *went out* at five o'clock.
Le train *est arrivé* à l'heure.	The train *arrived* on time.
Mon poisson rouge *est mort*.	My goldfish *has died*.
Vous *étiez parti* avant mon arrivée.	You *had left* before I arrived.
On *était* tous *retournés* chez lui.	We *had* all *gone back* to his place.
Je *serais parti* sans lui . . .	I *would have left* without him . . .
– Où est Patrick?	– Where's Patrick?
– Il *sera parti* pour Rome.	– He'*ll have set off* for Rome.

6c   Se laver, *to wash (oneself)*
Reflexive -er verb

Present participle	**Past participle**
me lavant /te lavant /se lavant /	lavé
nous lavant /vous lavant	

Imperative

lave-toi! (tu)   lavez-vous! (vous)   lavons-nous! (nous)

Present	**Perfect**
je me lave	je me suis lavé/lavée
tu te lave	tu t'es lavé/lavée
il/elle se lave	il s'est lavé
on se lave	elle s'est lavée
nous nous lavons	on s'est lavé
vous vous lavez	nous nous sommes lavés/lavées
ils/elles se lavent	vous vous êtes lavé/lavée/
	lavés/lavées
	ils se sont lavés
	elles se sont lavées

Imperfect	**Simple past**
je me lavais	je me lavai
tu te lavais	tu te lavas
il/elle se lavait	il/elle se lava
on se lavait	on se lava
nous nous lavions	nous nous lavâmes
vous vous laviez	vous vous lavâtes
ils/elles se lavaient	ils/elles se lavèrent

Past perfect	**Past anterior**
je m'étais lavé(-e)	je me fus lavé(-e)
tu t'étais lavé(-e)	tu te fus lavé(-e)
il s'était lavé	il se fut lavé
elle s'était lavée	elle se fut lavée
on s'était lavé	on se fut lavé
nous nous étions lavés(-es)	nous nous fûmes lavés(-es)
vous vous étiez lavé(-e/-s/-es)	vous vous fûtes lavé(-e/-s/-es)
ils se. sont lavés	ils se furent lavés
elles se sont lavées	elles se furent lavées

Future
je me laverai
tu te laveras
il/elle se lavera
on se lavera
nous nous laverons
vous vous laverez
ils/elles se laveront

Conditional
je me laverais
tu te laverais
il/elle se laverait
on se laverait
nous nous laverions
vous vous laveriez
ils/elles se laveraient

Present subjunctive
que je me lave
que tu te laves
qu'il/elle se lave
qu'on se lave
que nous nous lavions
que vous vous laviez
qu'ils/elles se lavent

Imperfect subjunctive
que je me lavasse
que tu te lavasses
qu'il/elle se lavât
qu'on se lavât
que nous nous lavassions
que vous vous lavassiez
qu'ils/elles se lavassent

Future perfect
je me serai lavé(-e)
tu te seras lavé(-e)
il se sera lavé
elle se sera lavée
on se sera lavé
nous nous serons lavés(-es)
vous vous serez lavé(-e/-s/-es)
ils se seront lavés
elles se seront lavées

Conditional perfect
je me serais lavé(-e)
tu te serais lavé(-e)
il se serait lavé
elle se serait lavée
on se serait lavé
nous nous serions lavés(-es)
vous vous seriez lavé(-e/-s/-es)
ils se seraient lavés
elles se seraient lavées

Perfect subjunctive
que je me sois lavé(-e)
que tu te sois lavé(-e)
qu'il se soit lavé
qu'elle se soit lavée
qu'on se soit lavé
que nous nous soyons lavés(-es)
que vous vous soyez lavé(-e/-s/-es)
qu'ils se soient lavés
qu'elles se soient lavées

Pluperfect subjunctive
que je me fusse lavé (-e)
que te fusses lavé(-e)
qu'il se fût lavé
qu'elle se fût lavée
qu'on se fût lavé
que nous nous fussions lavés (-es)
que vous fussiez lavé(-e/-s/-es)
qu'ils se fussent lavés
qu'elles se fussent lavées

Notes

1. All reflexive verbs in French use **être** in compound tenses, and the rules for agreement of the past participle apply as with nonreflexive verbs using **être**, *where the reflexive pronoun is the direct object of the verb.* (In verbs where the reflexive pronoun is the indirect object, there is no agreement of the past particple.)

2. Full alternatives according to gender (masculine or feminine) and number (singular or plural) are given for the perfect tense; in the other compound tenses the alternatives are given in abbreviated form.

3. It is possible to make masculine or feminine plural agreement for **on s'est lavés/-es**, where the sense is clearly plural.

Le matin	*In the morning*
Je *me réveille* **normalement vers sept heures. Je** *me lève* **vite. J'écoute le bulletin météo en** *me rasant.* **Puis** *je me brosse* **les dents et je** *me lave* **la figure avant de** *m'habiller.*	I normally *wake up* around seven. I *get up* quickly. I listen to the weather report while *shaving*. Then I *brush* my teeth and *wash* my face before *getting dressed*.
Elle *s'est réveillée* **vers sept heures.**	She *woke up* around seven o'clock.
Elle *s'est demande* **pourquoi le chien hurlait.**	She *wondered* why the dog was howling.
Je *m'entends* **bien avec mes parents.**	I *get on* well with my parents.
Je *m'entendais* **bien avec ma grand'mère.**	I *used to get on* well with my grandmother.
Les jeunes *se sont* **bien** *amusés* **en Italie.**	The young people *enjoyed themselves* in Italy.
Sans lui, on *se serait* **bien** *amusés.*	Without him, we *would have enjoyed* ourselves.
Installez-vous **ici, près de la fenêtre.**	*Sit here*, near the window.
Les ouvriers *s'étaient mis* **à réparer le toit.**	The workmen *had started* repairing the roof.
Recueillez-vous **un instant avant de quitter cette cathédrale.**	*Meditate* a moment before leaving this cathedral.

6d   Avoir, *to have*
Auxiliary verb

Present participle	**Past participle**
ayant	eu

Imperative

aie! (tu)   ayez! (vous)   ayons! (nous)

Present	**Perfect**
j'ai	j'ai eu
tu as	tu as eu
il/elle a	il/elle a eu
on a	on a eu
nous avons	nous avons eu
vous avez	vous avez eu
ils/elles ont	ils ont eu

Imperfect	**Simple past**
j'avais	j'eus
tu avais	tu eus
il/elle avait	il/elle eut
on avait	on eut
nous avions	nous eûmes
vous aviez	vous eûtes
ils/elles avaient	ils/elles eurent

Past perfect	**Past anterior**
j'avais eu	j'eus eu
tu avais eu	tu eus eu
il/elle avait eu	il/elle eut eu
on avait eu	on eut eu
nous avions eu	nous eûmes eu
vous aviez eu	vous eûtes eu
ils/elles avaient eu	ils/elles eurent eu

Future	**Future perfect**
j'aurai	j'aurai eu
tu auras	tu auras eu
il/elle aura	il/elle aura eu
on aura	on aura eu
nous aurons	nous aurons eu
vous aurez	vous aurez eu
ils/elles auront	ils/elles auront eu

Conditional	**Conditional perfect**
j'aurais	j'aurais eu
tu aurais	tu aurais eu
il/elle aurait	il/elle aurait eu
on aurait	on aurait eu
nous aurions	nous aurions eu
vous auriez	vous auriez eu
ils/elles auraient	ils/elles auraient eu

Present subjunctive	**Perfect subjunctive**
que j'aie	que j'aie eu
que tu aies	que tu aies eu
qu'il/elle ait	qu'il/elle ait eu
qu'on ait	qu'on ait eu
que nous ayons	que nous ayons eu
que vous ayez	que vous ayez eu
qu'ils/elles aient	qu'ils/elles aient eu

Imperfect subjunctive	**Pluperfect subjunctive**
que j'eusse	que j'eusse eu
que tu eusses	que tu eusses
qu'il/elle eût	qu'il/elle eût eu
qu'on eût	qu'on eût eu
que nous eussions	que nous eussions eu
que vous eussiez	que vous eussiez eu
qu'ils/elles eussent	qu'ils/elles eussent eu

Notes

1. **Avoir** is used as the auxiliary verb for the majority of verbs in compound tenses.

2. Note the impersonal phrase **il y a**, meaning "there is" and "there are" used in all common tenses. **Il y a** also means "ago," and in this use is invariable.

3. Note also the idiomatic expressins using **avoir: avoir faim** (to be hungry), **avoir chaud** (to be hot), etc. [➤ Verb index.]

J'*ai* dix-sept ans.	I'*m* seventeen.
Chez moi j'*ai* une machine à laver et un lave-vaisselle.	At home I *have* a washing machine and a dishwasher.

J'*ai* deux frères.	I *have* two brothers.
Quand j'étais petite, j'*avais* une belle poupée.	When I was little, I *had* a lovely doll.
En ville il y *a* deux cinémas.	There *are* two movie houses in town.
Il y *a* deux ans, je suis allé visiter le Louvre.	I went to visit the Louvre two years ago.
Il y *a eu* un accident.	There's *been* an accident.
Combien d'étudiants y *aurait*-il?	How many students *would* there *be*?
Nous *avons* besoin de votre aide.	We need your help.
J'*ai* sommeil.	I'm sleepy.
J'*ai eu* de la chance.	I've been lucky (I've *had* some luck).
Elle *aura* une soixantaine d'années.	She'll *be* about sixty.
J'*avais* peur du chien des voisins.	I *was* afraid of the neighbors' dog.
Le train partit sans qu'il *eût* le temps de lui dire au revoir.	The train left without his *having* time to say good-bye to her.

Examples of auxiliary use

Je n'*ai* pas encore acheté de magnétoscope.	I *have*n't yet bought a video recorder.
Je n'*aurais* jamais pensé à cela.	I *would* never *have* thought of that.
Il n'*avait* pas préparé son discours.	He *had*n't prepared his speech.
Dès qu'il *eut* vu la fille, il partit.	As soon as he *had* seen the girl, he left.
Je regrette qu'il ne t'*ait* pas invité.	I'm sorry he *did*n't invite you.
Ce journaliste n'*aurait* pas écrit ça!	That journalist *would* not *have* written that!
Il *aura* fallu des années pour tout remettre en ordre.	It *will have* taken years to put everything straight.

6e   Etre, *to be*

Auxiliary verb used in some compound tenses and for the passive

Present	*Perfect*
je suis	j'ai été
tu es	tu as été
il/elle est	il/elle a été
on est	on a été
nous sommes	nous avons été
vous êtes	vous avez été
ils/elles sont	ils/elles ont été

Imperfect	*Simple past*
j'étais	je fus
tu étais	tu fus
il/elle était	il/elle fut
on était	on fut
nous étions	nous fûmes
vous étiez	vous fûtes
ils/elles étaient	ils/elles furent

Past perfect	*Past anterior*
j'avais été	j'eus été
tu avais été	tu eus été
il/elle avait été	il/elle eut été
on avait été	on eut été
nous avions été	nous eûmes été
vous aviez été	vous eûtes été
ils/elles avaient été	ils/elles eurent été

Present participle	*Past perfect*
étant	été

Future	*Future perfect*
je serai	j'aurai été
tu seras	tu auras été
il/elle sera	il/elle aura été
on sera	on aura été
nous serons	nous aurons été
vous serez	vous aurez été
ils/elles seront	ils/elles auront été

Conditional	*Conditional perfect*
je serais	j'aurais été
tu serais	tu aurais été
il/elle serait	il/elle aurait été
on serait	on aurait été
nous serions	nous aurions été
vous seriez	vous auriez été
ils/elles seraient	ils/elles auraient été

Present subjunctive	*Perfect subjunctive*
que je sois	que j'aie été
que tu sois	que tu aies été
qu'il/elle soit	qu'il/elle ait été
qu'on soit	qu'on ait été
que nous soyons	que nous ayons été
que vous soyez	que vous ayez été
qu'ils/elles soient	qu'ils/elles aient été

Imperfect subjunctive	*Pluperfect subjunctive*
que je fusse	que j'eusse été
que tu fusses	que tu eusses été
qu'il/elle fût	qu'il/elle eût été
qu'on fût	qu'on eût été
que nous fussions	que nous eussions été
que vous fussiez	que vous eussiez été
qu'ils/elles fussent	qu'ils/elles eussent été

Notes

1. **être** is used as the auxiliary verb in compound tenses for all reflexive verbs, as well as the following thirteen intransitive verbs of motion, and their compounds:

aller	**venir**
partir	**arriver**
monter	**descendre**
sortir	**entrer**
mourir	**naître**
rester	**retourner**
tomber	

These form six pairs of verbs denoting movement in opposite directions, plus **tomber**.

2. Note that the auxiliary uses of **être** are in the formation of compound tenses, and in the passive voice [➤4c (ii), 5c (v)].

3. There is no French equivalent for the English progressive continuous present form, as in "I am writing." For this, either the simple present tense is used, or the expression **être en train de faire**, if the continuity is to be stressed.

Examples of use as linking verb

Je *suis* de nationalité britannique.	I *am* British.
Il *est* ingénieur.	He*'s* an engineer.
Nous *sommes* très déçus.	We*'re* very disappointed.
Les livres *sont* dans le sac.	The books *are* in the bag.
Quand j'*étais* petite, j'*étais* très timide.	When I *was* little, I *was* very shy.
Il *est* cinq heures.	It*'s* five o'clock.
On *sera* à Paris le 20 octobre.	We*'ll be* in Paris on the 20th of October.
Les chants d'oiseaux *seront* bientôt remplacés par des bruits mécaniques.	Birdsong *will* soon *be* replaced by the noise of machinery.
Je *serais* très contente de partir.	I *should be* very pleased to leave.
Elle a dit qu'elle *aurait été* très contente de partir.	She said she *would have been* very pleased to leave.

Examples of auxiliary use

Je *suis* arrivé avant toi.	I arrived before you.
Ils *étaient* partis à huit heures.	They had left at eight.
Je me *suis* levé avant six heures.	I got up before six.
Il ne *serait* pas parti sans les autres.	He wouldn't have left without the others.
Bien que je *sois* tombé de l'échelle, je ne me *suis* pas fait mal.	Although I fell off the ladder, I didn't hurt myself.
Nous *sommes* arrivés à un point critique.	We've reached a critical point.
Il croyait qu'on *était* arrivés à un point critique.	He thought we'd reached a critical point.
On se *serait* déjà arrêtés, si le patron n'était pas arrivé!	We would have stopped already if the boss hadn't arrived!
Ces tarifs ont *été* négociés avec chaque chaîne.	These rates have been negotiated with each TV channel.

6f   Etre blessé, *to be hurt*

*Full conjugation of the passive using the verb **être***

Imperative
sois . . . (tu)   soyez . . . (vous)   soyons . . . (nous)

Present
je suis blessé(-e)
tu es blessé(-e)
il est blessé
elle est blessée
on est blessé
nous sommes blessés(-es)
vous êtes blessé(-e/-s/-es)
ils sont blessés
elles sont blessées

Perfect
j'ai été blessé(-e)
tu as été blessé(-e)
il a été blessé
elle a été blessée
on a été blessé
nous avons été blessés(-es)
vous avez été blessé(-e/-s/-es)
ils ont été blessés
elles ont été blessées

Imperfect
j'étais blessé(-e)
tu étais blessé(-e)
il était blessé
elle était blessée
on était blessé
nous étions blessés(-es)
vous étiez blessé(-e/-s/-es)
ils étaient blessés
elles étaient blessées

Simple past
je fus blessé(-e)
tu fus blessé(-e)
il fut blessé
elle fut blessée
on fut blessé
nous fûmes blessés(-es)
vous fûtes blessé(-e/-s/-es)
ils furent blessés
elles furent blessées

Notes

1. The verb forms presented on other pages are all in the ordinary form, known as the "active voice." The "passive voice," or "passive" [➤5c (v)] is used when the verb's action is done to the subject by another agent, known or implied.

2. It is formed in French as in English by using the full range of tenses of the verb **être** (to be) [➤**être**] and the past participle. Any transitive verb can be used passively.

3. Note again differences between the two languages where verbs do not have the same patterns of use in French as in English. A passive construction is impossible with verbs such as **donner** because, in the active voice, the person receiving is not a direct object, but an indirect object.

Donner un cadeau *à* quelqu'un.   Give a present to someone.
Téléphoner *à* quelqu'un.   Telephone someone.

4. The imperative can be found occasionally.
Sois béni!   Bless you!

Present participle	*Past participle*
étant blessé(-e/-s/-es)	été blessé(-e/-s/-es)

Past perfect	*Past anterior*
j'avais été blessé(-e)	j'eus été blessé(-e)
Future	*Future perfect*
je serai blessé(-e)	j'aurai été blessé(-e)
Conditional	*Conditional perfect*
je serais blessé(-e)	j'aurais été blessé(-e)
Present subjunctive	*Perfect subjunctive*
que je sois blessé(-e)	que j'aie été blessé(-e)
Imperfect subjunctive	*Pluperfect subjunctive*
que je fusse blessé(-e)	que j'eusse été blessé(-e)

Je *suis aimé.*	I *am loved.*
Toutes les places *ont été prises*	All the seats *have been taken.*
Je regrette que la maison *soit vendue.*	I'm sorry the house *is sold.*
J'ai peur qu'il *ait été blessé.*	I'm afraid he'*s been injured.*
Le livre a *été retrouvé* mais il *était abîmé.*	The book *was found* but it *was ruined.*
Les fleurs *ont été données.*	The flowers *were given.*
On m'a donné les fleurs.	I was given the flowers.
On m'a téléphoné.	I was telephoned.

7 -er verbs

allumer

7a Parler, *to speak*
Regular -er verb

Imperative
parle! (tu)   parlez! (vous)   parlons! (nous)

Present	**Perfect**
je parle	j'ai parlé
tu parles	tu as parlé
il/elle parle	il/elle a parlé
on parle	on a parlé
nous parlons	nous avons parlé
vous parlez	vous avez parlé
ils/elles parlent	ils/elles ont parlé

Imperfect	**Simple past**
je parlais	je parlai
tu parlais	tu parlas
il/elle parlait	il/elle parla
on parlait	on parla
nous parlions	nous parlâmes
vous parliez	vous parlâtes
ils/elles parlaient	ils/elles parlèrent

Similar verbs

aimer	like	**jurer**	swear
briser	break	**louer**	hire, rent
chercher	look for	**montrer**	show
demander	ask	**oublier**	forget
écouter	listen (to)	**présenter**	present
fermer	shut	**trouver**	find
gronder	scold	**vérifier**	check
hésiter	hesitate	**verser**	pour
inviter	invite		

Notes

1. This is the pattern for the regular **-er** verb conjugation (➤also full conjugation of **marcher**, 6a).

2. This is by far the largest group of verbs and is the conjugation into which newly created verbs are added.

3. On the following pages are conjugations of -er verbs that have slight spelling modifications in certain forms.

4. -ier verbs follow the pattern above, which produces forms with -ii- in the imperfect indicative and present subjunctive:

Nous appréciions; vous appréciiez.

Present participle	**Past participle**
parlant	parlé

Past perfect	**Past anterior**
j'avais parlé	j'eus parlé
Future	**Future perfect**
je parlerai	j'aurai parlé
Conditional	**Conditional perfect**
je parlerais	j'aurais parlé
Present subjunctive	**Perfect subjunctive**
que je parle	que j'ai parlé
Imperfect subjunctive	**Pluperfect subjunctive**
que je parlasse	que j'eusse parlé

Conversation à sept heures du matin	**A conversation at seven o'clock in the morning**
– Qu'est-ce que tu *cherches?*	– What are you *looking for*?
– Je *cherche* mon stylo. Je l'*ai laissé* sur la table.	– I'*m looking for* my pen. I *left* it on the table.
– Alors *regarde* sous la table!	– Then look under the table.
– J'y *ai* déjà *regardé.*	– I'*ve* already *looked* there.
– Eh bien, tu *demanderas* à ta soeur! Elle te *prêtera* un stylo.	– Well, you *must ask* your sister. She'*ll lend* you a pen.
– Impossible! elle est encore fâchée parce que j'ai abîmé le stylo qu'elle *a acheté* hier matin. Pendant que j'*étudiais* ces lettres, elle *comptait* ses crayons et ses stylos!	– Impossible. She's still angry because I ruined the pen she *bought* yesterday. While I *was studying* those letters, she *was counting* her pens and pencils.
– Si tu ne *trouves* pas ton stylo à toi, tu vas en *acheter* un autre tout de suite!	– If you don't *find* your pen, you're going *to buy* another straight away.

43

7b   Aller, *to go*
Irregular -er verb

Imperative
va! (tu)   allez! (vous)   allons! (nous)

Present
je vais
tu vas
il/elle va
on va
nous allons
vous allez
ils/elles vont

Perfect
je suis allé/allée
tu es allé/allée
il est allé
elle est allée
on est allé
nous sommes allés/allées
vous êtes allé/allée/allés/allées
ils sont allés
elles sont allées

Imperfect
j'allais
tu allais
il/elle allait
on allait
nous allions
vous alliez
ils/elles allaient

Simple past
j'allai
tu allas
il/elle alla
on alla
nous allâmes
vous allâtes
ils/elles allèrent

Notes

1. **Aller** is the only verb of its type, and is the only irregular -er verb.
2. It is used with the infinitive as an immediate future tense, like English: e.g., je vais faire . . ., "I am going to do . . ." This form is extremely common in speech.

Examples of use as a full verb

- Où **vas-tu?**
- **Je vais au cinéma.**
- **Moi, j'y suis allée hier.**
- **On y serait allés à Noël.**

- Where are you going?
- I'm going to the movies/cinema.
- I went there yesterday myself.
- We would have gone there at Christmas.

Present participle allant	*Past participle* allé
Past perfect j'étais allé(-e)	*Past anterior* je fus allé(-e)
Future j'irai	*Future perfect* je serai allé(-e)
Conditional j'irais	*Conditional perfect* je serais allé(-e)
Present subjunctive que j'aille	*Perfect subjunctive* que je sois allé(-e)
Imperfect subjunctive que j'allasse	*Pluperfect subjunctive* que je fusse allé(-e)

Examples of use with an infinitive to express the immediate future

Qu'est-ce qu'on *va faire* demain?	What *are* we *going to do* tomorrow?
On *va passer* la matinée au musée.	We're *going to spend* the morning at the museum.
Ils *vont arriver* à midi.	They're *going to arrive* at noon.
On *allait passer* l'après-midi à la plage, mais il a plu.	We were *going to spend* the afternoon at the beach, but it rained.

7c   Appeler, *to call*

Regular -er verb; consonant doubles before mute ending and in future and conditional tenses

Imperative

appelle! (tu)   appelez! (vous)   appelons! (nous)

Present	**Perfect**
j'appelle	j'ai appelé
tu appelles	tu as appelé
il/elle appelle	il/elle a appelé
on appelle	on a appelé
nous appelons	nous avons appelé
vous appelez	vous avez appelé
ils/elles appellent	ils ont appelé

Imperfect	**Simple past**
j'appelais	j'appelai
tu appelais	tu appelas
il/elle appelait	il/elle appela
on appelait	on appela
nous appelions	nous appelâmes
vous appeliez	vous appelâtes
ils/elles appelaient	ils/elles appelèrent

Similar verbs

rappeler	remind	**rejeter**	reject
se rappeler	remember	**projeter**	project
jeter	throw	**ruisseler**	flow

Notes

The majority of verbs in **-eler** and **-eter** are spelled this way. The doubling of the letter **-l-** or **-t-** occurs when the vowel **-e-** is an open sound, as in English "let"; that is, when the following ending is not pronounced, and also throughout the future tense. (▶**acheter**, 7d, for those using **è** instead of **-tt-**, **-ll-**.)

Present participle	*Past participle*
appelant	appelé

Past perfect	*Past anterior*
j'avais appelé	j'eus appelé
Future	*Future perfect*
j'appellerai	j'aurai appelé
Conditional	*Conditional perfect*
j'appellerais	j'aurais appelé
Present subjunctive	*Perfect subjunctive*
que j'appelle	que j'aie appelé
Imperfect subjunctive	*Pluperfect subjunctive*
que j'appelasse	que j'eusse appelé

– Je m'*appelle* Marcel.
Comment vous *appelez*-vous?

– I'm *called* Marcel.
What's your name?

Je l'ai *appelée* hier soir.

I *called* her yesterday evening.

**Je crois qu'on *rejettera*
ma suggestion.**

I think they'*ll reject* my
suggestion.

**"*Rappelle*-toi, Barbara,
Il pleuvait sans cesse sur
Brest ce jour-là . . ."**
Paroles (Jacques Prévert)

"Do you remember, Barbara,
It was raining endlessly
on Brest that day . . ."

47

7d   Acheter, *to buy*

Regular -er verb requiring -è- before mute ending and in future and conditional tenses

---

Imperative
achète! (tu)   achetez! (vous)   achetons! (nous)

Present	**Perfect**
j'achète	j'ai acheté
tu achètes	tu as acheté
il/elle achète	il/elle a acheté
on achète	on a acheté
nous achetons	nous avons acheté
vous achetez	vous avez acheté
ils/elles achètent	ils/elles ont acheté

Imperfect	**Simple past**
j'achetais	j'achetai
tu achetais	tu achetas
il/elle achetait	il/elle acheta
on achetait	on acheta
nous achetions	nous achetâmes
vous achetiez	vous achetâtes
ils/elles achetaient	ils/elles achetèrent

Similar verbs

celer	conceal	marteler	hammer
ciseler	chisel	mener	lead
congeler	freeze	modeler	model
déceler	detect	peler	peel
dégeler	thaw	peser	weigh
geler	freeze	racheter	buy back
haleter	pant	semer	sow
lever	lift	surgeler	deep-freeze

Notes

1. Compounds of the verbs also follow the spelling pattern of **acheter; peler; mener; peser; lever;** and **semer.**

Present participle	*Past participle*
achetant	acheté

Past perfect	*Past anterior*
j'avais acheté	j'eus acheté
Future	*Future perfect*
j'achèterai	j'aurai acheté
Conditional	*Conditional perfect*
j'achèterais	j'aurais acheté
Present subjunctive	*Perfect subjunctive*
que j'achète	que j'aie acheté
Imperfect subjunctive	*Pluperfect subjunctive*
que j'achetasse	que j'eusse acheté

Je me *lève* vers sept heures.

I *get up* around seven.

Je *sème* à tout vent.
(Motto of Larousse publishing house.)

I *sow* in all directions.

Tu nous *mènes* où?

Where *are* you *leading* us?

Au supermarché

At the supermarket

– Bonjour, madame. Excusez-moi. J'*ai acheté* ce paquet de petits pois *congelés* hier, mais je les *ai pesés* chez moi et ils ne *pèsent* pas 200 grammes.

– Hello, ma'am. Excuse me. I *bought* this packet of *frozen* peas yesterday, but I *weighed* them at home and they *do*n't *weigh* 200g.

– Désolée, monsieur. Quand j'*aurai pelé* ces pommes de terre, je *me lèverai* pour vous chercher un autre paquet.

– Terribly sorry, sir. When I'*ve peeled* these potatoes, I'*ll get up* and find you another pack.

7e   Céder, to give way, cede
Regular -er verb changing -é- to -è-

Imperative

cède! (tu)   cédez! (vous)   cédons! (nous)

Present	**Perfect**
je cède	j'ai cédé
tu cèdes	tu as cédé
il/elle cède	il/elle a cédé
on cède	on a cédé
nous cédons	nous avons cédé
vous cédez	vous avez cédé
ils/elles cèdent	ils ont cédé

Imperfect	**Simple past**
je cédais	je cédai
tu cédais	tu cédas
il/elle cédait	il/elle céda
on cédait	on céda
nous cédions	nous cédâmes
vous cédiez	vous cédâtes
ils/elles cédaient	ils/elles cédèrent

Similar verbs

accélérer	speed up	**intégrer**	include
adhérer	adhere	**interpréter**	interpret
célébrer	celebrate	**précéder**	precede
déléguer	delegate	**régler**	settle
espérer	hope	**succéder**	succeed

Notes

1. Any verb having **-é-** before the last syllable of the infinitive follows this pattern. There are many combinations: **-ébrer; -écer; -écher; -éder; -égler; -égner; -égrer; -éguer; -éler; -émer; -éner; -éper; -équer; -érer; -éser; -éter; -étrer; -évrer; -éyer.**
2. The **-è-** occurs in the present tenses, when the ending is not heard, and in the singular imperative.

Répétez après moi . . .   *Repeat after me . . .*

Je ne veux pas que tu   I don't want you *to repeat*
répètes ça aux autres!   that to the others!

Present participle cédant	*Past participle* cédé

Past perfect j'avais cédé	*Past anterior* j'eus cédé
Future je céderai	*Future perfect* j'aurai cédé
Conditional je céderais	*Conditional perfect* j'aurais cédé
Present subjunctive que je cède	*Perfect subjunctive* que j'aie cédé
Imperfect subjunctive que je cédasse	*Pluperfect subjunctive* que j'eusse cédé

Vous n'*avez* pas *complété* le travail.

You *haven't finished* the work.

J'*espérais* te voir au bureau.

I *was hoping* to see you at the office.

Il *a abrégé* son voyage.

He *cut short* his journey.

J'*interpréterai* ce vers de poésie d'après le contexte.

I *shall interpret* this line of poetry according to the context.

L'anniversaire
– J'*espère* que tu *célébreras* tes vingt ans en nous invitant tous au resto!

The birthday
– I *hope* you *will celebrate* your twentieth birthday by inviting us all to eat out!

– Bien sûr, mais je te *délègue* la responsabilité de réserver la table!

– Of course, but I'*m delegating* you to reserve the table.

– Ah bon! Et je suppose que je dois *régler* l'addition après!

– Oh right! And I suppose I have to *pay* the bill after!

7f   Employer, *to work, employ*
*Regular **-er** verb ending in **-oyer** or **-uyer***

Imperative
emploie! (tu)   employez! (vous)   employons! (nous)

Present	Perfect
j'emploie	j'ai employé
tu emploies	tu as employé
il/elle emploie	il/elle a employé
on emploie	on a employé
nous employons	nous avons employé
vous employez	vous avez employé
ils/elles emploient	ils/elles ont employé

Imperfect	Simple past
j'employais	j'employai
tu employais	tu employas
il/elle employait	il/elle employa
on employait	on employa
nous employions	nous employâmes
vous employiez	vous employâtes
ils/elles employaient	ils/elles employèrent

Similar verbs

appuyer	lean; press	**noyer**	drown
broyer	grind	**ployer**	bend; sag
ennuyer	bore	**tutoyer**	address someone as "tu"
essuyer	wipe	**vouvoyer**	address someone as "vous"

Notes

1. Verbs in **-oyer** and **-uyer** follow this pattern.
2. **Envoyer** and **renvoyer** differ in the future and conditional tenses with irregular forms: **j'enverrai/je renverrai**, "I will send/resend."

Present participle employant	**Past participle** employé

Past perfect j'avais employé	**Past anterior** j'eus employé
Future j'employerai	**Future perfect** j'aurai employé
Conditional j'employerais	**Conditional perfect** j'aurais employé
Present subjunctive employe	**Perfect subjunctive** que j'aie employé
Imperfect subjunctive que j'employasse	**Pluperfect subjunctive** que j'eusse employé

J'*enverrai* ce paquet à ma soeur la semaine prochaine.	I *shall send* this package to my sister next week.
On peut se *tutoyer* maintenant.	We can *call* each other *"tu"* now.
***As*-tu bien *essuyé* les verres?**	*Have* you *dried* the glasses properly?
Elle m'*envoie* le journal régional tous les samedis.	She *sends* me the local paper every Saturday.
***Délayez* bien la farine dans le lait.**	*Mix* the flour well into the milk.
On fait très peu pour *enrayer* le chômage.	They're not doing much *to curb* unemployment.

7g   Manger, *to eat*
Regular -er verb ending in -ger

Imperative
mange! (tu)   mangez! (vous)   *mangeons*! (nous)

Present
je mange
tu manges
il/elle mange
on mange
nous *mangeons*
vous mangez
ils/elles mangent

Perfect
j'ai mangé
tu as mangé
il/elle a mangé
on a mangé
nous avons mangé
vous avez mangé
ils/elles ont mangé

Imperfect
je *mangeais*
tu *mangeais*
il/elle *mangeait*
on *mangeait*
nous mangions
vous mangiez
ils/elles *mangeaient*

Simple past
je *mangeai*
tu *mangeas*
il/elle *mangea*
on *mangea*
nous *mangeâmes*
vous *mangeâtes*
ils/elles mangèrent

Similar verbs

arranger	arrange	**juger**	judge
bouger	move	**outrager**	anger
déranger	disturb	**partager**	share
enrager	enrage	**plonger**	dive
loger	house	**ranger**	to tidy up

Notes
1. Italicized forms show the extra -e- in spelling.
2. All verbs ending in -ger are in this large group.

Present participle	**Past participle**
mangeant	mangé

Past perfect	**Past anterior**
j'avais mangé	j'eus mangé
Future	**Future perfect**
je mangerai	j'aurai mangé
Conditional	**Conditional perfect**
je mangerais	j'aurais mangé
Present subjunctive	**Perfect subjunctive**
que je mange	que j'aie mangé
Imperfect subjunctive	**Pluperfect subjunctive**
que je *mangeasse*	que j'eusse mangé

Il *plongea* dans la piscine et *nagea* jusqu'à l'autre bord.

He *dived* into the swimming pool and *swam* to the other side.

Une tragédie en miniature
– Qu'est-ce qu'il a, ton hamster? Il ne *bouge* plus.

A mini-tragedy
– What's the matter with your hamster? He's not *moving* any more.

– Je ne sais pas. Je voudrais bien qu'il *mange* quelque chose. La semaine dernière il *mangeait* très bien; mais depuis mardi il *n'a rien mangé* du tout.
– Eh bien, ramasse-le! Ça ne le *dérangera* pas.
– Tu as raison. Et de toute façon il ne *rongera* plus rien. Il est mort.

– I don't know. I really wish he'*d eat* something. Last week he *was eating* very well; but since Tuesday he *hasn't eaten* a thing.

– Well, pick him up! It *won't disturb* him.
– You're right. And anyway he *won't gnaw* anything else. He's dead.

7h   Placer, *to put, place*
Regular -er verb ending in -cer

Imperative
place! (tu)   placez! (vous)   *plaçons!* (nous)

Present
je place
tu places
il/elle place
on place
nous *plaçons*
vous placez
ils/elles placent

Perfect
j'ai placé
tu as placé
il/elle a placé
on a placé
nous avons placé
vous avez placé
ils/elles ont placé

Imperfect
je *plaçais*
tu *plaçais*
il/elle *plaçait*
on *plaçait*
nous placions
vous placiez
ils/elles *plaçaient*

Simple past
je *plaçai*
tu *plaças*
il/elle *plaça*
on *plaça*
nous *plaçâmes*
vous *plaçâtes*
ils/elles placèrent

Similar verbs

annoncer	announce	**relancer**	throw back
commencer	begin	**remplacer**	replace
dénoncer	denounce	**renoncer**	renounce
effacer	rub out	**retracer**	retrace
lancer	throw; launch	**sucer**	suck
prononcer	pronounce	**tracer**	trace
recommencer	begin again		

Notes

1. The italicized forms indicate the requirement to write **ç** before vowels **a**, **o**, and **u**. Hence the cedilla is written in all parts of the imperfect indicative and imperfect subjunctive, and in the simple past except in the third-person plural; in the present participle; and in the first-person plural present tense and imperative. (Compare the parallel use of **-ge-** in verbs of the **-ger** group ►**manger**, 7g, where exactly the same forms require the extra **-e-**.)
2. All verbs ending in **-cer** follow this pattern.

Present participle	Past participle
plaçant	placé

Past perfect	Past anterior
j'avais placé	j'eus placé

Future	Future perfect
je placerai	j'aurai placé

Conditional	Conditional perfect
je placerais	j'aurais placé

Present subjunctive	Perfect subjunctive
que je place	que j'aie placé

Imperfect subjunctive	Pluperfect subjunctive
que je *plaçasse*	que j'eusse placé

Commençons!

Let's begin!

C'est elle qui m'*a remplacé*.

She's the one who *replaced* me.

"Et la mer *efface* sur le sable les pas des amants désunis" (*Les Feuilles Mortes,* Jacques Prévert)

"And the sea *washes away* in the sand the footprints of parted lovers"

Ne *recommence* pas, je t'en supplie!

Don't *do that again*, I'm begging you.

Edward VIII *renonça* à la couronne britannique en 1938. Son frère le *remplaça*.

Edward VIII *renounced* the British crown in 1938. His brother *replaced* him.

7i   Payer, *to pay*
*Regular -**er** verb ending in -**ayer***

Imperative
pay!/paie! (tu)   payez! (vous)   payons! (nous)

Present
je paye/paie
tu payes/paies
il/elle paye/paie
on paye/paie
nous payons
vous payez
ils/elles payent/paient

Perfect
j'ai payé
tu as payé
il/elle a payé
on a payé
nous avons payé
vous avez payé
ils/elles ont payé

Imperfect
je payais
tu payais
il/elle payait
on payait
nous payions
vous payiez
ils/elles payaient

Simple past
je payai
tu payas
il/elle paya
on paya
nous payâmes
vous payâtes
ils/elles payèrent

Similar verbs

déblayer   clear away   **essayer**   try
délayer   mix; thin down   **étayer**   prop up
enrayer   stop; check   **rayer**   scratch out;
                                                     strike out;
                                                     erase

Notes

1. Verbs in **-ayer** have always had the choice of spelling: either to keep the letter **-y-** throughout, or to have a letter **-i-** before silent **-e** (**-es**, **-ent**) in the present, future and conditional tenses.

Present participle	Past participle
payant	payé

Past perfect	Past anterior
j'avais payé	j'eus payé

Future	Future perfect
je payerai/paierai	j'aurai payé

Conditional	Conditional perfect
je payerais/paierais	j'aurais payé

Present subjunctive	Perfect subjunctive
que je paye/paie	que j'aie payé

Imperfect subjunctive	Pluperfect subjunctive
que je payasse	que j'eusse payé

Je peux *essayer* ce pantalon?	May I *try* these pants *on*?
J'ai *payé* les billets, mais il faut que je *paie* le repas.	I've *paid* for the tickets, but I must *pay* for the meal.
Tu *essaieras de* te mettre en contact avec lui?	*Will* you *try* and contact him?
Il *a rayé* son nom.	He's *crossed* his name out.
Avant de jouer au football, nous *déblayons* le terrain.	Before playing soccer, we *are clearing* the ground *(of obstacles)*.
Il *délaie* son discours en donnant beaucoup d'exemples.	He's *spinning out* his speech by giving lots of examples.

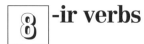 -ir verbs

8a   Finir, *to finish*
Regular -ir verb

Imperative

finis! (tu)   finissez! (vous)   finissons! (nous)

Present

je finis
tu finis
il/elle finit
on finit
nous finissons
vous finissez
ils/elles finissent

Perfect

j'ai fini
tu as fini
il/elle a fini
on a fini
nous avons fini
vous avez fini
ils/elles ont fini

Imperfect

je finissais
tu finissais
il/elle finissait
on finissait
nous finissions
vous finissiez
ils/elles finissaient

Simple past

je finis
tu finis
il/elle finit
on finit
nous finîmes
vous finîtes
ils/elles finirent

Past perfect

j'avais fini
tu avais fini
il/elle avait fini
on avait fini
nous avions fini
vous aviez fini
ils/elles avaient fini

Past anterior

j'eus fini
tu eus fini
il/elle eut fini
on eut fini
nous eûmes fini
vous eûtes fini
ils/elles eurent fini

Present participle	Past participle
finissant	fini

Future
je finirai
tu finiras
il/elle finira
on finira
nous finirons
vous finirez
ils/elles finiront

Future perfect
j'aurai fini
tu auras fini
il/elle aura fini
on aura fini
nous aurons fini
vous aurez fini
ils/elles auront fini

Conditional
je finirais
tu finirais
il/elle finirait
on finirait
nous finirions
vous finiriez
ils/elles finiraient

Conditional perfect
j'aurais fini
tu aurais fini
il/elle aurait
on aurait fini
nous aurions fini
vous auriez fini
ils/elles auraient fini

Present subjunctive
que je finisse
que tu finisses
qu'il/elle finisse
qu'on finisse
que nous finissions
que vous finissiez
qu'ils/elles finissent

Perfect subjunctive
que j'aie fini
que tu aies fini
qu'il/elle ait fini
qu'on ait fini
que nous ayons fini
que vous ayez fini
qu'ils/elles aient fini

Imperfect subjunctive
que je finisse
que tu finisses
qu'il/elle finît
qu'on finît
que nous finissions
que vous finissiez
qu'ils/elles finissent

Pluperfect subjunctive
que j'eusse fini
que tu eusses fini
qu'il/elle eût fini
qu'on eût fini
que nous eussions fini
que vous eussiez fini
qu'ils/elles eussent fini

Similar verbs

accomplir	achieve	**franchir**	cross
amortir	deaden; cushion	**réfléchir**	reflect; ponder
applaudir	applaud	**réussir**	succeed
avertir	warn	**surgir**	appear suddenly
choisir	choose		

Change-of-state verbs

appauvrir	impoverish	**jaunir**	go yellow
blanchir	turn white	**réunir**	gather together
démolir	demolish	**rougir**	go red
enrichir	enrich	**vieillir**	grow old
établir	establish	**unir**	unite
guérir	cure; heal		

Notes

1. The regular **-ir** conjugation with **-iss-** is a large group.
2. It includes verbs implying some kind of development or change of state.

Au grand magasin
– Les enfants, je vous *avertis* qu'on part dans deux minutes.
– Oh maman! je n'*ai* pas *fini*. Je n'*ai* rien *choisi*.
– Et moi, maman? Il faut que je *réfléchisse!* Trouver un cadeau pour Papa, ce n'est pas facile.
– Eh bien, on n'*a* pas *accompli* grand-chose ce matin.
– C'est vrai, mais si le prof ne m'*avait* pas *puni*, on aurait eu beaucoup plus de temps pour *choisir*.

On *avait établi* un petit commerce, mais cela n'*a* pas *réussi*.

Les moteurs de l'avion *vrombissaient* au décollage.

Je ne voudrais pas qu'on *démolisse* le vieux musée.

At the department store
– Children, I'*m warning* you that we're leaving in two minutes.
– Oh Mom, I *haven*'t *finished*. I *haven*'t *chosen* anything.
– And what about me, Mom? I have to *think about this*. Finding a present for Dad isn't easy.
– Well, we *haven*'t *achieved* much this morning.
– That's true, but if the teacher *had*n't *punished* me, we would have had a lot more time *to choose*.

They *had set up* a small business, but it *did*n't *succeed*.

The plane's engines *were roaring* on takeoff.

I wouldn't like them to *knock down* the old museum.

8b   Acquérir, *to acquire*
Irregular -ir verb

Imperative
acquiers! (tu)   acquérez! (vous)   acquérons! (nous)

Present
j'acquiers
tu acquiers
il/elle acquiert
on acquiert
nous acquérons
vous acquérez
ils/elles acquièrent

Perfect
j'ai acquis
tu as acquis
il/elle a acquis
on a acquis
nous avons acquis
vous avez acquis
ils/elles ont acquis

Imperfect
j'acquérais
tu acquérais
il/elle acquérait
on acquérait
nous acquérions
vous acquériez
ils/elles acquéraient

Simple past
j'acquis
tu acquis
il/elle acquit
on acquit
nous acquîmes
vous acquîtes
ils/elles acquirent

Similar verbs

conquérir   conquer   **reconquérir**   reconquer

Notes

1. The main difficulties in this verb are in the present tenses, as well as the future and conditional.

J'*ai acquis* cette table chez un brocanteur.

I *acquired* this table at a secondhand dealer's.

Où veux-tu que j'*acquière* un vélo à cette heure-ci?

Where do you expect me to *get* a bike from at this time of day?

Present participle	**Past participle**
acquérant	acquis

Past perfect	**Past anterior**
j'avais acquis	j'eus acquis
Future	**Future perfect**
j'acquerrai	j'aurai acquis
Conditional	**Conditional perfect**
j'acquerrais	j'aurais acquis
Present subjunctive	**Perfect subjunctive**
que j'acquière	que j'aie acquis
que tu acquières	
qu'il/elle acquière	
qu'on acquière	
que nous acquérions	
que vous acquériez	
qu'ils/elles acquièrent	
Imperfect subjunctive	**Pluperfect subjunctive**
que j'acquisse	que j'eusse acquis

Jules César *conquit* la Gaule en 58 av.J-C.	Julius Caesar *conquered* Gaul in 58 B.C.
Tu *acquerras* des tableaux?	*Will* you *purchase* some paintings?
Ces antiquités *ont acquis* beaucoup de valeur.	These antiques *have appreciated* a lot in value.
Ce Lothario *conquiert* tous les coeurs des dames.	That Lothario *wins* all the ladies' hearts.
Sans la trahison, nous *aurions reconquis* notre liberté.	If we hadn't been betrayed, we *would have won back* our freedom.

8c   Cueillir, *to pick*
Irregular -ir verb

Imperative

cueille! (tu)   cueillez! (vous)   cueillons! (nous)

Present	**Perfect**
je *cueille*	j'ai cueilli
tu *cueilles*	tu as cueilli
il/elle cueille	il/elle a cueilli
on cueille	on a cueilli
nous cueillons	nous avons cueilli
vous cueillez	vous avez cueilli
ils/elles cueillent	ils/elles ont cueilli

Imperfect	**Simple past**
je *cueillais*	je cueillis
tu *cueillais*	tu cueillis
il/elle *cueillait*	il/elle cueillit
on *cueillait*	on cueillit
nous *cueillions*	nous cueillîmes
vous *cueilliez*	vous cueillîtes
ils/elles *cueillaient*	ils/elles cueillirent

Similar verbs

acceillir   welcome   **recueillir**   pick again

Notes

1. Italicized forms show differences from regular **-ir** verbs.
2. This group, like the **ouvrir** group, has a mixture of forms from the **-er** and **-ir** conjugations.
3. **Assaillir** (to assail) and **défaillir** (to faint, falter) are conjugated like **cueillir** in all forms except the future and conditional tenses, where the form is **j'assaillirai**.

"Cueillez dès aujourd'hui les roses de la vie." *(Ronsard, sixteenth century)*	Gather ye rosebuds while ye may. *(Literally, "Gather the roses of life today.")*
Voici les pommes que j'*ai* **cueillies ce matin.**	These are the apples I *picked* this morning.

Present participle	**Past participle**
cueillant	cueilli

Past perfect

j'avais cueilli

Past anterior

j'eus cueilli

Future

je *cueillerai*

tu *cueilleras*

Future perfect

j'aurai cueilli

Conditional

je *cueillerais*

Conditional perfect

j'aurais cueilli

Present subjunctive

que je *cueille*

Perfect subjunctive

que j'aie cueilli

Imperfect subjunctive

que je cueillisse

Pluperfect subjunctive

que j'eusse cueilli

L'hôtel peut *accueillir* un grand nombre de touristes.

The hotel can *accommodate* a large number of tourists.

On m'*a accueilli* avec chaleur.

They *welcomed* me warmly.

Je l'*accueillerai* chez moi.

I *shall welcome* him into my home.

Dans six mois; il *aura recueilli* son héritage.

In six months he *will have come into* his inheritance.

Le compositeur Vaughan Williams *recueillait* régulièrement les vieilles chansons folkloriques qu'il entendait.

The composer Vaughan Williams regularly *noted down* the old folk songs he heard.

On l'*a assailli* de questions après le discours.

They *bombarded* him with questions after the speech.

Elle *défaille* de faim.

She'*s fainting* with hunger.

8d   Courir, *to run*
Irregular -ir verb

Imperative

cours! (tu)	courez! (vous)	courons! (nous)

Present

je cours
tu cours
il/elle court
on court
nous courons
vous courez
ils/elles courent

Perfect

j'ai couru
tu as couru
il/elle a couru
on a couru
nous avons couru
vous avez couru
ils/elles ont couru

Imperfect

je courais
tu courais
il/elle courait
on courait
nous courions
vous couriez
ils/elles couraient

Simple past

je courus
tu courus
il/elle courut
on courut
nous courûmes
vous courûtes
ils/elles coururent

Similar verbs

accourir	run up; rush up	**recourir**	run again
concourir	compete	**secourir**	help; assist
parcourir	cover; travel		

.

Present participle	*Present participle*
courant	couru

Past perfect	*Past anterior*
j'avais couru	j'eus couru
Future	*Future perfect*
je courrai	j'aurai couru
Conditional	*Conditional perfect*
je courrais	j'aurais couru
Present subjunctive	*Perfect subjunctive*
que je coure	que j'aie couru
Imperfect subjunctive	*Pluperfect subjunctive*
que je courusse	que j'eusse couru

J'*ai couru*. Je suis essouflé.

I'*ve been running*. I'm out of breath.

Allez, *courez!*

Come on, *run!*

Il *a parcouru* le monde.

He'*s been* all over the world.

Je *recourrai* au patron.

I *shall appeal* to the boss.

On *aurait concouru* à ce projet, mais l'argent manquait.

We *would have cooperated* on that project, but money was short.

Il *secourait* toujours les amis qui avaient des problèmes financiers.

He *always helped* friends who had financial problems.

8e   Dormir, *to sleep*
Irregular -ir verb

Imperative
dors! (tu)   *dormez!* (vous)   *dormons!* (nous)

Present
je *dors*
tu *dors*
il/elle *dort*
on *dort*
nous *dormons*
vous *dormez*
ils/elles *dorment*

Perfect
j'ai dormi
tu as dormi
il/elle a dormi
on a dormi
nous avons dormi
vous avez dormi
ils/elles ont dormi

Imperfect
je *dormais*
tu *dormais*
il/elle *dormait*
on *dormait*
nous *dormions*
vous *dormiez*
ils/elles *dormaient*

Simple past
je dormis
tu dormis
il/elle dormit
on dormit
nous dormîmes
vous dormîtes
ils/elles dormirent

Similar verbs

s'endormir   go to sleep   **se rendormir**   go back to sleep

Notes

1. Italicized forms show differences from model verb **finir** (➤8a).

– *Avez*-vous bien *dormi?*

– Did you sleep well?

– Oui, je *me suis* très vite *endormi*. Mais mon mari ne *dort* jamais bien.

– Yes *I went to sleep* very quickly. But my husband never *sleeps* well.

– Il s'est réveillé pendant la nuit?

– Did he wake up in the night?

– Oui, et il ne *s'est* pas *rendormi* avant six heures.

– *Yes*, and he didn't *get back* to *sleep* until six o'clock.

Present participle	**Past participle**
dormant	dormi

Past perfect	**Past anterior**
j'avais dormi	j'eus dormi
Future	**Future perfect**
je dormirai	j'aurai dormi
Conditional	**Conditional perfect**
je dormirais	j'aurais dormi
Present subjunctive	**Perfect subjunctive**
que je *dorme*	que j'aie dormi
Imperfect subjunctive	**Pluperfect subjunctive**
que je dormisse	que j'eusse dormi

Dormez **bien, les enfants!**	*Sleep* well, children.
Tu *dormiras* **bien après un petit verre de cognac.**	You'*ll sleep* well after a small glass of brandy.
Ne faites pas de bruit – les gosses *se seront endormis!*	Don't make a noise – the kids *will have gone to sleep.*
On *se serait rendormis* **s'il n'y avait pas eu tous ces trains qui passaient.**	We *would have gone back to sleep* if all those trains hadn't been going by.
Elle *s'était* **vite** *endormie.*	She *had fallen asleep* quickly.

71

8f   Faillir, *to almost do, to fail*
Irregular -ir verb

Imperative
—

Present
—

Perfect
j'ai failli
tu as failli
il/elle a failli
on a failli
nous avons failli
vous avez failli
ils/elles ont failli

Imperfect
—

Simple past
je faillis
tu faillis
il/elle faillit
on faillit
nous faillîmes
vous faillîtes
ils/elles faillirent

Notes

1. This verb exists only in past tenses.

Present participle	*Past participle*
faillant	failli

Past perfect	*Past anterior*
j'avais failli	j'eus failli

Future	*Future perfect*
—	j'aurai failli

Conditional	*Conditional perfect*
—	j'aurais failli

Present subjunctive	*Perfect subjunctive*
—	que j'aie failli

Imperfect subjunctive	*Pluperfect subjunctive*
—	que j'eusse failli

J'*ai failli* réussir.	I *almost* succeeded.
Il *a failli* tomber.	He *almost* fell.
On *a failli* perdre tout notre argent.	We *nearly* lost all our money.

Notes

1. The idiom **faillir à quelque chose** means "to be lacking, to fail in something."

Il *faillit* à son devoir.	He *failed* in his duty.
Son courage lui *faillit*.	Her courage *failed* her.

8g   Fuir, *to flee*
Irregular -ir verb

Imperative

fuis! (tu)   fuyez! (vous)   fuyons! (nous)

Present	**Perfect**
je fuis	j'ai fui
tu fuis	tu as fui
il/elle fuit	il/elle a fui
on fuit	on a fui
nous fuyons	nous avons fui
vous fuyez	vous avez fui
ils/elles fuient	ils/elles ont fui

Imperfect	**Simple past**
je fuyais	je fuis
tu fuyais	tu fuis
il/elle fuyait	il/elle fuit
on fuyait	on fuit
nous fuyions	nous fuîmes
vous fuyiez	vous fuîtes
ils/elles fuyaient	ils/elles fuirent

Similar verbs

s'enfuir   run away; flee

Notes

1. The **-y-** in forms with an audible ending is the main feature of this verb.
2. **S'enfuir** (flee from; run away) is conjugated in the same way (with **être** in compound tenses).

Present participle	**Past participle**
fuyant	fui

Past perfect	**Past anterior**
j'avais fui	j'eus fui
Future	**Future perfect**
je fuirai	j'aurai fui
Conditional	**Conditional perfect**
je fuirais	j'aurais fui
Present subjunctive	**Perfect subjunctive**
que je fuie	que j'aie fui
Imperfect subjunctive	**Pluperfect subjunctive**
que je fuisse	que j'eusse fui

Fuyons!	Let's *run for it!*
Il *s'est enfui* à toute vitesse.	He *ran away* as fast as he could.
Les réfugiés *fuient* devant les soldats.	The refugees *are fleeing* from the soldiers.
Le temps *fuit.*	Time *flies.*
Le beau temps *a fui.*	The fine weather's *gone.*

8h Mourir, *to die*
Irregular *-ir* verb

Imperative
meurs! (tu) mourez! (vous) mourons! (nous)

Present	Perfect
je meurs	je suis mort
tu meurs	tu es mort
il/elle meurt	il est mort/elle est morte
on meurt	on est mort
nous mourons	nous sommes morts
vous mourez	vous êtes mort(-e/-s/-es)
ils/elles meurent	ils sont morts/elles sont mortes

Imperfect	Simple past
je mourais	je mourus
tu mourais	tu mourus
il/elle mourait	il/elle mourut
on mourait	on mourut
nous mourions	nous mourûmes
vous mouriez	vous mourûtes
ils/elles mouraient	ils/elles moururent

Notes

1. The present tenses and the future and conditional, as well as the simple past and imperfect subjunctive, are irregular forms.
2. The past participle is irregular but well known in its use as the adjective "dead."
3. **Mourir** takes **être** in compound tenses, as does **naître** (to be born).

Il *est mort.*	He is *dead/has died.*
Jeanne d'Arc *mourut* en 1431.	Joan of Arc *died* in 1431.
On *a failli mourir* de peur.	We *nearly died* of fright.
C'est *à mourir* de rire.	It's *enough to make you die* laughing.
Il *devait mourir* plus tard de ses blessures.	He *was to die* later from his wounds.
On attend qu'il *meure.*	We're waiting for him to *die.*

Present participle	*Past participle*
mourant	mort

Past perfect	*Past anterior*
j'étais mort(-e)	je fus mort(-e)
Future	*Future perfect*
je mourrai	je serai mort(-e)
Conditional	*Conditional perfect*
je mourrais	je serais mort(-e)
Present subjunctive	*Perfect subjunctive*
que je meure	que je sois mort(-e)
Imperfect subjunctive	*Pluperfect subjunctive*
que je mourusse	que je fusse mort(-e)

Sans les soins de mon médicin, je *serais mort* il y a bien longtemps.	Without my doctor's care, I *would have died* ages ago.
Bien des enfants du Tiers Monde *meurent* avant l'âge de cinq ans.	Many children in the Third World *die* before the age of five.
Quelle tragédie que Chopin *soit mort* si jeune!	What a tragedy that Chopin *died* so young!

8i   Ouvrir, *to open*
Irregular -ir verb

Imperative

ouvre! (tu)   *ouvrez!* (vous)   *ouvrons!* (nous)

Present	**Perfect**
j'*ouvre*	j'ai *ouvert*
tu *ouvres*	tu as *ouvert*
il/elle *ouvre*	il/elle a *ouvert*
on *ouvre*	on a *ouvert*
nous *ouvrons*	nous avons *ouvert*
vous *ouvrez*	vous avez *ouvert*
ils/elles *ouvrent*	ils/elles ont *ouvert*

Imperfect	**Simple past**
j'*ouvrais*	j'ouvris
tu *ouvrais*	tu ouvris
il/elle *ouvrait*	il/elle ouvrit
on *ouvrait*	on ouvrit
nous *ouvrions*	nous ouvrîmes
vous *ouvriez*	vous ouvrîtes
ils/elles *ouvraient*	ils/elles ouvrirent

Similar verbs

couvrir	cover	**rouvrir**	open again
découvrir	discover	**souffrir**	suffer
offrir	offer		

Notes

1. Italicized forms show differences from model verb **finir** (➤8a).
2. This group displays a mixture of forms from the **-er** and **-ir** conjugations.

Present participle	Past participle
ouvrant	ouvert

Past perfect	Past anterior
j'avais *ouvert*	j'eus *ouvert*

Future	Future perfect
j'ouvrirai	j'aurai *ouvert*

Conditional	Conditional perfect
j'ouvrirais	j'aurais *ouvert*

Present subjunctive	Perfect subjunctive
que j'*ouvre*	que j'aie *ouvert*
que tu *ouvres*	

Imperfect subjunctive	Pluperfect subjunctive
que j'ouvrisse	que j'eusse *ouvert*

Ouvrez les fenêtres!

Open the windows!

Qu'est-ce qu'on t'*a offert* comme cadeau?

What present *did* they *give* you?

D'ici on *découvre* toute la ville.

You *can see* the whole town from here.

La police *a découvert* deux kilos de cannabis dans la voiture.

The police *discovered* two kilos of cannabis in the car.

Va *ouvrir*!

Go and *open* the door!

Le bureau *ouvre* à quelle heure?

What time *does* the office *open*?

Il nous *offrait* de séjourner chez lui.

He *offered* to put us up at his place. (Literally, *He was offering us a stay at his house.*)

Maintenant il *aura découvert* son erreur.

He *will have discovered* his mistake by now.

8j   Sentir, *to feel*
Irregular -ir verb

Imperative
sens! (tu)   *sentez!* (vous)   *sentons!* (nous)

Present	Perfect
je *sens*	j'ai senti
tu *sens*	tu as senti
il/elle *sent*	il/elle a senti
on *sent*	on a senti
nous *sentons*	nous avons senti
vous *sentez*	vous avez senti
ils/elles *sentent*	ils/elles ont senti

Imperfect	Simple past
je *sentais*	je sentis
tu *sentais*	tu sentis
il/elle *sentait*	il/elle sentit
on *sentait*	on sentit
nous *sentions*	nous sentîmes
vous *sentiez*	vous sentîtes
ils/elles *sentaient*	ils/elles sentirent

Similar verbs

mentir	lie; tell lies	**se repentir**	repent
partir	leave; go away	**sortir**	go out
ressentir	feel; experience		

Notes

1. Italicized forms show differences from model verb **finir** (➤8a).
2. **Sortir** and **partir**, plus their compounds, are also in this group, though these are all conjugated with **être** in compound tenses.

Present participle	Past participle
sentant	senti

Past perfect	Past anterior
j'avais senti	j'eus senti

Future	Future perfect
je sentirai	j'aurai senti

Conditional	Conditional perfect
je sentirais	j'aurais senti

Present subjunctive	Perfect subjunctive
que je *sente*	que j'aie senti
que tu *sentes*	
qu'il/elle *sente*	

Imperfect subjunctive	Pluperfect subjunctive
que je sentisse	que j'eusse senti

Je ne *me sens* pas très bien aujourd'hui.

I don't *feel* very well today.

Ce n'est pas vrai – tu m'*as menti*.

It isn't true – you *lied* to me.

. . . il est permis de *mentir* aux enfants quand c'est pour leur bien.
La Gloire de mon père (Marcel Pagnol)

. . . you are allowed *to lie* to children when it's for their own good.

"*Repens-toi*, Dieu te pardonnera!"
(Line from traditional song about St Nicholas)

"*Repent,* God will forgive you!"

Il *est sorti* tout à l'heure.

He just *went out*.

Le bateau *partira* à quatorze heures.

The boat *will leave* at 2:00 P.M.

8k   Tenir, *to hold*
Irregular -ir verb

Imperative

tiens! (tu)   tenez! (vous)   tenons! (nous)

Present	**Perfect**
je tiens	j'ai tenu
tu tiens	tu as tenu
il/elle tient	il/elle a tenu
on tient	on a tenu
nous tenons	nous avons tenu
vous tenez	vous avez tenu
ils/elles tiennent	ils/elles ont tenu

Imperfect	**Simple past**
je tenais	je tins
tu tenais	tu tins
il/elle tenait	il/elle tint
on tenait	on tint
nous tenions	nous tînmes
vous teniez	vous tîntes
ils/elles tenaient	ils/elles tinrent

Past perfect	**Past anterior**
j'avais tenu	j'eus tenu

Similar verbs

abstenir (s')	refrain; abstain	**maintenir**	maintain
appartenir	belong	**obtenir**	obtain
contenir	contain; hold; take	**retenir**	hold back
détenir	detain; hold	**soutenir**	support;
entretenir	maintain; keep; support		sustain

Notes

1. **Venir** and all its compounds are also in this group, but are conjugated with **être** in compound tenses (except **prévenir**, which is conjugated with **avoir**). Compounds are **convenir**; **devenir**; **intervenir**; **souvenir (se)**; **survenir**; and **redevenir**.
2. **Venir de faire** is an idiomatic expression meaning "to have done."

| **Present participle** | **Past participle** |
| tenant | tenu |

Future
je tiendrai

Future perfect
j'aurai tenu

Conditional
je tiendrais

Conditional perfect
j'aurais tenu

Present subjunctive
que je tienne
que tu tiennes
qu'il/elle tienne
qu'on tienne
que nous tenions
que vous teniez
qu'ils/elles tiennent

Perfect subjunctive
que j'aie tenu

Imperfect subjunctive
que je tinsse
que tu tinsses
qu'il tînt
que nous tinssions
que vous tinssiez
qu'ils/elles tinssent

Pluperfect subjunctive
que j'eusse tenu

Tu *viens* avec moi?

Are you *coming* with me?

Il *tenait à* faire votre connaissance.

He really *wanted to* meet you.

Il *est devenu* facteur.

He *became* a mailman.

Demain elle va *soutenir* sa thèse.

Tomorrow she's going to defend her thesis.

Je ne sais pas ce qui *me retient* de vous casser la figure.
La Gloire de mon père (Marcel Pagnol)

I don't know what'*s stopping* me from smashing your face in.

Examples of the use of **venir de faire:**
Le train *venait de partir.*

The train *had just left.*

'*Vient de paraître*'.

Just out/just published.

81   Vêtir, *to dress*

Irregular -ir verb

Imperative

vêts! (tu)	vêtez! (vous)	vêtons! (nous)

Present	**Perfect**
je vêts	j'ai vêtu
tu vêts	tu as vêtu
il/elle vêt	il/elle a vêtu
on vêt	on a vêtu
nous vêtons	nous avons vêtu
vous vêtez	vous avez vêtu
ils/elles vêtent	ils/elles ont vêtu

Imperfect	**Simple past**
je vêtais	je vêtis
tu vêtais	tu vêtis
il/elle vêtait	il/elle vêtit
on vêtait	on vêtit
nous vêtions	nous vêtîmes
vous vêtiez	vous vêtîtes
ils/elles vêtaient	ils/elles vêtirent

Similar verbs

dévêtir	undress	**revêtir**	put on; take on

Notes

1. The reflexive verb means "to get dressed," and is more usual with compound tenses conjugated with **être**, in common with all reflexive verbs.

Present participle vêtant	**Past participle** vêtu

Past participle j'avais vêtu	**Past anterior** j'eus vêtu
Future je vêtirai	**Future perfect** j'aurai vêtu
Conditional je vêtirais	**Conditional perfect** j'aurais vêtu
Present subjunctive que je vête	**Perfect subjunctive** que j'aie vêtu
Imperfect subjunctive que je vêtisse	**Pluperfect subjunctive** que j'eusse vêtu

Elle *s'est vêtue* en noir.	She *dressed* in black.
Revêts-toi vite!	Quick! *Put your clothes back on!*

-re verbs

9a   Vendre, *to sell*
Regular -re verb

Imperative
vends! (tu)   vendez! (vous)   vendons! (nous)

Present
je vends
tu vends
il/elle vend
on vend
nous vendons
vous vendez
ils/elles vendent

Perfect
j'ai vendu
tu as vendu
il/elle a vendu
on a vendu
nous avons vendu
vous avez vendu
ils/elles ont vendu

Imperfect
je vendais
tu vendais
il/elle vendait
on vendait
nous vendions
vous vendiez
ils/elles vendaient

Simple past
je vendis
tu vendis
il/elle vendit
on vendit
nous vendîmes
vous vendîtes
ils/elles vendirent

Past perfect
j'avais vendu
tu avais vendu
il/elle avait vendu
on avait vendu
nous avions vendu
vous aviez vendu
ils/elles avaient vendu

Past anterior
j'eus vendu
tu eus vendu
il/elle eut vendu
on eut vendu
nous eûmes vendu
vous eûtes vendu
ils/elles eurent vendu

Present participle	**Future perfect**
vendant	vendu

Future
je vendrai
tu vendras
il/elle vendra
on vendra
nous vendrons
vous vendrez
ils/elles vendront

Future perfect
j'aurai vendu
tu auras vendu
il/elle aura vendu
on aura vendu
nous aurons vendu
vous aurez vendu
ils/elles auront vendu

Conditional
je vendrais
tu vendrais
il/elle vendrait
on vendrait
nous vendrions
vous vendriez
ils/elles vendraient

Conditional perfect
j'aurais vendu
tu aurais vendu
il/elle aurait vendu
on aurait vendu
nous aurions vendu
vous auriez vendu
ils/elles auraient vendu

Present subjunctive
que je vende
que tu vendes
qu'il/elle vende
qu'on vende
que nous vendions
que vous vendiez
qu'ils/elles vendent

Perfect subjunctive
que j'aie vendu
que tu aies vendu
qu'il/elle ait vendu
qu'on ait vendu
que nous ayons vendu
que vous ayez vendu
qu'ils/elles aient vendu

Imperfect subjunctive
que je vendisse
que tu vendisses
qu'il/elle vendît
qu'on vendît
que nous vendissions
que vous vendissiez
qu'ils/elles vendissent

Pluperfect subjunctive
que j'eusse vendu
que tu eusses vendu
qu'il/elle eût vendu
qu'on eût vendu
que nous eussions vendu
que vous eussiez vendu
qu'ils/elles eussent vendu

Similar verbs

attendre	wait (for)	**prétendre**	claim
dépendre	depend	**répandre**	spread
descendre	to come/go down;	**répondre**	answer
	to take down	**rendre**	give back, render
entendre	hear	**suspendre**	hang, suspend
pendre	hang	**tondre**	cut (lawn)
pondre	lay (eggs)		

Notes

1. A large group of verbs follows this pattern of the regular **-re** conjugation.

2. There are, however, a lot of verbs with infinitives in **-re** which are irregular.

3. **Rompre** (to break) is conjugated like **vendre**, except that the third person singular of the present tense is **il rompt**, etc. Compounds **corrompre** (to corrupt, taint) and **interrompre** (to interrupt) follow this pattern.

4. **Vaincre** (to win, conquer) is conjugated like **vendre**, except that it requires **-qu-** in the plural of the present indicative and in all parts of the imperfect tenses, the simple past and the present subjunctive. **Convaincre** (to convince) has the same forms.

5. **Descendre** can be used as an inhansitive verb, using **être** as its auxilliary, or as a transitive verb, using **avoir** as its auxilliary.

– **Qu'est-ce que vous *attendez*?**

– What are you *waiting for?*

– **J'*ai entendu dire* qu'on allait vendre des cassettes et des CD ici au marché.**

– I've heard they're going to sell cassettes and CDs here in the market.

– **C'*est* vrai? A quelle heure?**

– *Is* that right? What time?

– **Je ne sais pas. Ça *dépend* . . .**

– I don't know. It *depends* . . .

– **Nous *descendions de* l'autobus quand le gangster l'*a descendu*.**

– We *were getting off* the bus when the gangster *shot* him *dead*. (*Literally, "felled him," "took him down."*)

9b Boire, *to drink*
Irregular -re verb

Imperative

bois! (tu)   buvez! (vous)   buvons! (nous)

Present
je bois
tu bois
il/elle boit
on boit
nous buvons
vous buvez
ils/elles boivent

Perfect
j'ai bu
tu as bu
il/elle a bu
on a bu
nous avons bu
vous avez bu
ils/elles ont bu

Imperfect
je buvais
tu buvais
il/elle buvait
on buvait
nous buvions
vous buviez
ils/elles buvaient

Simple past
je bus
tu bus
il/elle but
on but
nous bûmes
vous bûtes
ils/elles burent

Notes

1. This is the only verb of its type.

Present participle	*Past participle*
buvant	bu

Past perfect	*Past anterior*
j'avais bu	j'eus bu
Future	*Future perfect*
je boirai	j'aurai bu
Conditional	*Conditional perfect*
je boirais	j'aurais bu
Present subjunctive	*Perfect subjunctive*
que je boive	que j'aie bu
Imperfect subjunctive	*Pluperfect subjunctive*
que je busse	que j'eusse bu

J'en *boirai* cinq ou six bouteilles (Traditional song *Chevaliers de la table ronde*)

I'*ll drink* five or six bottles . . .

Il *a* trop *bu*.

He'*s had* too much to *drink*.

Tu *bois* du thé?

Do you *drink* tea?

Je ne *bois* pas d'alcool.

I *don't drink* alcohol.

Tant il *but* et mangea, le pauvre saint homme, qu'il mourut pendant la nuit . . .

So much *did* he eat and *drink,* the poor holy man, that he died during the night . . .

Allons boire un petit coup. (*Lettres de mon moulin,* Alphonse Daudet)

Let's go and have a drink.

9c Conclure, *to conclude*
Irregular -re verb

Imperative
conclus! (tu)   concluez! (vous)   concluons! (nous)

Present
je conclus
tu conclus
il/elle conclut
on conclut
nous concluons
vous concluez
ils/elles concluent

Perfect
j'ai conclu
tu as conclu
il/elle a conclu
on a conclu
nous avons conclu
vous avez conclu
ils/elles ont conclu

Imperfect
je concluais
tu concluais
il/elle concluait
on concluait
nous concluions
vous concluiez
ils/elles concluaient

Simple past
je conclus
tu conclus
il/elle conclut
on conclut
nous conclûmes
vous conclûtes
ils/elles conclurent

Similar verbs
exclure   turn out, put out   **inclure**   insert, include

Notes
1. **Inclure** (to insert, include) is conjugated like **conclure**, the only differences being that the past participle is **inclus**.

Present participle concluant	*Past participle* conclu

Past perfect j'avais conclu	*Past anterior* j'eus conclu
Future je conclurai	*Future perfect* j'aurai conclu
Conditional je conclurais	*Conditional perfect* j'aurais conclu
Present subjunctive que je conclue	*Perfect subjunctive* que j'aie conclu
Imperfect subjunctive que je conclusse	*Pluperfect subjunctive* que j'eusse conclu

Marché *conclu!*	It's a deal!
Les jurés *ont conclu* à sa culpabilité.	The jury *decided* he was guilty.
Vous trouverez *ci-inclus* le dossier que j'ai préparé.	You will find *enclosed* the file I prepared.
On *conclut* le traité de Versailles en 1919.	The treaty of Versailles *was signed* in 1919.
J'*ai conclu* mon article en donnant des statistiques.	I'*ve concluded* my article by giving some statistics.
On *exclut* votre participation à ce projet.	They *are refusing* to let you join in this project.
Il n'*est* pas *exclu* que je fasse partie du groupe.	It'*s* not *out of the question* for me to join the group.

9d   Conduire, *to drive, lead*
Irregular -re verb ending in -uire

Imperative
conduis! (tu)   conduisez! (vous)   conduisons! (nous)

Present	**Perfect**
je conduis	j'ai conduit
tu conduis	tu as conduit
il/elle conduit	il/elle a conduit
on conduit	on a conduit
nous conduisons	nous avons conduit
vous conduisez	vous avez conduit
ils/elles conduisent	ils/elles ont conduit

Imperfect	**Simple past**
je conduisais	je conduisis
tu conduisais	tu conduisis
il/elle conduisait	il/elle conduisit
on conduisait	on conduisit
nous conduisions	nous conduisîmes
vous conduisiez	vous conduisîtes
ils/elles conduisaient	ils/elles conduisirent

Similar verbs

construire	construct; build	**nuire**	harm
cuire	cook	**produire**	produce
introduire	introduce	**réduire**	reduce
luire	gleam; shine	**traduire**	translate

Notes

1. Verbs in this group include compounds of the verbs listed here (e.g., **reconstruire**, "to reconstruct.")
2. The past participles of **luire** and **nuire** are **lui** and **nui.**

Au restaurant	*At the restaurant*
– **Et le steak, vous le *prenez* comment?**	– How would you *like* your steak?
– **Bien *cuit*.**	– Well *done*.

Present participle	**Past participle**
conduisant	conduit
Past perfect	**Past anterior**
j'avais conduit	j'eus conduit
Future	**Future perfect**
je conduirai	j'aurai conduit
Conditional	**Conditional perfect**
je conduirais	j'aurais conduit
Present subjunctive	**Perfect subjunctive**
que je conduise	que j'aie conduit
Imperfect subjunctive	**Pluperfect subjunctive**
que je conduisisse	que j'eusse conduit

– Tiens! Je ne savais pas qu'on *avait construit* cet immeuble!
– Oui, c'est une compagnie italienne qui l'*a construit* et c'est moi qui *ai traduit* touts les documents.
– Ah bon? Mais tu *conduis* trop vite, tu sais.

– Wow! I didn't know they'*d built* that apartment house.
– Yes, it's an Italian company that *built it*, and I was the one who *translated* all the documents.
– Oh yes? But you'*re driving* too fast, you know.

– Quelle est cette lumière qui *luit* là-bas?
– Je crois que c'est l'aurore boréale que *produit* ces couleurs.

– What's that light *glowing* over there?
– I think it's the aurora borealis that's producing those colors.

9e   Connaître, *to know*
Irregular -re verb

Imperative

connais! (tu)   connaissez! (vous)   connaissons! (nous)

Present	**Perfect**
je connais	j'ai connu
tu connais	tu as connu
il/elle connaît	il/elle a connu
on connaît	on a connu
nous connaissons	nous avons connu
vous connaissez	vous avez connu
ils connaissent	ils/elles ont connu

Imperfect	**Simple past**
je connaissais	je connus
tu connaissais	tu connus
il/elle connaissait	il/elle connut
on connaissait	on connut
nous connaissions	nous connûmes
vous connaissiez	vous connûtes
ils/elles connaissaient	ils/elles connurent

Similar verbs

apparaître	appear
comparaître	appear (in court)
disparaître	disappear
paraître	to seem, appear
reconnaître	recognize

Notes

1. All compounds of **connaître** and **paraître** follow the pattern of **connaître**.

Present participle	*Past participle*
connaissant	connu

Past perfect	*Past anterior*
j'avais connu	j'eus connu
Future	*Future perfect*
je connaîtrai	j'aurai connu
Conditional	*Conditional perfect*
je connaîtrais	j'aurais connu
Present subjunctive	*Perfect subjunctive*
que je connaisse	que j'aie connu
Imperfect subjunctive	*Pluperfect subjunctive*
que je connusse	que j'eusse connu

Les causes de ce désastre ne sont pas encore connues.	The causes of this disaster *are*n't yet *known*.
Tu *connais* cet homme?	*Do* you *know* that man?
Il l'*a connue* à Paris.	He *met* her in Paris.
Je la *connaissais* déjà depuis cinq ans.	I'*d* already *known* her for five years.
Il doit *comparaître* devant le tribunal.	He has *to appear* before the court.
Il *parait* qu' ils *s'étaient connus* . . .	It *seems* that they *had got to know each other* . . .

9f   Coudre, *to sew*
Irregular -re verb

Imperative

couds! (tu)   cousez! (vous)   cousons! (nous)

Present	**Perfect**
je couds	j'ai cousu
tu couds	tu as cousu
il/elle coud	il/elle a cousu
on coud	on a cousu
nous cousons	nous avons cousu
vous cousez	nous avez cousu
ils/elles cousent	ils/elles ont cousu

Imperfect	**Simple past**
je cousais	je cousis
tu cousais	tu cousis
il/elle cousait	il/elle cousit
on cousait	on cousit
nous cousions	nous cousîmes
vous cousiez	vous cousîtes
ils/elles cousaient	ils/elles cousirent

Similar verbs

découdre	unpick
recoudre	sew up/back on again

Present participle cousant	**Past participle** cousu

Past perfect j'avais cousu	**Past anterior** j'eus cousu
Future je coudrai	**Future perfect** j'aurai cousu
Conditional je coudrais	**Conditional perfect** j'aurais cousu
Present subjunctive que je couse	**Perfect subjunctive** que j'aie cousu
Imperfect subjunctive que je cousisse	**Pluperfect subjunctive** que j'eusse cousu

Elle *a cousu* le bouton à la chemise.	She *sewed* the button on the shirt.
Tu pourrais me *recoudre* cet ourlet?	Could you *sew up* this seam *again* for me?
Elle *coud* une robe.	She'*s making* a dress.
Elle *avait recousu* tout le devant de la jupe.	She *had resewn* all the front of the skirt.
Je *découdrais* tout ça, si j'avais le temps.	I'*d undo* all that stitching, if I had the time.

9g Croire, *to believe*
Irregular -re verb

Imperative

crois! (tu)   croyez! (vous)   croyons! (nous)

Present	**Perfect**
je crois	j'ai cru
tu crois	tu as cru
il/elle croit	il/elle a cru
on croit	on a cru
nous croyons	nous avons cru
vous croyez	vous avez cru
ils/elles croient	ils/elles ont cru

Imperfect	**Simple past**
je croyais	je crus
tu croyais	tu crus
il/elle croyait	il/elle crut
on croyait	on crut
nous croyions	nous crûmes
vous croyiez	vous crûtes
ils/elles croyaient	ils/elles crurent

Notes

1. This is the only verb of this type.

Present participle	*Past participle*
croyant	cru

Past perfect	*Past anterior*
j'avais cru	j'eus cru
Future	*Future perfect*
je croirai	j'aurai cru
Conditional	*Conditional perfect*
je croirais	j'aurais cru
Present subjunctive	*Perfect subjunctive*
que je croie	que j'aie cru
que nous croyions	
Imperfect subjunctive	*Pluperfect subjunctive*
que je crusse	que j'eusse cru

– Tu *crois* qu'il arrivera bientôt?	– *Do* you *think* he'll arrive soon?
– Non, je ne *crois* pas.	– No, I *don*'t *think* so.
Je *croyais* qu'il allait te prêter mille euros.	I thought he was going to lend you a thousand euros.
Croyez-vous en Dieu?	*Do* you *believe* in God?
Je n'*aurais* jamais *cru* . . .	I *would* never *have thought* . . .

9h   Dire, *to say*
Irregular -re verb

Imperative

dis! (tu)   dites! (vous)   disons! (nous)

Present	**Perfect**
je dis	j'ai dit
tu dis	tu as dit
il/elle dit	il/elle a dit
on dit	on a dit
nous disons	nous avons dit
vous dites	vous avez dit
ils/elles disent	ils/elles ont dit

Imperfect	**Simple past**
je disais	je dis
tu disais	tu dis
il/elle disait	il/elle dit
on disait	on dit
nous disions	nous dîmes
vous disiez	vous dîtes
ils/elles disaient	ils/elles dirent

Similar verbs

contredire	contradict
interdire	forbid; prohibit
frire	fry
prédire	foretell, predict

Notes

1. Note similarities and differences between **dire**, **écrire**, **lire**.
2. **Suffire** (be sufficient) is conjugated like **dire**, except that the present indicative tense is **vous suffisez**, and the past participle is **suffi**.
3. **Frire** (fry) is found mainly in the past participle, **frit** (fried), and in the expression **faire frire** (fry food).

Que *dis*-tu?	What *do* you *say*?
	What *are* you *saying*?
Je lui *ai dit* de venir me voir.	I *told* him to come and see me.
***Dites*-lui bonjour de ma part.**	*Say* hello to her from me.

Present participle	Past participle
disant	dit

Past perfect	Past anterior
j'avais dit	j'eus dit

Future	Future perfect
je dirai	j'aurai dit

Conditional	Conditional perfect
je dirais	j'aurais dit

Present subjunctive	Perfect subjunctive
que je dise	que j'aie dit

Imperfect subjunctive	Pluperfect subjunctive
que je disse	que j'eusse dit

Il n'*a* rien *dit*.

He *did*n't *say* a thing.
(He *said* nothing.)

– On se voit à quelle heure?
– *Disons* cinq heures.

– What time shall we meet?
– *Let's say* five.

Et je *dirais* même plus . . .

And I'*d even go so far as to say* . . .

Louis X (*dit* le Hutin)

Louis X (*called* "the Quarrelsome")

Il n'y a plus rien *à dire*.

There's nothing more *to say*.

Comment *dit*-on en français . . ?

How do you *say* in French . . ?

Cela te *dit* d'aller au cinéma?

Do you *feel like* going to
the movies?

– Ça te *dit* quelque chose,
cette adresse?
– Non, ça ne me *dit* rien.

– Does that address *mean*
anything to you?
– No, it doesn't *ring a bell*.

– Veux-tu des pommes frites?
– Non, merci. Mon médecin me
les a interdites.

– Do you want some French fries?
– No, thanks. My doctor has
forbidden me (to eat) them.

9i   Ecrire, *to write*
Irregular -re verb

Imperative
écris! (tu)   écrivez! (vous)   écrivons! (nous)

Present
j'écris
tu écris
il/elle écrit
on écrit
nous écrivons
vous écrivez
ils/elles écrivent

Perfect
j'ai écrit
tu as écrit
il/elle a écrit
on a écrit
nous avons écrit
vous avez écrit
ils/elles ont écrit

Imperfect
j'écrivais
tu écrivais
il/elle écrivait
on écrivait
nous écrivions
vous écriviez
ils/elles écrivaient

Simple past
j'écrivis
tu écrivis
il/elle écrivit
on écrivit
nous écrivîmes
nous écrivîtes
ils/elles écrivirent

Similar verbs

circonscrire	contain; confine
décrire	describe
inscrire	note down; write down
prescrire	prescribe; stipulate
proscrire	ban; prohibit
récrire	write down again
réinscrire	reinscribe; reregister
retranscrire	retranscribe
souscrire	subscribe
transcrire	copy out; transcribe; transliterate

Present participle	*Past participle*
écrivant	écrit

Past perfect	*Past anterior*
j'avais écrit	j'eus écrit
Future	*Future perfect*
j'écrirai	j'aurai écrit
Conditional	*Conditional perfect*
j'écrirais	j'aurais écrit
Present subjunctive	*Perfect subjunctive*
que j'écrive	que j'aie écrit
Imperfect subjunctive	*Pluperfect subjunctive*
que j'écrivisse	que j'eusse écrit

Écris-moi vite.	*Write* soon.
Je lui *ai écrit* la semaine dernière.	I *wrote* to him last week.
Il faut que j'*écrive* une lettre.	I *must write* a letter.
Décrivez les voleurs.	*Describe* the thieves.
Ne pas dépasser la dose *prescrite*.	Do not exceed the *recommended* dose.

9j   Faire, *to do, make*
Irregular -re verb

Imperative
fais! (tu)   faites! (vous)   faisons! (nous)

Present	**Perfect**
je fais	j'ai fait
tu fais	tu as fait
il/elle fait	il/elle a fait
on fait	on a fait
nous faisons	nous avons fait
vous faites	vous avez fait
ils/elles font	ils/elles ont fait

Imperfect	**Simple past**
je faisais	je fis
tu faisais	tu fis
il/elle faisait	il/elle fit
on faisait	on fit
nous faisions	nous fîmes
vous faisiez	vous fîtes
ils/elles faisaient	ils/elles firent

Similar verbs

contrefaire	imitate, mimic
défaire	dismantle
redéfaire	undo, take off, unpick again
refaire	redo
satisfaire	satisfy
surfaire	overrate, overprice

Que *fais*-tu?	What *are* you *doing?*
Je *fais* mes devoirs.	I'*m doing* my homework.
Il *fait* la vaisselle tous les jours.	He *does* the dishwashing every day.
J'aime *faire du cheval.*	I like *horseback-riding.*
Faites le plein!	*Fill* up the tank!

Present participle	Past participle
faisant	fait

Past perfect	**Past anterior**
j'avais fait	j'eus fait
Future	**Future perfect**
je ferai	j'aurai fait
Conditional	**Conditional perfect**
je ferais	j'aurais fait
Present subjunctive	**Perfect subjunctive**
que je fasse	que j'aie fait
Imperfect subjunctive	**Pluperfect subjunctive**
que je fisse	que j'eusse fait

Il *fait* chaud.	It's hot (weather).
Quel temps *a*-t-il *fait* hier?	What *was* the weather like yesterday?
Tous les matins, on *faisait* une promenade ensemble.	Every morning we *used to* go for a walk together.
Que *feriez*-vous si votre père vendait la maison?	What *would you do* if your father sold the house?
Qu'est-ce tu *aurais fait* si je n'étais pas arrivé?	What *would* you *have done* if I hadn't arrived?
Je vais *faire du ski.*	I'm going *skiing.*
Que veux-tu que je *fasse?*	What do you want me to *do?*
Cela te *fera* du bien.	That *will do* you *good.*

9k Lire, *to read*
Irregular -re verb

Imperative
lis! (tu)   lisez! (vous)   lisons! (nous)

Present
je lis
tu lis
il/elle lit
on lit
nous lisons
vous lisez
ils/elles lisent

Perfect
j'ai lu
tu as lu
il/elle a lu
on a lu
nous avons lu
vous avez lu
ils/elles ont lu

Imperfect
je lisais
tu lisais
il/elle lisait
on lisait
nous lisions
vous lisiez
ils/elles lisaient

Simple past
je lus
tu lus
il/elle lut
on lut
nous lûmes
vous lûtes
ils/elles lurent

Similar verbs

élire   elect
réélire   reelect
relire   reread

Present participle	**Past participle**
lisant	lu

Past perfect	**Past anterior**
j'avais lu	j'eus lu

Future	**Future perfect**
je lirai	j'aurai lu

Conditional	**Conditional perfect**
je lirais	j'aurais lu

Present subjunctive	**Perfect subjunctive**
que je lise	que j'aie lu

Imperfect subjunctive	**Pluperfect subjunctive**
que je lusse	que j'eusse lu

Tu _as lu_ le journal?

Have you _read_ the paper?

Je _lis_ beaucoup de romans policiers.

I _read_ a lot of thrillers.

On l'_a élu_ président.

He _was elected_ president.

J'aimerais bien _relire_ Le Rouge et le Noir.

I'd really like to _read_ Le Rouge et le Noir _again_.

Lisez à haute voix . . .

Read aloud . . .

Tu sais _lire?_

Can you _read?_

Il alla prendre un abécédaire et je _lus_ sans difficulté plusieurs pages.
La Gloire de mon père
(Marcel Pagnol)

He went and got an alphabet book and I _read_ several pages without difficulty.

109

91   Mettre, *to put*
Irregular *-re* verb

Imperative

mets! (tu)   mettez! (vous)   mettons! (nous)

Present	**Perfect**
je *mets*	j'ai *mis*
tu *mets*	tu as *mis*
il/elle *met*	il/elle a *mis*
on *met*	on a *mis*
nous mettons	nous avons *mis*
vous mettez	vous avez *mis*
ils/elles mettent	ils/elles ont *mis*

Imperfect	**Simple past**
je mettais	je *mis*
tu mettais	tu *mis*
il/elle mettait	il/elle *mit*
on mettait	on *mit*
nous mettions	nous *mîmes*
vous mettiez	vous *mîtes*
ils/elles mettaient	ils/elles *mirent*

Similar verbs

admettre	admit	**permettre**	allow
commettre	commit	**promettre**	promise
compromettre	compromise	**réadmettre**	readmit
démettre	dislocate	**remettre**	put again
émettre	give/send out; emit	**retransmettre**	transmit again
entremettre (s')	mediate; intervene	**soumettre**	subject; subjugate
omettre	omit	**transmettre**	transmit

Notes

1. Italicized forms show differences from model verb **vendre** (➤9a).
2. **Battre** (to beat) and its compounds **combattre** (to combat), **abattre** (to slaughter; to dishearten) and others are conjugated exactly as **mettre** in all forms but the past participle, which is **battu (combattu, abattu)**.

Present participle	Past participle
mettant	mis

Past Perfect	Past anterior
j'avais *mis*	j'eus *mis*

Future	Future perfect
je mettrai	j'aurai *mis*

Conditional	Conditional perfect
je mettrais	j'aurais *mis*

Present subjunctive	Perfect subjunctive
que je *mette*	que j'aie *mis*

Imperfect subjunctive	Pluperfect subjunctive
que je *misse*	que j'eusse *mis*

Mettez-vous à ma place!	*Put* yourself in my position!
Où *as*-tu *mis* les billets?	Where *did* you *put* the tickets?
Je te *promets* qu'on ira à Paris.	I *promise* you we'll go to Paris.
Il ne veut rien *admettre*.	He won't *admit* a thing.
On ne me *permet* pas de sortir après neuf heures.	I'm not *allowed* to go out after nine.
On ne lui *permet* pas de sortir le soir.	They don't *allow* her to go out in the evening.
Je lui *ai permis* de m'accompagner.	I *allowed* him to go with me.
Va *mettre* la table!	Go and *lay* the table!
On *se bat*!	They're *fighting*!

9m   Moudre, *to grind*
Irregular -re verb

Imperative
mouds! (tu)   moulez! (vous)   moulons! (nous)

Present
je mouds
tu mouds
il/elle moud
on moud
nous moulons
vous moulez
ils/elles moulent

Perfect
j'ai moulu
tu as moulu
il/elle a moulu
on a moulu
nous avons moulu
vous avez moulu
ils/elles ont moulu

Imperfect
je moulais
tu moulais
il/elle moulait
on moulait
nous moulions
vous mouliez
ils/elles moulaient

Simple past
je moulus
tu moulus
il/elle moulut
on moulut
nous moulûmes
vous moulûtes
ils/elles moulurent

Similar verbs

émoudre   sharpen; grind
remoudre   grind again

Notes

1. The forms are very similar to those of **coudre**, the intervening consonant being **-l-** in **moudre** (**-s-** in **coudre**).

Present participle	***Past participle***
moulant	moulu

Past perfect	***Past anterior***
j'avais moulu	j'eus moulu
Future	***Future perfect***
je moudrai	j'aurai moulu
Conditional	***Conditional perfect***
je moudrais	j'aurais moulu
Present subjunctive	***Perfect subjunctive***
que je moule	que j'aie moulu
Imperfect subjunctive	***Pluperfect subjunctive***
que je moulusse	que j'eusse moulu

Je vais *moudre* du café.	I'm going *to grind* some coffee.
On l'*a moulu* de coups.	They *beat* him up.
Elle *moulait* du café pour ses invités.	She *was grinding* some coffee for her guests.
Il a dit qu'*il moudrait* du café pour ce soir.	He said he *would grind* some coffee for this evening.
Je *mouds* un peu de poivre.	I'*m grinding* a little pepper.

9n   Naître, *to be born*
Irregular -re verb

Imperative
nais! (tu)   naissez! (vous)   naissons! (nous)

Present
je nais
tu nais
il/elle naît
on naît
nous naissons
vous naissez
ils/elles naissent

Perfect
je suis né(-e)
tu es né(-e)
il est né
elle est née
on est né
nous sommes nés/nées
vous êtes né/née/nés/nées
ils sont nés
elles sont nées

Imperfect
je naissais
tu naissais
il/elle naissait
on naissait
nous naissions
vous naissiez
ils/elles naissaient

Simple past
je naquis
tu naquis
il/elle naquit
on naquit
nous naquîmes
vous naquîtes
ils/elles naquirent

Similar verbs

renaître   be born again; reborn, revived;
                            spring up again

Notes

1. This verb is not often found in the present or imperfect tenses; it appears most often found are the perfect and simple past forms.
2. It is conjugated with **être** in compound tenses.

Present participle	**Past participle**
naissant	né

Past perfect	**Past anterior**
j'étais né(-e)	je fus né(-e)

Future	**Future perfect**
je naîtrai	je serai né(-e)

Conditional	**Conditional perfect**
je naîtrais	je serais né(-e)

Present subjunctive	**Perfect subjunctive**
que je naisse	que je sois né(-e)

Imperfect subjunctive	**Pluperfect subjunctive**
que je naquisse	que je fusse né(-e)

– **Quel est votre lieu de naissance?**

– What is your place of birth?

– **Je *suis né* à Marseille.**

– I *was born* in Marseille.

Il *est né*, le divin enfant . . .
(*French traditional carol*)

He *is born*, the divine child . . .

Je ne savais pas qu'il *était né* en Corse.

I didn't know he *was born* in Corsica.

Tous nos enfants *sont nés* au Canada.

All our children *were born* in Canada.

9o Peindre, *to paint*
Irregular -re verb ending in -indre

Imperative

peins! (tu)   peignez! (vous)   peignons! (nous)

Present	**Perfect**
je peins	j'ai peint
tu peins	tu as peint
il/elle peint	il/elle a peint
on peint	on a peint
nous peignons	nous avons peint
vous peignez	vous avez peint
ils/elles peignent	ils/elles ont peint

Imperfect	**Simple past**
je peignais	je peignis
tu peignais	tu peignis
il/elle peignait	il/elle/on peignit
on peignait	on peignit
nous peignions	nous peignîmes
vous peigniez	vous peignîtes
ils/elles peignaient	ils/elles peignirent

Similar verbs

craindre	fear
dépeindre	depict
éteindre	extinguish, put out
étreindre	embrace, hug
plaindre	pity
(re)joindre	join (again)
repeindre	repaint

Notes

1. **Se plaindre** (to complain), a reflexive verb (conjugated with **être** in compound tenses), follows the same pattern.
2. **Craindre** and **plaindre** take **craint** and **plaint** as their past participles.
3. **Rejoindre** takes **rejoint** as its past participle.

Present participle	**Past participle**
peignant	peint

Past perfect	**Past anterior**
j'avais peint	j'eus peint

Future	**Future perfect**
je peindrai	j'aurai peint

Conditional	**Conditional perfect**
je peindrais	j'aurais peint

Present subjunctive	**Perfect subjunctive**
que je peigne	j'aie peint

Imperfect subjunctive	**Pluperfect subjunctive**
que je peignisse	que j'eusse peint

Franchement, je le *plains*.	Quite honestly, I *feel sorry for* him.
De quoi te *plains*-tu?	What are you *complaining* about?
J'*ai repeint* l'appartement.	I'*ve repainted* the apartment.
Monet *peignait* très souvent sa femme.	Monet often *painted* his wife.
Elle a eteint sa cigarette.	She put out her cigarette.
"Pour faire le portrait d'un oiseau *peindre* d'abord une cage avec une porte ouverte." *Paroles* (Jacques Prévert)	"To paint a portrait of a bird, first *paint* a cage with an open door."
Nous nous *sommes rejoints* à Nice.	We *rejoined each other* in Nice.
Que *craignez vous*?	What *are you afraid of*?

9p   Plaire, *to please*
Irregular -re verb

Imperative
plais! (tu)   plaisez! (vous)   plaisons! (nous)

Present
je plais
tu plais
il/elle plaît
on plaît
nous plaisons
vous plaisez
ils/elles plaisent

Perfect
j'ai plu
tu as plu
il/elle a plu
on a plu
nous avons plu
vous avez plu
ils ont plu

Imperfect
je plaisais
tu plaisais
il/elle plaisait
on plaisait
nous plaisions
vous plaisiez
ils/elles plaisaient

Simple past
je plus
tu plus
il/elle plut
on plut
nous plûmes
vous plûtes
ils/elles plurent

Similar verbs

déplaire   displease
taire   be silent

Notes

1. **Taire** has no accent on the third-person singular present tense: **il se tait**..

Present participle plaisant	*Past participle* plu

Past perfect j'avais plu	*Past anterior* j'eus plu
Future je plairai	*Future perfect* j'aurai plu
Conditional je plairais	*Conditional perfect* j'aurais plu
Present subjunctive que je plaise	*Perfect subjunctive* que j'aie plu
Imperfect subjunctive que je plusse	*Pluperfect subjunctive* que j'eusse plu

S'il vous *plaît*.	*Please.*
Il me *plaît* beaucoup.	I *like* him a lot. (*Literally,* "He *pleases me.*")
Taisez-vous, les enfants.	*Be quiet*, children.
Ils *se sont tus*.	They *fell silent*.
Ça me *plairait* beaucoup que tu viennes.	I'*d* really *like* you to come.
J'ai essayé de lui *plaire*.	I *tried* to please her.

9q Prendre, *to take*
Irregular -re verb

Imperative
prends! (tu) prenez! (vous) prenons! (nous)

Present
je prends
tu prends
il/elle prend
on prend
nous prenons
vous prenez
ils/elles prennent

Perfect
j'ai pris
tu as pris
il/elle a pris
on a pris
nous avons pris
vous avez pris
ils/elles ont pris

Imperfect
je prenais
tu prenais
il/elle prenait
on prenait
nous prenions
vous preniez
ils/elles prenaient

Simple past
je pris
tu pris
il/elle prit
on prit
nous prîmes
vous prîtes
ils/elles prirent

Similar verbs

apprendre learn
(s')éprendre fall in love
comprendre understand; consist of

entreprendre begin; undertake embark upon
réapprendre relearn
reprendre resume; recapture
surprendre surprise

Qu'est-ce que tu *prends*? What are you *having* (to drink)?

J'ai toujours mal à la tête, mais j'*ai pris* des comprimés. I have still got a headache, but I've *taken* some tablets.

Où *as*-tu *appris* à nager? Where *did* you *learn* to swim?

Present participle	**Past participle**
prenant	pris

Past perfect
j'avais pris

Past anterior
j'eus pris

Future
je prendrai

Future perfect
j'aurai pris

Conditional
je prendrais

Conditional perfect
j'aurais pris

Present subjunctive
que je prenne
que tu prennes
qu'il/elle prenne
qu'on prenne
que nous prenions
que vous preniez
qu'ils/elles prennent

Perfect subjunctive
que j'aie pris

Imperfect subjunctive
que je prisse

Pluperfect subjunctive
que j'eusse pris

Tu veux un biscuit?
Prends-en deux!

Do you want a biscuit?
Take two!

J'aime ce pull
— je le _prends_.

I like this sweater
— I'll _take_ it.

Cela lui _apprendra_ à vivre.

That _will teach_ him a lesson.

Le service n'est pas _compris_.

Service is not _included_.

Quand il parle anglais,
personne ne le _comprend_.

When he speaks English,
no one _understands_ him.

Je n'_ai_ rien _compris_
— comment veux-tu que je
comprenne?

I _did_n't _understand_ a thing
— how to you expect me to
understand?

9r   Résoudre, *to resolve*
Irregular -re verb

Imperative
résous! (tu)   résolvez! (vous)   résolvons! (nous)

Present
je résous
tu résous
il/elle résout
on résout
nous résolvons
vous résolvez
ils/elles résolvent

Perfect
j'ai résolu
tu as résolu
il/elle a résolu
on a résolu
nous avons résolu
vous avez résolu
ils/elles ont résolu

Imperfect
je résolvais
tu résolvais
il/elle résolvait
on résolvait
nous résolvions
vous résolviez
ils/elles résolvaient

Simple past
je résolus
tu résolus
il/elle résolut
on résolut
nous résolûmes
vous résolûtes
ils/elles résolurent

Similar verbs

absoudre   absolve; pardon
dissoudre   dissolve

Present participle	**Past participle**
résolvant	résolu

Past perfect	**Past anterior**
j'avais résolu	j'eus résolu
Future	**Future perfect**
je résoudrai	j'aurai résolu
Conditional	**Conditional perfect**
je résoudrais	j'aurais résolu
Present subjunctive	**Perfect subjunctive**
que je résolve	que j'aie résolu
Imperfect subjunctive	**Pluperfect subjunctive**
que je résolusse	que j'eusse résolu

Il n'*a* pas *résolu* le problème.	He *has*n't *solved* the problem.
Je *me suis résolu* à quitter la compagnie.	I *made up my mind* to leave the company.
Il faut faire *dissoudre* le sel dans de l'eau.	You have to *dissolve* the salt in water.
Elle *a résolu* de partir.	She'*s made up her mind* to leave.
Je vous *absous*!	I *forgive* you!

9s   Rire, *to laugh*
Irregular -re verb

Imperative
ris! (tu)   riez! (vous)   rions! (nous)

Present
je ris
tu ris
il/elle rit
on rit
nous rions
vous riez
ils/elles rient

Perfect
j'ai ri
tu as ri
il/elle a ri
on a ri
nous avons ri
vous avez ri
ils ont ri

Imperfect
je riais
tu riais
il/elle riait
on riait
nous riions
vous riiez
ils/elles riaient

Simple past
je ris
tu ris
il/elle rit
on rit
nous rîmes
vous rîtes
ils/elles rirent

Similar verbs

sourire   smile

Present participle riant	**Past participle** ri

Past perfect j'avais ri	**Past anterior** j'eus ri
Future je rirai	**Future perfect** j'aurai ri
Conditional je rirais	**Conditional perfect** j'aurais ri
Present subjunctive que je rie	**Perfect subjunctive** que j'aie ri
Imperfect subjunctive que je risse	**Pluperfect subjunctive** que j'eusse ri

"Tu *souriais,*
et moi je *souriais* de même."
Barbara (Jacques Prévert)

"You *were smiling,*
and I *smiled* too."

Rira bien qui *rira* le dernier.

He who *laughs* last *laughs* best.

Ne *riez* pas.

Don't *laugh.*

On s'est tordu de *rire.*

We cracked up laughing.

On *a* bien *ri.*

We *had* a good *laugh.*

Elle *riait* de lui.

She *was laughing* at him.

Tu *ris* — pourquoi?

You'*re laughing* — why?

Ils *rient* aux éclats!

They'*re roaring with laughter!*

9t soustraire, *to subtract*
Irregular -re verb

Imperative
soustrais! (tu)   soustrayez! (vous)   soustrayons! (nous)

Present
je soustrais
tu soustrais
il/elle soustrait
on soustrait
nous soustrayons
vous soustrayez
ils/elles soustraient

Perfect
j'ai soustrait
tu as soustrait
il/elle a soustrait
on a soustrait
nous avons soustrait
vous avez soustrait
ils/elles ont soustrait

Imperfect
je soustrayais
tu soustrayais
il/elle soustrayait
on soustrayait
nous soustrayions
vous soustrayiez
ils/elles soustrayaient

Simple past
—

Similar verbs

abstraire	abstract
distraire	entertain; divert
extraire	extract

Present participle	**Past participle**
soustrayant	soustrait

Past perfect   **Past anterior**
j'avais soustrait   j'eus soustrait

Future   **Future perfect**
je soustrairai   j'aurai soustrait

Conditional   **Conditional perfect**
je soustrairais   j'aurais soustrait

Present subjunctive   **Perfect subjunctive**
que je soustraie   que j'aie soustrait

Imperfect subjunctive   **Pluperfect subjunctive**
—   que j'eusse soustrait

On *trait* les vaches à cinq heures.   We *milk* the cows at five o'clock.

J'aime regarder la télé   I like watching TV for
pour me *distraire.*   *entertainment.*

On *extrait* le charbon ici.   They *mine* coal here.

Dans le passé on *extrayait*   In the past they *quarried*
le marbre.   marble.

Tu m'*as distrait.*   You *distracted* me.

Soustrayez dix dollars de   *Subtract* ten dollars from
notre compte.   our bill.

9u   Suivre, *to follow*
Irregular -re verb

Imperative
suis! (tu)   suivez! (vous)   suivons! (nous)

Present	**Perfect**
je suis	j'ai suivi
tu suis	tu as suivi
il/elle suit	il/elle a suivi
on suit	on a suivi
nous suivons	nous avons suivi
vous suivez	vous avez suivi
ils/elles suivent	ils/elles ont suivi

Imperfect	**Simple past**
je suivais	je suivis
tu suivais	tu suivis
il/elle suivait	il/elle suivit
on suivait	on suivit
nous suivions	nous suivîmes
vous suiviez	vous suivîtes
ils/elles suivaient	ils/elles suivirent

Similar verbs

poursuivre   pursue

Notes

1. **S'ensuivre** (to result, ensue) is also conjugated this way (using **être** in compound tenses).
2. There is rarely confusion between the two meanings of **je suis** (I am/I follow); the context normally makes the sense clear.

Present participle	**Past participle**
suivant	suivi
Past perfect	**Past anterior**
j'avais suivi	j'eus suivi
Future	**Future perfect**
je suivrai	j'aurai suivi
Conditional	**Conditional perfect**
je suivrais	j'aurais suivi
Present subjunctive	**Perfect subjunctive**
que je suive	que j'aie suivi
Imperfect subjunctive	**Pluperfect subjunctive**
que je suivisse	que j'eusse suivi

Suivez-moi, s'il vous plaît!	*Follow* me, please.
Ce chien nous *suit* depuis une heure.	This dog *has been following* us for an hour.
La police *a poursuivi* les voleurs.	The police *pursued* the thieves
A suivre.	*To be continued.*
Il *a été poursuivi* en justice.	He *was prosecuted.*

9v   Vaincre, *to defeat*
Irregular -re verb

Imperative

vaincs! (tu)   vainquez! (vous)   vainquons! (nous)

Present
je vaincs
tu vaincs
il/elle vainc
on vainc
nous vainquons
vous vainquez
ils/elles vainquent

Perfect
j'ai vaincu
tu as vaincu
il/elle a vaincu
on a vaincu
nous avons vaincu
vous avez vaincu
ils/elles ont vaincu

Imperfect
je vainquais
tu vainquais
il/elle vainquait
on vainquait
nous vainquions
vous vainquiez
ils/elles vainquaient

Simple past
je vainquis
tu vainquis
il/elle vainquit
on vainquit
nous vainquîmes
vous vainquîtes
ils/elles vainquirent

Similar verbs

convaincre   convince

Notes

1. In front of a vowel (except **-u-**) the **-c-** of **vaincre** changes to **-qu-**.

Present participle	**Past participle**
vainquant	vaincu

Past perfect	**Past anterior**
j'avais vaincu	j'eus vaincu

Future
je vaincrai

Future perfect
j'aurai vaincu

Conditional
je vaincrais

Conditional perfect
j'aurais vaincu

Present subjunctive
que je vainque

Perfect subjunctive
que j'aie vaincu

Imperfect subjunctive
que je vainquisse

Pluperfect subjunctive
que j'eusse vaincu

Il m'*a convaincu* d'abandonner le projet.
He *convinced* me to give up the project.

Nous *avons vaincu!*
We *won!*

Je ne *suis* pas *convaincu.*
I'*m* not *convinced.*

Nous *vaincrons!*
We *shall win!*

Il *va vaincre* la maladie.
He *will overcome* the illness.

Il *était vaincu* d'avance.
He *was defeated* before he started.

Wellington *vainquit* à Waterloo.
Wellington *won* at Waterloo.

9w   Vivre, *to live*
   Irregular -re verb

Imperative
vis! (tu)   vivez! (vous)   vivons! (nous)

Present
je vis
tu vis
il/elle vit
on vit
nous vivons
vous vivez
ils/elles vivent

Perfect
j'ai vécu
tu as vécu
il/elle a vécu
on a vécu
nous avons vécu
vous avez vécu
ils/elles ont vécu

Imperfect
je vivais
tu vivais
il/elle vivait
on vivait
nous vivions
vous viviez
ils/elles vivaient

Simple past
je vécus
tu vécus
il/elle vécut
on vécut
nous vécûmes
vous vécûtes
ils/elles vécurent

Similar verbs

revivre   live again
survivre   survive

Present participle	**Past participle**
vivant	vécu

Past perfect	**Past anterior**
j'avais vécu	j'eus vécu
Future	**Future perfect**
je vivrai	j'aurai vécu
Conditional	**Conditional perfect**
je vivrais	j'aurais vécu
Present subjunctive	**Perfect subjunctive**
que je vive	que j'aie vécu
Imperfect subjunctive	**Pluperfect subjunctive**
que je vécusse	que j'eusse vécu

Tant que je *vivrai* . . .	As long as I *live* . . .
Il *a vécu* à Rome.	He *lived* in Rome.
En 1883, Gauguin *vivait* à Paris	In 1883, Gauguin *was living* in Paris.
On a juste de quoi *vivre.*	We have just enough *to live* on.
Nous *vivons* chez nos parents.	We *live* at our parents' house.
Pétrarque *vécut* en Provence.	Petrarch *lived* in Provence.
Ils n'*avaient* jamais *vécu* à Paris.	They *had* never *lived* in Paris.
Je ne crois pas qu'il sur*vive* très longtemps.	I don't think he'*ll survive* for long.

-oir verbs

10a   s'asseoir, *to sit down*
Irregular reflexive verb in -oir

Imperative
assieds-toi! (tu)   asseyez-vous! (vous)   asseyons-nous (nous)

Present
je m'assieds (m'assois)
tu t'assieds (t'assois)
il/elle s'assied (s'assoit)
on s'assied (s'assoit)
nous nous asseyons
vous vous asseyez
ils/elles s'asseyent (assoient)

Perfect
je me suis assis(-e)
tu t'es assis(-e)
il s'est assis
elle s'est assise
on s'est assis
nous nous sommes assis(-es)
vous vous êtes assis(-e)(-es)
ils se sont assis
elles se sont assises

Imperfect
je m'asseyais
tu t'asseyais
il/elle s'asseyait
on s'asseyait
nous nous asseyions
vous vous asseyiez
ils/elles s'asseyaient

Simple past
je m'assis
tu t'assis
il/elle s'assit
on s'assit
nous nous assîmes
vous vous assîtes
ils/elles s'assirent

Notes

1. This verb is the only one of its kind. Where two forms exist, the first is more common; those with **-oi-** are much less common.

Present participle asseyant/assoyant	*Past participle* assis

Past perfect
je m'étais assis(-e)

Past anterior
je me fus assis(-e)

Future
je m'asseyerai or
je m'assiérai

Future perfect
je me serai assis(-e)

Conditional
je m'asseyerais or
je m'assoirais

Conditional perfect
je me serais assis(-e)

Present subjunctive
que je m'asseye or
que je m'assoie

Perfect subjunctive
que je me sois assis(-e)

Imperfect subjunctive
que je m'assisse

Pluperfect subjunctive
que je me fusse assis(-e)

**Asseyons-nous devant le feu,
où il fait chaud.**

Lets sit down in front of the fire,
where it's warm.

Asseyez-vous, les enfants.

Sit down, children.

Je *me suis assis* devant lui.

I *sat down* in front of him.

Où voulez-vous *vous asseoir?*

Where do you want to *sit?*

10b   Devoir, *to have to*
Irregular modal verb in -oir

Imperative

| dois! (tu) | devez! (vous) | devons! (nous) |

Present
je dois
tu dois
il/elle doit
on doit
nous devons
vous devez
ils/elles doivent

Perfect
j'ai dû
tu as dû
il/elle a dû
on a dû
nous avons dû
vous avez dû
ils/elles ont dû

Imperfect
je devais
tu devais
il/elle devait
on devait
nous devions
vous deviez
ils/elles devaient

Simple past
je dus
tu dus
il/elle dut
on dut
nous dûmes
vous dûtes
ils/elles durent

Notes

1. The imperative is rarely found.
2. If the past participle requires a feminine agreement, the spelling is **due.**
3. As a full verb, **devoir** means "to owe."
4. It is the only verb of its type, though similarities with **pouvoir** and **vouloir** will be obvious (➤10e, 10k).

Examples of use as a full verb

| **Je lui *dois* 50 euros.** | I *owe* her 50 euros. |
| **Il me *devait* 60 euros.** | He *owed* me 60 euros. |

136

Present participle	Past participle
devant	dû

Past perfect	Past anterior
j'avais dû	j'eus dû

Future	Future perfect
je devrai	j'aurai dû

Conditional	Conditional perfect
je devrais	j'aurais dû

Present subjunctive	Perfect subjunctive
que je doive	que j'aie dû

Imperfect subjunctive	Pluperfect subjunctive
que je dusse	que j'eusse dû

Examples of use as a modal verb

Tu *dois* y arriver avant huit heures.	You *must* get there by eight o'clock.
On *doit* écouter les instructions.	We *must* listen to the instructions.
On *devra* partir à l'aube.	We'*ll have to* leave at dawn.
Il *a dû* travailler jusqu'à minuit.	He *had to* work until midnight.
Il *a dû* avoir un accident.	He *must have* had an accident.
Elle *devait* l'accompagner en vacances.	She *was supposed* to go on vacation with him.
On *devrait* téléphoner tout de suite.	Someone *ought to* phone immediately.
Tu *aurais dû* lui offrir des fleurs.	You *ought to have* given her some flowers.

10c Falloir, *to have to*
Irregular impersonal modal verb in -oir

Imperative

—

| **Present** | **Perfect** |
| il faut | il a fallu |

| **Imperfect** | **Simple past** |
| il fallait | il fallut |

Notes

1. This verb only exists in the third-person singular, and covers meanings from "it is necessary," "one must", to "we have to", "you have to."
2. **Il me faut** means "I need." (The addition of the personal indirect object pronoun personalizes the meaning.)

Il *faut* appeler les pompiers.	We *have to* call the fire department.
Il *faut* arriver à l'heure.	You *must* arrive on time.
Il *faut* que je voie mes cousins.	I *must* see my cousins.
Il *a fallu* nettoyer la maison.	We *had to* clean the house (and we did).
Il *faudrait* acheter du pain.	We *ought to* buy some bread.

Present participle	*Past participle*
—	fallu

Past perfect	*Past anterior*
il avait fallu	il eut fallu

Future	*Future perfect*
il faudra	il aura fallu

Conditional	*Conditional perfect*
il faudrait	il aurait fallu

Present subjunctive	*Perfect subjunctive*
qu'il faille	qu'il ait fallu

Imperfect subjunctive	*Pluperfect subjunctive*
qu'il fallût	qu'il eut fallu

Si Dieu n'existait pas, il faudrait l'inventer. (Voltaire)	If God did not exist, we *would have* to invent him.
Il me faut des oeufs.	I *need* some eggs.
Il ne faut pas courir!	We don't *need* to run!
Il ne faut jamais nager seul.	You *should* never swim alone.
Il aurait fallu téléphoner plus tôt.	Someone *ought to have* phoned earlier.
Il fallut signer l'Armistice en juin 1940.	It *was necessary* to sign the Armistice in June 1940.

10d   Pleuvoir, *to rain*
Irregular impersonal verb in -oir

Imperative
—

| **Present** | **Perfect** |
| il pleut | il a plu |

| **Imperfect** | **Simple past** |
| il pleuvait | il plut |

Notes

1. This impersonal verb is normally only found in the third-person singular. Occasionally a figurative usage may give rise to a plural verb. Example: **Les coups de fusil pleuvent sur les hommes**, "Gunfire rained down on the men."
2. There are no other verbs like it.

Present participle pleuvant	**Past participle** plu

Past perfect il avait plu	**Past anterior** il eut plu
Future il pleuvra	**Future perfect** il aura plu
Conditional il pleuvrait	**Conditional perfect** il aurait plu
Present subjunctive qu'il pleuve	**Perfect subjunctive** qu'il ait plu
Imperfect subjunctive qu'il plût	**Pluperfect subjunctive** qu'il eût plu

Il *pleut*.	It's *raining*.
Il va *pleuvoir*.	It's going *to rain*.
Il a *plu* hier.	It *rained* yesterday.
J'espère qu'il ne *pleuvra* pas au mois de juillet.	I hope it *won't rain* in July.
Il *pleuvait* toute la journée.	It *was raining* all day long.
Il a dit qu'il *pleuvrait*.	He said it *would rain*.
Elle m'a dit qu'il *avait plu* longtemps.	She told me it *had rained* for a long time.

10e   Pouvoir, *to be able*
Irregular modal verb in -oir

Imperative

—

Present	Perfect
je peux/je puis	j'ai pu
tu peux	tu as pu
il/elle peut	il/elle a pu
on peut	on a pu
nous pouvons	nous avons pu
vous pouvez	vous avez pu
ils/elles peuvent	ils/elles ont pu

Imperfect	Simple past
je pouvais	je pus
tu pouvais	tu pus
il/elle pouvait	il/elle put
on pouvait	on put
nous pouvions	nous pûmes
vous pouviez	vous pûtes
ils/elles pouvaient	ils/elles purent

Notes

1. There are no other verbs like **pouvoir**, though similarities with **devoir** and **vouloir** will be evident (➤10b, 10k, respectively).
2. The various tenses of **pouvoir** convey a full variety of meanings.
3. **Puis-je?** "May I?" is going out of use and is often considered old-fashioned.

Present participle	**Past participle**
pouvant	pu
Past perfect	**Past anterior**
j'avais pu	j'eus pu
Future	**Future perfect**
je pourrai	j'aurai pu
Conditional	**Conditional perfect**
je pourrais	j'aurais pu
Present subjunctive	**Perfect subjunctive**
que je puisse	que j'aie pu
que nous puissions	
Imperfect subjunctive	**Pluperfect subjunctive**
que je pusse	que j'eusse pu

Je *peux* entrer?	*May* I come in?
Il ne *peut* pas fermer cette fenêtre.	He *can*'t close that window.
On *peut* aller à la patinoire.	We *can* go to the skating rink.
On *pourra* y aller en voiture.	We'*ll be able to* go there by car.
Il *pourrait* pleuvoir plus tard.	It *might* rain later.
***Pourriez*-vous me passer le sel?**	*Could* you pass me the salt?
À l'époque on *pouvait* y acheter toutes sortes de choses.	At the time you *could* buy all sorts of things there.
Tu *aurais pu* me le dire!	You *could have* told me!
J'*ai pu* réparer la serrure.	I'*ve managed* to fix the lock.
Je regrette qu'on ne *puisse* plus y aller.	I'm sorry you *can*'t go there any more.

10f Promouvoir, *to promote, encourage*
Irregular verb in -oir

Imperative

promeus! (tu)   promouvez! (vous)   promouvons! (nous)

Present	**Perfect**
je promeus	j'ai promu
tu promeus	tu as promu
il/elle promeut	il/elle a promu
on promeut	on a promu
nous promouvons	nous avons promu
vous promouvez	vous avez promu
ils/elles promeuvent	ils/elles ont promu

Imperfect	**Simple past**
je promouvais	je promus
tu promouvais	tu promus
il/elle promouvait	il/elle promut
on promouvait	on promut
nous promouvions	nous promûmes
vous promouviez	vous promûtes
ils promouvaient	ils promurent

Similar verbs

émouvoir   affect; disturb; arouse
mouvoir   move

Notes

1. **Promouvoir** is found most frequently in the infinitive and compound tenses.

Present participle	**Past participle**
promouvant	promu

Past perfect	**Past anterior**
j'avais promu	j'eus promu

Future	**Future perfect**
je promouvrai	j'aurai promu

Conditional	**Conditional perfect**
je promouvrais	j'aurais promu

Present subjunctive	**Perfect subjunctive**
que je promeuve	que j'aie promu

Imperfect subjunctive	**Pluperfect subjunctive**
que je promusse	que j'eusse promu

On m'*a promu.*	I've been *promoted.*
Il faut *promouvoir* l'étude des langues vivantes.	It's necessary to *encourage* the study of modern languages.
Je *suis ému.*	I *am overcome* (*with emotion*).
Cette musique m'*a* toujours *ému.*	This music *has* always *moved* me.
La misère de ces pauvres gens l'*émouvait* profondément.	The poverty of those poor folk *moved* him deeply.
Les grèves de 1995 *émurent* profondément la population Française.	The strike in 1995 deeply *troubled* the French people.

10g Recevoir, *to receive*
Irregular -oir verb ending in -cevoir

Imperative

reçois! (tu)   recevez! (vous)   recevons! (nous)

Present	**Perfect**
je reçois	j'ai reçu
tu reçois	tu as reçu
il/elle reçoit	il/elle a reçu
on reçoit	on a reçu
nous recevons	nous avons reçu
vous recevez	vous avez reçu
ils/elles reçoivent	ils/elles ont reçu

Imperfect	**Simple past**
je recevais	je reçus
tu recevais	tu reçus
il/elle recevait	il/elle reçut
on recevait	on reçut
nous recevions	nous reçûmes
vous receviez	vous reçûtes
ils/elles recevaient	ils/elles reçurent

Similar verbs

apercevoir	notice; see	**concevoir**	imagine; conceive
décevoir	deceive; disappoint	**percevoir**	perceive; detect; make out

Notes

1. As usual the cedilla is required whenever **c** precedes **o** or **u**.

Present participle	***Past participle***
recevant	reçu

Past perfect	***Past anterior***
j'avais reçu	j'eus reçu
Future	***Future perfect***
je recevrai	j'aurai reçu
Conditional	***Conditional perfect***
je recevrais	j'aurais reçu
Present subjunctive	***Perfect subjunctive***
que je reçoive	que j'aie reçu
qu'ils/elles reçoivent	
Imperfect subjunctive	***Pluperfect subjunctive***
que je reçusse	que j'eusse reçu

Le courier	*The mail*
– Tous les matins, je *reçois* au moins trois factures.	– Every morning I *receive* at least three bills.
– Qu'est-ce que vous *avez reçu* ce matin?	– What *have* you *received* this morning?
– Rien! Mais je n'*ai* pas encore *aperçu* le facteur.	– Nothing! But I *have*n't yet *caught sight of* the mailman/ postman.
Tu *recevras* ma lettre demain.	You'*ll receive* my letter tomorrow.
Tu l'*aurais reçue* ce matin si je l'avais postée en ville.	You *would have received* it this morning if I'd posted it in town.
On *a reçu* le maire.	They *entertained* the mayor.
D'ici on *aperçoit* le sommet de la montagne.	From here you *can* just *glimpse* the mountain top.

10h   Savoir, *to know*
Irregular modal verb in *-oir*

Imperative

sache! (tu)   sachez! (vous)   sachons! (nous)

Present	**Perfect**
je sais	j'ai su
tu sais	tu as su
il/elle sait	il/elle a su
on sait	on a su
nous savons	nous avons su
vous savez	vous avez su
ils/elles savent	ils/elles ont su

Imperfect	**Simple past**
je savais	je sus
tu savais	tu sus
il/elle savait	il/elle sut
on savait	on sut
nous savions	nous sûmes
vous saviez	vous sûtes
ils/elles savaient	ils/elles surent

Notes

1. This verb is important in two areas: (i) it is used for knowing a fact; (ii) it also has the meaning of "to be able," in the sense of having acquired a skill.

2. It should not be used for knowing people, countries, or works of art, music, theater, literature etc., where the correct verb is **connaître** (➤9e).

Examples of use as a full verb

– **Quelle heure est-il?**	– What time is it?
– **Je ne *sais* pas.**	– I *don't know.*
Je ne *savais* pas qu'il était à New York.	I *didn't know* he was in New York.
Je ne veux pas qu'on *sache* mon nom.	I don't want anyone to *know* my name.
Il *a su* son nom.	He *found out* her name.

Present participle	Past participle
sachant	su

Past perfect	Past anterior
j'avais su	j'eus su

Future	Future perfect
je saurai	j'aurai su

Conditional	Conditional perfect
je saurais	j'aurais su

Present subjunctive	Perfect subjunctive
que je sache	que j'aie su
que nous sachions	

Imperfect subjunctive	Pluperfect subjunctive
que je susse	que j'eusse su

Examples of use as a full verb

On ne *sait* jamais.	You never *know*.
Il *saura* les détails demain.	He'*ll know* the details tomorrow.
Finalement, on *sut* que Dreyfus était innocent.	In the end, people *learnt* that Dreyfus was innocent.
Il m'a dit qu'il n'*avait* pas *su* le numéro de la maison.	He told me he *had*n't *known* the house number.

Example of use as a modal verb

Je ne *saurais* pas le dire.	I *could*n't say.
Tu *sais* jouer du piano?	*Can* you play the piano?
Vous *savez* nager?	*Can* you swim?
A cette époque je ne *savais* pas jouer du violon.	At that time I *could*n't play the violin.

10i   Valoir, *to be worth*
Irregular verb in -oir

Imperative

vaux! (tu)   valez! (vous)   valons! (nous)

Present	**Perfect**
je vaux	j'ai valu
tu vaux	tu as valu
il/elle vaut	il/elle a valu
on vaut	on a valu
nous valons	nous avons valu
vous valez	vous avez valu
ils/elles valent	ils/elles ont valu

Imperfect	**Simple past**
je valais	je valus
tu valais	tu valus
il/elle valait	il/elle valut
on valait	on valut
nous valions	nous valûmes
vous valiez	vous valûtes
ils/elles valaient	ils/elles valurent

Similar verbs

équivaloir	be equivalent; amount to
prévaloir	prevail
revaloir	pay back

Notes

1. Impersonal usage: **il vaut mieux**, "it is better."

Present participle	Past participle
valant	valu

Past perfect	Past anterior
j'avais valu	j'eus valu

Future	Future perfect
ja vaudrai	j'aurai valu

Conditional	Conditional perfect
je vaudrais	j'aurais valu

Present subjunctive	Perfect subjunctive
que je vaille	que j'aie valu
que tu vailles	
qu'il/elle vaille	
qu'on vaille	
que nous valions	
que vous valiez	
qu'ils/elles vaillent	

Imperfect subjunctive	Pluperfect subjunctive
que je valusse	que j'eusse valu

Ça *vaut* combien?	How much is that *worth?*
Ce tableau *vaut* un million.	That painting is *worth* a million.
Ce film *vaut* la peine d'être vu.	That movie is *worth* seeing.
Ce type ne *vaut* pas cher.	That guy's not much *good.*
Ce café ne *vaut* pas le brésilien.	This coffee's not *as good* as the Brazilian.
Cette affaire lui *a valu* bien des soucis.	That matter *caused* him a lot of worry.
Il *vaut mieux* partir.	It*'s better* to leave.
Il *vaudrait mieux* partir tout de suite.	It *would be better* to leave at once.

10j   Voir, *to see*
Irregular verb in -oir

Imperative

vois! (tu)	voyez! (vous)	voyons! (nous)

Present	**Perfect**
je vois	j'ai vu
tu vois	tu as vu
il/elle voit	il/elle a vu
on voit	on a vu
nous voyons	nous avons vu
vous voyez	vous avez vu
ils voient	ils ont vu

Imperfect	**Simple past**
je voyais	je vis
tu voyais	tu vis
il/elle voyait	il/elle vit
on voyait	on vit
nous voyions	nous vîmes
vous voyiez	vous vîtes
ils/elles voyaient	ils/elles virent

Similar verbs

entrevoir	glimpse
prévoir	foresee; predict
revoir	see again

Notes

1. The future and conditional tenses of **prévoir** are **je prévoirai** and **je prévoirais**, respectively.
2. **Pourvoir** (to provide) is also similarly conjugated: **je pourvoirai** in the future tense; **je pourvoirais** in the conditional; and **je pourvus** in the simple past, **que je pourvusse** in the imperfect subjunctive.

Present participle	Past participle
voyant	vu

Past perfect	Past anterior
j'avais vu	j'eus vu

Future	Future perfect
je verrai	j'aurai vu

Conditional	Conditional perfect
je verrais	j'aurais vu

Present subjunctive	Perfect subjunctive
que je voie	que j'aie vu

Imperfect subjunctive	Pluperfect subjunctive
que je visse	que j'eusse vu

Devant le cinéma

– **Tu *as vu* ce film?**

– **Non. Je vais le *voir* demain.**

Outside the movies

– *Have* you *seen* that film?

– No, I'm going to *see* it tomorrow.

A la maison

– **Je n'ai pas encore nettoyé la cuisine.**

– **Ça *se voit*!**

At home

– I haven't cleaned the kitchen yet.

– That's *obvious!*

Au musée

– **Je suis désolée que vous n'*ayez* pas *vu* l'exposition d'art breton.**

– **Ça ne fait rien! On la *verra* à Paris.**

At the museum

– I'm so sorry you *didn't see* the Breton art exhibit.

– Never mind. We'*ll see it* in Paris.

10k Vouloir, *to want, wish*
Irregular modal verb in *-oir*

Imperative

veuille! (tu)   veuillez! (vous)   voulons! (nous)

Present	**Perfect**
je veux	j'ai voulu
tu veux	tu as voulu
il/elle veut	il/elle a voulu
on veut	on a voulu
nous voulons	nous avons voulu
vous voulez	vous avez voulu
ils/elles veulent	ils/elles ont voulu

Imperfect	**Simple past**
je voulais	je voulus
tu voulais	tu voulus
il/elle voulait	il/elle voulut
on voulait	on voulut
nous voulions	nous voulûmes
vous vouliez	vous voulûtes
ils/elles voulaient	ils/elles voulurent

Notes

1. This is the only verb of its type, though the patterns of **devoir** and **pouvoir** are similar (➤10b, 10e). Notice that the present indicative tense has irregular forms in the singular and the third-person plural, while the first- and second-persons plural have the stem of the infinitive.
2. The imperative is used as a courtesy in such phrases as **Veuillez agréer, monsieur, l'expression de mes sentiments distingués** (Yours truly); **Veuillez répondre tout de suite** (Please be so good as to reply immediately).
3. Used transitively, **vouloir** means "to want (something)."

Examples of use as a full verb

Tu *veux* une glace?	*Do* you *want* an ice cream cone?
Je *voudrais* cinq kilos de pommes de terre.	I'd *like* five kilos of potatoes.

Present participle	**Past participle**
voulant	voulu

Past perfect	**Past anterior**
j'avais voulu	j'eus voulu

Future	**Future perfect**
je voudrai	j'aurai voulu

Conditional	**Conditional perfect**
je voudrais	j'aurais voulu

Present subjunctive	**Perfect subjunctive**
que je veuille	que j'aie voulu
que nous voulions	

Imperfect subjunctive	**Pluperfect subjunctive**
que je voulusse	que j'eusse voulu

Examples of use as a modal verb

Je *veux* regarder ce film.	I *want* to watch that film.
Il ne *veut* pas aller en Espagne.	He *doesn*'t *want* to go to Spain.
Voulez-vous vérifier la pression des pneus?	*Will* you check the tire pressure?
Voulez-vous me téléphoner ce soir?	*Will* you phone me this evening?
Je *voudrais* voir le chef de personnel.	I'*d like* to see the personnel manager.
Elle ne *veut* rien faire.	She *won*'t do a thing.
J'*aurais voulu* assister à leur mariage.	I *would have liked* to go to their wedding.
Jules César *voulut* envahir la Bretagne.	Julius Caesar *wanted* to invade Britain.

C
SUBJECT INDEX

Subject index

The following subjects are covered in PART A, "Verbs in French: their functions and uses,"

D

VERB INDEX

Verb index

There are over 2,200 entries in this section.

Each verb, or verbal expression, is given in French, with its English meaning; a note as to whether it is transitive (tr), intransitive (intr), or reflexive (ref); and its conjugation group.

Verbs that are set out in PART B, "Model French Verbs" are noted ☐M.

The thirteen verbs and their compounds that are conjugated with **être** in compound tenses are marked with an asterisk (*). Reflexive verbs are not thus marked, as all reflexive verbs are conjugated with **être** in compound tenses.

Verbs that begin with **h-** are marked ᵗ**h** if they require no liaison (aspirate h).

Abbreviations: **qch – quelque chose; qqn – quelqu'un.**

A   **abandonner** (tr)   give up, abandon 7a
abasourdir (tr)   dumbfound, bewilder 8a
abattre (tr)   slaughter 9l
abîmer (tr)   spoil 7a
abolir (tr)   abolish 8a
abonder (intr)   be abundant, abound 7a
abonner, s' (ref)   subscribe 7a
aborder (tr)   reach, approach 7a
aboutir (intr)   work out well 8a
aboutir à (intr)   result in 8a
aboyer (intr)   bark 7f
abriter (tr)   shelter (someone) 7a
abriter, s' (ref)   take shelter 7a
absenter, s' (ref)   be absent, absent oneself 7a

absorber (tr)   take over, absorb 7a
absoudre (tr)   absolve 9r
abstenir de, s' (ref)   keep off, abstain, refrain from 8k

abuser de (tr)   misuse 7a
accélérer (tr & intr)   accelerate 7g
accepter (tr)   agree to, accept 7a
accommoder de qch. s' (ref)   make the best of 7a
accompagner (tr)   accompany 7a
accomplir (tr)   fulfil, achieve 8a

accorder (tr)	grant (request), tune (instrument) 7a
accorder avec, s' (ref)	accord with 7a
accoster (tr)	accost 7a
accoucher de (tr)	give birth to 7a
accouder, s' (ref)	lean (on elbows) 7a
accoupler (tr)	couple 7a
accoupler, s' (ref)	mate 7a
accourir (vers/jusqu'à)(intr)	run to 8d
accrocher (tr)	hook, hang up 7a
accrocher à, s' (ref)	cling to 7a
accroupir, s' (ref)	squat, crouch 8a
accumuler (tr)	accumulate 7a
accuser réception de (tr)	acknowledge (receipt of) 7a
accuser (de) (tr)	accuse, charge (with crime) 7a
acheter (tr)	buy, purchase 7d ⊡M
adquérir (tr)	acquire, get 8b ⊡M
acquitter (tr)	acquit 7a
adapter (tr)	adapt 7a
additionner (tr)	add up 7a
adhérer (intr)	adhere, stick to, join 7e
admettre (tr)	admit, grant to be true 9l
administrer (tr)	administer 7a
administrer un médicament (tr)	dose 7a
admirer (tr)	admire 7a
adonner à, s' (ref)	become addicted 7a
adopter (tr)	adopt 7a
adorer (tr)	worship, adore 7a
adosser à, s' (ref)	lean up against 7a
adresser (tr)	address 7a
adresser à, s' (ref)	address 7a
aérer (tr)	air 7e
affaiblir, s' (ref)	weaken 8a
affairer, s' (ref)	bustle 7a
affecter (tr)	affect 7a
affirmer (tr)	affirm 7a
affliger (tr)	afflict, distress 7g
affranchir (tr)	stamp (letters) 8a
affréter (tr)	charter (plane) 7e
affronter (tr)	stand up to 7a
agenouiller, s' (ref)	kneel (down) 7a
aggraver, s' (ref)	get worse 7a
agir (intr)	act, take action 8a
agir de, s' (ref)	be a matter of, be about 8a
il s'agit d'un homme qui . . .	*it's about a man who . . .*

agiter (tr)	wave (flag) 7a
agiter, s' (ref)	get worked up 7a
agrafer (tr)	staple 7a
agrandir (tr)	enlarge 8a
agrandir, s' (ref)	grow larger 8a
aider (tr)	aid, help 7a
aider beaucoup (tr)	do a lot for 7a
aider, s' (ref)	help oneself 7a
aigrir (tr)	sour 8a
aiguiser (tr)	sharpen 7a
aimer (tr)	like, love 7a
ajourner (tr)	adjourn 7a
ajouter (tr)	add, build on (to house) 7a
ajouter (des détails) (tr)	sketch in 7a
alarmer (tr)	alarm 7a
alerter (tr)	alert 7a
aliéner (tr)	alienate 7e
aligner (tr)	align, line up 7a
allaiter (tr)	suckle, breast-feed 7a
alléger (tr)	lighten, alleviate
***aller** (intr)	go, suit 7b M
je vais aller (intr)	*I'm going to go*
***aller à la pêche** (intr)	go fishing 7b
***aller à l'école** (intr)	attend school 7b
***aller à pas furtifs** (intr)	go stealthily 7b
***aller à vélo** (intr)	go by bike, cycle 7b
***aller au lit** (intr)	go to bed 7b
***aller bien** (intr)	keep well 7b
***aller chercher** (tr)	fetch, go for 7b
aller de *x* a *y (intr)	range from *x* to *y* 7b
***aller en bateau** (intr)	sail 7b
***aller faire** (tr)	go doing 7b
***aller plus vite** (intr)	speed up 7b
***aller voir** (tr)	go and see, visit 7b
Allez! (intr)	*Come on!*
Allons y! (intr)	*Let's go!*
On y va? (intr)	*Shall we go?*
Il va jouer au football.	*He's going to play soccer.*
Comment ça va? (intr)	*How are you?*
Ça va bien, merci. (intr)	*I'm fine, thanks.*
Cette robe te va très bien. (intr)	*That dress really suits you.*
Ça ne va pas du tout. (intr)	*That won't do at all!*
Ça ira! (intr)	*Things will be ok!*
allier (tr)	ally, combine 7a
allier, s' (ref)	unite with,
	become allied with 7a

allonger (tr & intr)	stretch, lengthen 7g
allonger, s' (ref)	get longer 7g
allonger la sauce (tr)	thin sauce, "stretch it out" 7g
allouer (tr)	allow, allocate (funds) 7a
allumer (tr)	switch on, ignite, strike a match 7a
allumer, s' (ref)	light up, come on (lights) 7a
alterner (tr)	alternate 7a
amarrer (tr)	moor (boat) 7a
amasser (tr)	hoard 7a
améliorer (tr)	improve, upgrade 7a
amender (tr)	amend 7a
amortir (tr)	deaden, cushion 8a
amplifier (tr)	amplify 7a
amputer (tr)	amputate, cut off 7a
amuser (tr)	amuse 7a
amuser, s' (ref)	play around, have fun, enjoy oneself 7a
analyser (tr)	analyze 7a
anéantir (tr)	annihilate 8a
anesthésier (tr)	anesthetize 7a
animer (tr)	animate 7a
annexer (tr)	annex 7a
annoncer (tr)	announce 7h
annuler (tr)	annul, call off, cancel 7a
anticiper (tr)	anticipate 7a
apercevoir (tr)	sight, spot 10g
apercevoir de, s' (ref)	glimpse, notice 10g
aplanir (tr)	flatten 8a
apparaître (intr)	appear* 9e
appartenir (tr)	belong 8k
appeler (tr)	call, ring up 7c M
appeler par radio (tr)	call on the radio 7c
appeler sous les drapeaux (tr)	call up (for military service) 7c
appeler, s' (ref)	be called 7c
applaudir (tr)	clap, applaud 8a
appliquer (tr)	apply 7a
apporter (tr)	bring 7a
apprécier (tr)	enjoy, value 7a
apprendre (tr)	learn 9q
apprendre par coeur (tr)	learn by heart 9q
apprivoiser (tr)	tame 7a
approcher (tr & intr)	close in, bring close 7a
approcher, s' (ref)	approach 7a
approfondir (tr)	deepen 8a
approprier, s' (ref)	appropriate 7a

attendre avec impatience (tr)	look forward to 9a
attendre à, s' (ref)	expect 9a
atterrir (intr)	land 8a
attirer (tr)	attract, entice 7a
attirer, s' (ref)	incur 7a
attraper (tr)	catch 7a
attrister (tr)	sadden 7a
auditionner (tr)	audition 7a
augmenter (tr)	increase, raise, add to 7a
automatiser (tr)	automate 7a
autoriser (tr)	authorize, entitle 7a
avaler (tr)	swallow 7a
avancer (intr)	move forward 7h
avancer (tr)	advance, further, stick out 7h
avancer à toute vapeur (intr)	steam ahead 7h
avancer, s' (ref)	advance, move forward 7h
aventurer, s' (ref)	venture 7a
avérer, s' (ref)	turn out 7e
avertir (tr)	warn 8a
aveugler (tr)	blind 7a
avoir (tr)	have, have got 6d M
il y a (tr)	*there is, are*
Qu'est-ce qu'il y a? (tr)	*What's the matter?*
Il m'a eu. (tr)	*He tricked me (I was had).*
avoir besoin de (tr)	need 6d
avoir chaud (tr)	be hot, feel hot 6d
avoir des rapports avec (tr)	relate to 6d
avoir des rapports (sexuels) avec (tr)	have (sexual) intercourse with 6d
avoir faim (tr)	be hungry 6d
avoir froid (tr)	be cold, feel cold 6d
avoir honte (tr)	be ashamed 6d
avoir la diarrhée (tr)	have diarrhea 6d
avoir l'air (intelligent) (tr)	look (intelligent) 6d
avoir le mal de mer (tr)	be seasick 6d
avoir lieu (tr)	take place 6d
avoir l'intention de (faire) (tr)	intend to (do) 6d
avoir mal au coeur (tr)	feel sick 6d
avoir peur (tr)	be afraid 6d
avoir raison (tr)	be right 6d
avoir sept ans (tr)	be seven years old 6d
avoir soif (tr)	be thirsty 6d
avoir sommeil (tr)	be sleepy 6d
avoir tendance à (tr)	tend 6d
avoir tort (tr)	be wrong 6d

	avoir un accident (tr)	have an accident 6d
	avoir un compte à (tr)	bank with, at 6d
	avoir un point de vue (tr)	have a point of view 6d
	avouer (tr)	admit, confess 7a
	bagarrer, se (ref)	brawl 7a
B	baigner (se) (tr & ref)	bathe 7a
	bâiller (intr)	yawn, gape 7a
	bâillonner (tr)	gag, stifle 7a
	baiser (tr)	screw (have sex) 7a
	baisser (tr)	lower, come down 7a
	baisser, se (ref)	stoop 7a
	balader, se (ref)	stroll 7a
	balancer (tr)	swing 7h
	balancer, se (ref)	rock 7h
	balayer (tr)	sweep 7i
	bander (tr)	bandage 7a
	bannir (tr)	banish 8a
	baptiser (tr)	baptize 7a
	barrer (tr)	cancel out, cross out 7a
	barrer la porte (tr)	bar 7a
	barricader (tr)	barricade 7a
	baser sur (intr)	base on 7a
	battre (tr)	beat, thresh 9l
	battre du tambour (intr)	beat the drum 9l
	bavarder (intr)	gossip, chat 7a
	baver (intr)	dribble 7a
	bégayer (tr & intr)	stammer 7i
	bêler (intr)	bleat 7a
	bénir (tr)	bless 8a
	bétonner (tr)	concrete over 7a
	beugler (intr)	bellow 7a
	bifurquer (intr)	branch off, fork (road) 7a
	blanchir (tr)	bleach 8a
	blesser (tr)	wound, offend 7a
	blesser, se (ref)	hurt oneself 7a
	bloquer (tr)	block 7a
	blottir, se (ref)	huddle 8a
	bluffer (tr & intr)	bluff 7a
	boire (tr)	drink 9b [M]
	boire à petits coups (tr)	sip 9b
	boiter (intr)	limp 7a
	bombarder (tr)	bomb, shell 7a
	bomber (intr)	bulge 7a
	bondir (intr)	spring 8a

border (tr)	border 7a
boucher (tr)	cork, plug 7a
bouder (intr)	sulk 7a
bouger (tr & intr)	move, shift 7g
bouillir (intr)	boil 8a
bouillonner (intr)	bubble 7a
bourdonner (intr)	buzz, hum 7a
bourrer (tr)	stuff 7a
bourrer de (tr)	cram with 7a
bousculer, se (tr & ref)	jostle 7a
boutonner (tr)	button 7a
boxer (intr)	box 7a
boycotter (tr)	boycott 7a
braconner (intr)	poach (game) 7a
braiser (tr)	braise 7a
brancher (tr)	connect up to 7a
brasser (tr)	brew 7a
bricoler (tr & intr)	tinker around 7a
brider (tr)	bridle 7a
briller (intr)	shine 7a
broder (tr)	embroider 7a
broncher (intr)	flinch 7a
bronzer, se (ref)	tan 7a
brosser (tr)	brush 7a
brouiller (tr)	blur 7a
brouiller, se (ref)	fall out, quarrel 7a
brouter (tr)	graze 7a
broyer (tr)	grind, crush 7f
brûler (tr)	burn 7a
brûler légèrement (tr)	scorch 7a

C

cabrer se (ref)	rear up 7a
cacher (tr)	hide, conceal 7a
cajoler (tr)	coax 7a
calculer (tr)	calculate, compute 7a
caler (tr & intr)	wedge, stall 7a
câliner (tr)	cuddle, pet 7a
calmer (tr)	calm 7a
calmer, se (ref)	calm down 7a
calomnier (tr)	slander 7a
cambrioler (tr)	burgle 7a
camper (intr)	camp 7a
canaliser (tr)	channel 7a
capituler (intr)	capitulate 7a
capturer (tr)	capture 7a

classifier (tr)	classify 7a
cligner des yeux (intr)	wink, blink 7a
cloisonner (tr)	partition off 7a
clôturer (tr)	fence in, enclose 7a
clouer (tr)	nail down 7a
coasser (intr)	croak 7a
cocher (tr)	tick (on list) 7a
coexister (intr)	coexist 7a
cogner contre (intr)	knock against 7a
cohabiter (intr)	cohabit 7a
coincider (intr)	coincide 7a
collaborer (intr)	collaborate 7a
collectionner (tr)	collect 7a
coller (tr)	stick, glue 7a
colorier (tr)	color in 7a
combattre (tr)	fight 9l
combiner (tr)	combine 7a
commander (tr)	order (meal, etc.) 7a
commémorer (tr)	commemorate 7a
commencer (tr)	begin, start, make a start 7h
commettre (tr)	commit 9l
communier (intr)	receive communion 7a
communiquer (tr)	communicate 7a
comparaître (intr)	appear (in court) 9e
comparer (tr)	compare 7a
compiler (tr)	compile 7a
compléter (tr)	complete 7e
complimenter (tr)	compliment 7a
compliquer (tr)	complicate 7a
comploter (tr)	plot 7a
comporter se (tr)	behave 7a
composer (tr)	compose 7a
comprendre (tr)	understand, comprehend 9q
comprimer (tr)	compress 7a
compromettre (tr)	compromise 9l
compter (tr)	count 7a
compter sur (intr)	count on, depend on 7a
concéder (tr)	concede 7e
concentrer (tr)	concentrate 7a
concerner (tr)	concern 7a
concevoir (tr)	conceive, design 10g
conclure (tr)	conclude, close 9c $\boxed{\text{M}}$
concourir (tr)	compete, work together 8d
condamner (tr)	damn, condemn, blame 7a
condamner à une amende (tr)	levy a fine 7a
condenser (tr)	condense 7a

coopérer (tr & intr)	cooperate 7e
coordonner (tr)	coordinate 7a
copier (tr)	copy 7a
corder (tr)	string 7a
correspondre (tr)	correspond, write 9a
correspondre à (tr)	correspond to 9a
corriger (tr)	correct 7g
corroder (tr)	corrode 7a
corrompre (tr)	corrupt 9a
coucher, se (ref)	lie down 7a
coudre (tr)	sew,
	stitch 9f ⬚M⬚
couler (tr)	sink 7a
couper (tr)	cut, clip 7a
couper à travers (tr)	cut across 7a
couper la gorge à qqn (tr)	cut someone's throat 7a
couper ras les cheveux (tr)	crop (hair) 7a
courber (tr)	curve, bend 7a
courir (intr)	run, race 8d ⬚M⬚.
couronner (tr)	crown 7a
court-circuiter (tr)	short-circuit 7a
coûter (tr)	cost 7a
Ça coute cher.	*It's expensive.*
couver (tr)	hatch 7a
couvrir (tr)	cover 8i
couvrir d'ampoules, se (ref)	blister 8i
couvrir, se (ref)	put on one's hat, cover up;
	cloud over (sky) 8i
couvrir (d'un toit) (tr)	put a roof on 8i
cracher (tr)	spit 7a
crachiner (intr)	drizzle 7a
craindre (tr)	fear 9o
créditer (tr)	credit 7a
créer (tr)	create 7a
crépiter (intr)	crackle 7a
creuser (tr)	dig, sink (a well),
	hollow out 7a
crever (tr)	burst 7d
Je creve de faim!	*I'm starving!*
cribler de (tr)	riddle with 7d
crier (tr)	shout, cry out 7a
cristalliser, se (ref)	crystalize 7a
critiquer (tr)	criticize, censure 7a
croire (tr)	believe, think 9g ⬚M⬚
Je ne crois pas. (tr)	*I don't think so.*
croire en (intr)	believe in 9g

découvrir (tr)	uncover, discover 8i
décréter (tr)	decree 7e
décrire (tr)	describe 9i
décrocher (tr & intr)	take down, lift receiver 7a
dédier (tr)	dedicate 7a
dédommager pour (tr)	compensate for 7g
déduire (tr)	deduce, deduct 9d
défaillir (tr)	faint, falter 8c
défaire (tr)	undo, untie, unpack 9j
défendre (tr)	defend, forbid 9a
défier (tr)	challenge 7a
défiler (intr)	march past, parade 7a
définir (tr)	define 8a
déformer (tr)	distort, deform 7a
dégeler (tr & intr)	thaw 7d
dégivrer (tr)	de-ice, defrost (refrigerator) 7a
dégonfler (tr)	deflate 7a
dégoûter (tr)	disgust 7a
dégoutter (intr)	trickle 7a
dégrader (tr)	degrade, deface 7a
déguiser (se) (tr & ref)	disguise 7a
déjeuner (intr)	have lunch 7a
délayer (tr)	dilute; draw out (a story) 7i
déléguer (tr)	delegate 7e
délibérer (de) (intr & intr)	deliberate 7e
demander (tr)	ask, enquire, request 7a
Ça demande beaucoup de temps. (tr)	*That takes up a lot of time.*
demander (à qqn de faire qqc)	ask (someone to do something) 7a
demander des nouvelles (tr)	ask after 7a
demander, se (ref)	wonder 7a
démanger (intr)	itch 7g
démaquiller, se (ref)	remove makeup 7a
démarrer (tr & intr)	start 7a
démêler (tr)	disentangle 7a
déménager (intr)	move house 7a
démissionner (intr)	resign 7a
démolir (tr)	demolish 8a
démonter (tr)	take down, dismantle 7a
démontrer (tr)	show, demonstrate 7a
dénigrer (tr)	disparage 7a
dénoncer (tr)	denounce 7h
dénoter (tr)	denote 7a

dénoyauter (tr)	stone, pit 7a
dépasser (tr)	surpass, overtake 7a
dépêcher, se (ref)	hurry 7a
Dépéchez-vous! (ref)	*Hurry up!*
dépeindre (tr)	depict 9o
dépenser (tr)	spend 7a
déplacer (tr)	displace 7h
déplaire (tr)	displease 9p
déposer (tr)	deposit, dump 7a
dépouiller (tr)	strip 7a
déprécier (tr)	depreciate 7a
déprimer (tr)	depress 7a
déraisonner (intr)	rave 7a
déranger (tr)	disturb 7g
déraper (intr)	skid 7a
dériver de (tr)	be derived from 7a
dérober, se (ref)	back down 7a
désaltérer, se (ref)	quench 7e
désamorcer (tr)	defuse 7h
désapprouver (tr)	disapprove 7a
désarmer (tr)	disarm 7a
désavouer (tr)	disclaim 7a
***descendre** (intr)	come down 7b
descendre (tr)	bring down, carry down 9a
Le gangster l'a descendu. (tr)	*The gangster shot him dead.*
désenivrer (tr & intr)	sober up 7a
déserter (tr)	desert 7a
désespérer, se (ref)	despair 7e
déshabiller (tr)	undress (someone) 7a
déshabiller, se (ref)	get undressed 7a
désherber (tr)	weed 7a
déshériter (tr)	disinherit 7a
désinfecter (tr)	disinfect 7a
désintégrer, se (ref)	disintegrate 7e
désirer (tr)	desire 7a
désorganiser (tr)	disorganize 7a
desservir (tr)	clear away, clear table 8j
dessiner (tr)	draw 7a
détacher (tr)	detach 7a
détacher sur le fond, se (ref)	stand out against (the background) 7a
détailler (tr)	detail 7a
détendre, se (ref)	relax 9a
détériorer (tr)	deteriorate 7a
détériorer, se (ref)	worsen 7a

déterminer (tr)	determine 7a
déterminer la quantité de (tr)	quantify 7a
déterrer (tr)	dig up 7a
détester (tr)	hate 7a
détourner (tr)	divert 7a
détourner un avion (tr)	hijack 7a
détruire (tr)	destroy 9d
dévaliser (tr)	rob 7a
dévaluer (tr)	devalue 7a
dévaster (tr)	devastate 7a
développer (tr)	expand 7a
*devenir (intr)	become 7b
*devenir adulte (intr)	grow up 7b
dévier (tr & intr)	deviate 7a
deviner (tr)	guess 7a
dévisager (tr)	stare at 7g
dévisser (tr)	unscrew 7a
dévisser se (ref)	come unscrewed 7a
devoir (tr)	owe 10b M
devoir (tr)	have to, must 10b
devoir partir (tr)	be called away 10b
dévorer (tr)	devour 7a
diagnostiquer (tr)	diagnose 7a
dicter (tr)	dictate 7a
différencier (tr)	differentiate 7a
différer (intr)	differ 7e
différer de (intr)	be different 7e
digérer (tr)	digest 7e
diluer (tr)	dilute 7a
diminuer (tr & intr)	diminish, lessen 7a
dîner (intr)	dine 7a
dire (tr)	say, tell 9h M
dire au revoir (tr)	say good-bye, see off 9h
dire du mal de (tr)	speak ill of 9h
dire merci (tr)	say thank you 9h
dire, se (ref)	call, be said 9h
Comment ça se dit en français?	*How do you say that in French?*
diriger (tr)	direct 7g
diriger un orchestre (tr)	conduct orchestra 7g
diriger vers, se (ref)	make for 7g
discerner (tr)	discern 7a
discipliner (tr)	discipline 7a
disculper (tr)	exonerate 7a
discuter (tr & intr)	debate 7a
discuter de (tr)	discuss 7a

E

éblouir (tr)	dazzle 8a
ébrécher (tr)	chip 7e
écarter de, s' (ref)	get out of way of 7a
échanger (tr)	exchange 7g
échapper à (intr)	slip 7a
échapper de, s' (ref)	escape from 7a
échauffer, s' (ref)	warm up (for sport) 7a
échelonner (tr)	stagger, space out 7a
échouer à (intr)	fail 7a
éclabousser (tr)	splash, spatter 7a
éclaircir, s' (ref)	brighten up, clear up (weather) 8a
économiser (tr)	economize 7a
écorcher (tr)	skin 7a
écosser (tr)	shell 7a
écouter (tr)	listen 7a
écraser (tr)	crush 7a
écraser, s' (ref)	crash 7a
écrire (tr)	write 9i $\boxed{\text{M}}$
écrire pour une demande (tr)	write away for 9i
écrouler, s' (ref)	subside, collapse 7a
éditer (tr)	edit 7a
effacer (tr)	rub out, erase 7h
effleurer (tr)	brush against 7a
effondrer, s' (ref)	flop down 7a
effrayer (tr)	scare, frighten 7i
égaliser (tr)	equalize 7a
égaliser, s' (ref)	even out 7a
égarer, s' (ref)	stray, wander 7a
On s'est égaré. (ref)	*We got lost.*
égoutter, s' (ref)	drip 7a
élaborer (tr)	think out, work out (plan) 7a
élargir (tr)	widen, broaden 8a
électrifier (tr)	electrify 7a
élever (tr)	rear 7d
élever à la puissance *x* (tr)	raise to the power of *x* 7d
élever à, s' (ref)	amount to, add up to 7d
élever une objection contre (tr)	object 7d
éliminer (tr)	eliminate 7a
élire (tr)	elect 9k
éloigner (tr)	move something away from 7a
éloigner, s' (ref)	walk away, move away 7a
emballer (tr)	package 7a
embarquer (tr & intr)	embark 7a

engager, s' (ref)	commit oneself 7g
engloutir (tr)	gobble 8a
engraisser (tr)	fatten 7a
enivrer, s' (ref)	get drunk 7a
enlever (tr)	remove (clothes), lift, carry off 7d
enlever de sa coquille (tr)	shell 7d
ennuyer (tr)	bore 7f
ennuyer, s' (ref)	be bored, restless 7f
enrayer (tr)	curb, check 7i
enregistrer (tr)	record 7a
enregistrer sur magnéto-scope (tr)	video, record on video 7a
enrhumer, s' (ref)	catch cold 7a
enrichir (tr)	enrich 8a
enrouler (tr)	coil 7a
enseigner (tr)	teach 7a
entasser (tr)	heap, pile up, hoard 7a
entendre (tr)	hear, find out 9a
entendre, s' (ref)	get along with 9a
entendre bien avec, s' (ref)	get on well with 9a
enterrer (tr)	bury 7a
entortiller (tr)	twist 7a
entourer (tr)	surround 7a
entourer d'une haie (tr)	hedge 7a
entraîner (tr)	train 7a
entreprendre (tr)	undertake 9s
*entrer (intr)	go in, enter 7a
*entrer comme une flèche (intr)	shoot in 7a
*entrer dans une maison (intr)	join firm (business) 7a
*entrer en éruption (intr)	burst in 7a
*entrer en scène (intr)	come on (stage) 7a
*entrer rapidement (intr)	sweep in 7a
*entrer par effraction (intr)	break in, burgle 7a
*entrer dans l'armée (intr)	join up 7a
entretenir (tr)	maintain, service, provide for 8k
entretenir avec qqn, s' (ref)	confer, converse with 8k
entrouvrir (tr)	half-open 8i
envier (tr)	envy 7a
envoler, s' (ref)	fly away 7a
envoyer (tr)	send 7f
envoyer chercher (tr)	send for, summon 7f
envoyer la facture (tr)	bill 7f
envoyer par téléfax (tr)	fax 7f
envoyer (des suggestions) (tr)	write in 7f

être content (intr)	be pleased 6e
être contrarié (intr)	be annoyed, cross 6e
être contre (intr)	be against 6e
être d'accord (intr)	agree (with),
	be in agreement 6e
être dans le commerce (intr)	deal 6e
être détaché (intr)	be separate 6e
être dû à (intr)	be due to 6e
être écrivain (intr)	write 6e
être effrayé (intr)	be frightened 6e
être égal (intr)	not to matter 6e
Ça m'est égal. (intr)	*I don't care.* 6e
être en chômage (intr)	be unemployed 6e
être en colère (intr)	be angry 6e
être en expansion (intr)	boom 6e
être en grève (intr)	be on strike 6e
être en retard (intr)	be late 6e
être en séance (intr)	sit, be in session
	(court, parliament) 6e
être la vedette (intr)	star 6e
être mannequin (intr)	model 6e
être naufragé (intr)	be shipwrecked 6e
être nécessaire (intr)	be necessary 6e
être obligé de (intr)	be obliged to 6e
être parent de (intr)	be related to 6e
être patient/impatient (intr)	be patient/impatient 6e
être permis (intr)	be allowed 6e
être pour/contre (intr)	be for/against 6e
être pris de vertiges (intr)	feel dizzy 6e
être prudent (intr)	be careful 6e
en être quitte pour (intr)	get away with 6e
être reçu (intr)	pass (exam) 6e
être responsable de (intr)	be liable for 6e
être retardé (intr)	be delayed 6e
être retenu (intr)	be delayed 6e
être sage (intr)	behave 6e
être servi de (intr)	be served by 6e
être sur le point de (intr)	be about to 6e
être très impoli	
envers qqn (intr)	be rude to 6e
être valable (intr)	be valid 6e
étudier (tr)	study 7a
évacuer (tr)	evacuate 7a
évaluer (tr)	appraise 7a
évanouir, s' (ref)	faint 8a
évaporer, s' (ref)	evaporate, boil dry 7a

faciliter (tr)	facilitate 7a
façonner (tr)	fashion, tailor 7a
faillir (intr)	very nearly do, just miss doing 8f [M]
faire (tr)	do, make 9j [M]
Cela ne fait rien. (tr)	*That doesn't matter.*
faire accepter, se (ref)	get in, on 9j
faire apparaître (tr)	conjure up, make appear 9j
faire appel à (tr)	appeal to 9j
faire attention (tr)	pay attention 9j
faire attention à (tr)	attend to 9j
faire attention à qch (tr)	mind, watch out for 9j
faire bouillir (tr)	boil 9j
faire breveter (tr)	patent 9j
faire cadeau de (tr)	give away 9j
faire chanter (tr)	blackmail 9j
faire chauffer (tr)	heat 9j
faire cuire (au four) (tr)	bake 9j
faire de la gymnastique (tr)	do gymnastics 9j
faire de la peine à qqn	upset, distress somebody 9j
faire de la publicité (pour) (tr)	advertise 9j
faire de la voile (tr)	go sailing 9j
faire de l'escrime (tr)	fence (sport) 9j
faire de petits travaux (tr)	do odd jobs 9j
faire défiler (tr)	scroll (computer) 9j
faire demi-tour (tr)	turn back 9j
faire des affaires avec (tr)	do business with 9j
faire des courses (tr)	shop, go shopping 9j
faire des progrès (tr)	progress, make progress 9j
faire des recherches (tr)	research 9j
faire des signes (tr)	signal 9j
faire désintoxiquer, se (ref)	dry out, come off drugs 9j
faire don de (tr)	donate 9j
faire du bien à (tr)	benefit 9j
faire du bruit (tr)	rattle 9j
faire du commerce (tr)	trade 9j
faire du jogging (tr)	jog 9j
faire du mal à (tr)	hurt, harm 9j
faire du ski (tr)	ski, go skiing 9j
faire du stop (tr)	hitchhike 9j
Il fait du vent. (tr)	*It's windy.* (weather)
faire égoutter (tr)	strain 9j
faire entrer (tr)	show in, let in 9j

faire un régime (tr)	diet 9j
faire remarquer (tr)	remark, comment 9j
faire sauter (tr)	blow up 9j
faire sauter un plomb (tr)	blow a fuse (electrical) 9j
faire semblant de (tr)	pretend 9j
faire signe (tr)	sign 9j
faire signe à qqn (tr)	beckon 9j
faire signe de la main (tr)	wave 9j
faire sortir (tr)	send out 9j
faire suivre (tr)	send on (mail, luggage) 9j
faire sursauter (tr)	startle 9j
faire taire (tr)	silence 9j
faire tort à (tr)	harm 9j
faire un collage (tr)	cut and paste 9j
faire un don à (tr)	give charity 9j
faire un effort (tr)	make an effort 9j
faire un métier (tr)	do (trade, job) 9j
faire un pas (tr)	step 9j
faire un zoom (tr)	zoom 9j
faire une balade (tr)	go for a walk 9j
faire une demande (tr)	apply (for job) 9j
faire une enquête (tr)	carry out an inquiry 9j
faire une entorse, se (ref)	sprain 9j
faire une fausse couche (tr)	miscarry 9j
faire une mise en plis (tr)	set hair 9j
faire une offre de (tr)	bid 9j
faire une ordonnance (tr)	prescribe (medicine) 9j
faire une pause (tr)	pause 9j
faire une promenade (tr)	walk, go for a walk 9j
faire une radio de (tr)	X-ray 9j
faire une randonnée (tr)	ramble 9j
faire une remise de (tr)	discount 9j
faire une valise (tr)	pack 9j
faire voir, se (ref)	show up 9j
falloir (tr)	be necessary 10c M
Il ne faut pas fumer!	*You must not smoke!*
faner (intr)	fade 7a
fasciner (tr)	fascinate 7a
fatiguer (tr)	tire 7a
faufiler, se (ref)	slip 7a
favoriser (tr)	favor 7a
fêler (tr)	crack 7a
féliciter (tr)	congratulate 7a
fendre (tr)	split 9a
fermenter (tr & intr)	ferment 7a
fermer (tr)	close, shut 7a

fermer à clef (tr)	lock 7a
fermer à double tour (tr)	double-lock 7a
fermer au verrou (tr)	bolt down 7a
fermer avec une fermeture éclair (tr)	zip 7a
fermer définitivement (tr)	close down 7a
ferrer (tr)	shoe (horse) 7a
fêter (tr)	feast, celebrate 7a
feuilleter (tr)	browse, leaf through 7c
fiancer, se (ref)	get engaged 7h
fier à, se (ref)	trust 7a
filer (tr)	spin 7a
filer (intr)	clear off 7a
filmer (tr)	shoot 7a
filtrer (tr)	filter 7a
financer (tr)	finance 7h
finir (tr)	finish, end, wind up 8a M
finir de travailler (intr)	stop working 8a
fixer (tr)	fix 7a
fixer le prix (tr)	price 7a
flairer (tr)	scent 7a
flamber (intr)	blaze 7a
flâner (intr)	loiter 7a
flatter (tr)	flatter 7a
fleurir (intr)	flower 8a
flirter (intr)	flirt 7a
flotter (intr)	float 7a
fonctionner (intr)	work, function 7a
fonder (tr)	found 7a
fondre (tr)	melt 9a
forcer (tr)	force 7h
formater (tr)	format 7a
former (tr)	form 7a
fouetter (tr)	whip 7a
fouiller (tr)	search 7a
fournir (tr)	supply 8a
fracturer (tr)	fracture 7a
franchir (tr)	clear, get over (barrier), shoot rapids 8a
frapper (tr)	strike 7a
frauder (tr)	defraud 7a
frayer un passage, se (ref)	force one's way 7i
freiner (intr)	brake 7a
frémir (intr)	quiver 8a

fréquenter (tr)	frequent (place), date (person) 7a
friser (tr)	curl 7a
frissonner (intr)	shiver 7a
froisser (tr)	crumple, ruffle 7a
frotter (tr)	rub 7a
frotter au papier de verre (tr)	sandpaper 7a
frustrer (tr)	frustrate 7a
fuir (tr)	flee 8g $\boxed{M}$
fuire (intr)	leak 9d
fumer (intr)	steam, smoke 7a
fumer (tr)	smoke (cigarettes etc) 7a
fusionner (tr)	merge 7a

G

gâcher (tr)	make a mess of 7a
gagner (tr)	earn 7a
garantir (tr)	guarantee 8a
garder (tr)	guard 7a
garer (tr)	park 7a
gaspiller (tr)	waste 7a
gâter (tr)	spoil 7a
gaver, se (ref)	stuff 7a
gazouiller (intr)	twitter 7a
geler (intr)	freeze 7d
gémir (intr)	moan 8a
gêner (tr)	trouble, embarrass 7a
générer	generate 7e
gérer (tr)	manage 7e
germer (intr)	sprout 7a
gifler (tr)	slap 7a
glacer (tr)	ice 7h
glisser (intr)	slide 7a
gonfler (tr)	inflate 7a
gonfler, se (ref)	swell 7a
goûter (tr)	taste 7a
gouverner (tr)	govern, steer 7a
graisser (tr)	grease 7a
grandir (intr)	grow 8a
gratter (tr)	scrape 7a
graver (tr)	engrave 7a
greffer sur (tr)	graft onto 7a
grêler (intr)	hail 7a
griffer (tr)	scratch 7a
griffonner (tr)	scribble 7a
grignoter (tr)	nibble 7a
griller (tr)	grill 7a

imaginer (tr)	imagine 7a
imiter (tr)	imitate 7a
immigrer (intr)	immigrate 7a
immuniser (tr)	immunize 7a
importer (intr)	matter 7a
importuner (tr)	molest 7a
impressionner (tr)	impress 7a
imprimer (tr)	print 7a
incinérer (tr)	cremate 7e
inciser (tr)	incise 7a
inciter (tr)	stir 7a
incliner la tête (tr)	nod 7a
incliner, s' (ref)	bend 7a
incorporer (tr)	incorporate 7a
indiquer (tr)	point out/to 7a
infecter (tr)	infect 7a
infecter, s' (ref)	become infected 7a
influencer (tr)	influence 7h
informer (tr)	advise 7a
informer sur, s' (ref)	enquire, get information 7a
ingérer, s' (ref)	interfere, meddle 7e
initier (tr)	initiate 7a
injecter (qch a qqn) (tr)	inject 7a
inonder (tr)	flood 7a
inquiéter (tr)	worry, bother (someone) 7e
inquiéter, s' (ref)	worry 7e
inscrire, s' (à) (ref)	register, enrol (in) 9i
insérer (tr)	insert 7e
insister (intr)	insist 7a
inspirer (tr)	inhale 7a
installer (tr)	sit 7a
installer des micros cachés (tr)	bug 7a
installer, s' (ref)	settle down 7a
instruire (tr)	instruct 9d
insulter (tr)	insult 7a
intégrer (tr)	integrate 7e
intensifier (tr)	intensify 7a
intéresser (tr)	interest 7a
intéresser à, s' (ref)	be interested in 7a
interjeter appel (tr)	lodge an appeal 7c
interpréter (tr)	interpret, read 7e
interroger (tr)	interrogate 7g
interrompre (tr)	interrupt, come in 9a
interrompre son voyage (tr)	stop off (on a trip) 9a

	*intervenir (intr)	intervene, take place, occur 8i
	interviewer (tr)	interview 7a
	intriguer (intr)	scheme 7a
	introduire (tr)	introduce, show in 9d
	introduire progressive–ment (tr)	phase in, introduce gradually 9d
	inventer (tr)	invent 7a
	investir (tr)	invest 8a
	inviter (tr)	invite 7a
	ioniser (tr)	ionize 7a
	irriguer (tr)	irrigate 7a
	irriter (tr)	irritate 7a
	isoler de (tr)	isolate from 7a
J	jardiner (intr)	garden 7a
	jaunir (intr)	turn yellow 8a
	jeter (tr)	throw, cast 7c
	jeter, se (dans) (ref)	plunge into 7c
	jeter un coup d'oeil à (tr)	glance at 7c
	jeter un pont sur (tr)	build a bridge (over a river) 7c
	jeter une bombe (tr)	throw a bomb 7c
	joindre (tr)	connect 9o
	joncher (tr)	strew 7a
	jouer (tr)	gamble, stake 7a
	jouer (tr & intr)	act 7a
	jouer au football (intr)	play soccer 7a
	jouer d'un instrument (intr)	play an instrument 7a
	jouer un rôle (tr)	play a part 7a
	juger (tr)	judge 7g
	jurer (tr)	swear 7a
	justifier (tr)	justify 7a
K	kidnapper (tr)	kidnap 7a
	klaxonner (intr)	blow (car) horn 7a
L	labourer (tr)	till (soil) 7a
	lâcher (tr)	let loose 7a
	laisser (tr)	leave 7a
	laisser entrer (tr)	admit 7a
	laisser passer (tr)	let through 7a
	laisser tomber (tr)	drop 7a

laisser tromper, ne pas, se (ref)	see through 7a
Laissez-moi finir! (tr)	*Let me finish!*
lancer (tr)	fling 7h
lancer la balle (tr)	bowl 7h
languir (intr)	pine 8a
larguer les amarres (tr)	cast off 7a
larmoyer (intr)	snivel, tear up 7f
laver (tr)	wash 7a
laver, se (ref)	wash self 6c M
lécher (tr)	lick 7e
légaliser (tr)	legalize 7a
léguer (qch à qqn) (tr)	leave, bequeath 7e
lever (tr)	raise 7d
lever, se (ref)	stand up, get up 7d
libérer (tr)	set free 7e
lier (tr)	bind, tie 7a
lier d'amitié, se (ref)	make friends 7a
limer (tr)	file 7a
limiter (tr)	limit 7a
liquéfier (tr)	liquify 7a
lire (tr)	read 9k M
lire à haute voix (tr)	read aloud 9k
lisser (tr)	smooth 7a
livrer (tr)	deliver 7a
loger (tr)	house, accommodate 7g
loucher (intr)	squint 7a
louer (tr)	rent, hire 7a
louer à bail (tr)	lease out 7a
louer une place (tr)	reserve, book a seat 7a
lubrifier (tr)	oil 7a
luire (intr)	gleam 9d
lutter (intr)	wrestle 7a

M

mâcher (tr)	chew 7a
magnétiser (tr)	magnetize 7a
magnétoscoper (tr)	video 7a
maigrir (intr)	get thin 8a
maintenir (tr)	maintain 8k
maintenir, se (ref)	keep up 8k
maîtriser (tr)	master 7a
mal interpréter (tr)	misinterpret 7e
maltraiter (tr)	mistreat 7a
manger (tr)	eat 7g M
manier (tr)	handle 7a

mettre au lit, se (ref)	go to bed 9l
mettre au point (tr)	perfect, debug 9l
mettre à, se (ref)	take to, take up 9l
mettre à faire, se (ref)	start to do 9l
mettre à/en (tr)	store 9l
mettre de côté (tr)	put aside, save 9l
mettre en bocal (tr)	bottle 9l
mettre en communication (tr)	put through 9l
mettre en commun (tr)	pool 9l
mettre en faillite (tr)	bankrupt 9l
mettre en pratique (tr)	put into practice 9l
mettre en réserve (tr)	store 9l
mettre en scène (tr)	stage 9l
mettre la table (tr)	lay the table 9l
mettre le feu à (tr)	set fire to 9l
mettre les menottes à (tr)	handcuff 9l
mettre plus fort (tr)	turn up (radio, stereo) 9l
mettre pour la première fois (tr)	wear for first time 9l
mettre qch par écrit (tr)	put down in writing 9l
mettre sur le compte de qqn (tr)	charge (someone's account) 9l
mettre un index (tr)	index 9l
mettre en banque (tr)	bank 9l
miauler (intr)	mew 7a
migrer (intr)	migrate 7a
mimer (tr)	mime 7a
minuter (tr)	time 7a
moderniser (tr)	modernize 7a
modifier (tr)	modify 7a
moisir (intr)	go mouldy 8a
moissonner (tr)	reap 7a
monopoliser (tr)	monopolize 7a
*monter (intr)	rise 7a
monter (with auxiliary **avoir**) (tr)	take up, carry up 7a
*monter à cheval (intr)	ride a horse 7a
*monter dans (intr)	board 7a
*monter d'une classe (intr)	go up (in school) 7a
*monter en flèche (intr)	soar 7a
montrer (tr)	show 7a
mordre (tr)	bite 9a
motiver (tr)	motivate 7a
moudre (tr)	mill, grind 9m M
mouiller (tr)	wet 7a
mouler (tr)	mold 7a

opposer (tr)	oppose 7a
opposer à, s' (ref)	confront each other, rebel (against) 7a
orbiter (tr)	orbit 7a
ordonner (tr)	order, ordain 7a
organiser (tr)	organize 7a
osciller (intr)	oscillate 7a
oser (tr)	dare 7a
oublier (tr)	forget, overlook 7a
ouvrir (tr)	open, access a (computer) file 8i M
ouvrir sur (intr)	open on to 8i
ouvrir, s' (ref)	open 8i
ouvrir les veines, s' (ref)	slash one's wrists 8i
oxydiser (tr)	oxidize 7a
P **pâlir** (intr)	turn pale 8a
palper (tr)	feel 7a
panser (tr)	dress (wound), groom (horse) 7a
paraître (intr)	appear 9e
paralyser (tr)	paralyze 7a
parcourir (tr)	travel across, look through (book) 8d
pardonner (à qqn) (tr)	pardon, forgive someone 7a
paresser (intr)	laze about 7a
parier (tr)	bet 7a
parier sur (intr)	back, gamble on 7a
parler (tr & intr)	speak, talk 7a M
parler franchement (intr)	speak candidly 7a
partager (tr)	share, share out 7g
participer à (intr)	take part, join in 7a
***partir** (intr)	depart, set off, leave 8j
La fusée est partie. (intr)	*The rocket lifted off.*
***passer** (intr)	pass, drop in/by 7a
passer (tr)	pass, hand round 7a
passer au crible (tr)	screen 7a
***passer de mode** (intr)	go out of fashion 7a
passer de, se (ref)	dispense with, do without 7a
passer en contrebande (tr)	smuggle 7a
passer en revue (tr)	survey 7a
passer l'aspirateur (tr)	vacuum 7a
***passer par** (intr)	go through 7a
passer prendre (tr)	call for 7a
passer, se (ref)	occur 7a

195

pisser (intr)   piss, urinate 7a
     Son nez pisse le sang. (tr)   *Blood is pouring out of his nose.*

placer (tr)	place 7h M
plaindre (tr)	pity 9o
plaindre, se (ref)	complain 9o
plaire (à qqn) (intr)	please (someone) 9p M
plaisanter (intr)	joke, have a joke 7a
planer (intr)	glide 7a
planter (tr)	plant 7a
plâtrer (tr)	plaster 7a
pleurer (intr)	weep, cry 7a
pleuvoir (intr)	rain 10d M
plier (tr)	fold 7a
plisser (tr)	pleat 7a
plomber (tr)	seal, fill (tooth) 7a
plonger (tr & intr)	plunge 7g
poignarder (tr)	stab 7a
poinçonner (tr)	punch 7a
pointer à la sortie (intr)	clock out 7a
pointer à l'arrivée (intr)	clock in 7a
poivrer (tr)	pepper 7a
polir (tr)	polish, shine 8a
polluer (tr)	pollute 7a
polycopier (tr)	photocopy 7a
pomper (tr)	pump 7a
pondre (tr)	lay 9a
porter (tr)	wear, carry 7a
porter un toast à (tr)	toast (in champagne, etc) 7a
porter des fruits (tr)	bear fruit 7a
poser (tr)	fit 7a
poser une question (tr)	ask a question 7a
posséder (tr)	possess 7e
poster (tr)	mail 7a
potasser (intr)	study (hard), cram 7a
poudrer (tr)	powder 7a
pouffer de rire (intr)	giggle 7a
pourchasser (tr)	pursue 7a
pourrir (intr)	rot 8a
poursuivre (tr)	follow up 9u
poursuivre en justice (tr)	prosecute 9u
pourvoir (de) (tr)	provide (with) 10j
pourvoir en personnel (tr)	staff 10j
pousser (tr)	shove 7a

prétendre (tr)	allege 9a
prêter (tr)	lend 7a
prévaloir (sur) (intr)	prevail (over) 10i
prévoir (tr)	forecast 10j
prier (tr)	pray, beg 7a
priser (tr)	prize 7a
privatiser (tr)	privatize 7a
priver de, se (ref)	go without 7a
procéder (intr)	proceed 7e
procréer (tr)	procreate 7a
produire (tr)	produce 9d
profiter de (intr)	profit (from) 7a
profiter à (intr)	benefit (someone) 7a
programmer (tr)	program 7a
projeter (tr)	project 7c
prolonger (tr)	prolong 7g
promener (tr)	take for a walk 7d
promener se (ref)	go for a walk 7d
promettre (tr)	promise 9l
promouvoir (tr)	promote 10f [M]
prononcer (tr)	pronounce 7h
prononcer une condamnation (tr)	convict, sentence 7h
proposer (tr)	propose 7a
prospérer (intr)	thrive 7e
prostituer, se (ref)	prostitute oneself 7a
protéger (tr)	protect 7e/7g
protester (tr)	protest 7a
prouver (tr)	prove 7a
publier (tr)	issue 7a
puer (tr)	stink 7a
puiser (tr)	draw (water, resources) 7a
pulvériser (tr)	grind 7a
punir (tr)	punish 8a
purifier (tr)	purify 7a

Q

qualifier (tr)	qualify 7a
questionner (tr)	question, interrogate 7a

R

raccourcir (tr)	shorten 8a
raccourcir, se (ref)	become shorter 8a
raccrocher (intr)	hang up (the telephone) 7a
raconter (tr)	tell, relate (a story) 7a
radiodiffuser (tr)	broadcast 7a

recopier (tr)	write out 7a
recoucher (tr)	put back to bed 7a
recourir à (intr)	resort to,
	have recourse to 7c
recouvrer (tr)	recover, regain 7a
recouvrir (tr)	cover over,
	cover again, hide 8i
rectifier (tr)	rectify 7a
reculer (intr)	reverse, move back 7a
recupérer (tr)	salvage get back 7e
recycler (tr)	recycle 7a
rédiger (tr)	draw up, draft 7g
rédiger le compte-rendu (tr)	draft the report 7g
redoubler (tr)	increase, redouble;
	repeat year at school 7a
redouter (tr)	dread 7a
redresser (tr)	straighten, set upright 7a
redresser, se (ref)	sit up 7a
réduire (tr)	reduce, cut down 9d
réduire en esclavage (tr)	enslave 9d
refaire (tr)	redo 9j
refaire qqn de qch (tr)	do out of 9j
réfléchir (intr)	reflect 8a
réfléchir à (intr)	think over 8a
refléter (tr)	reflect (light) 7a
réfrigérer (tr)	refrigerate 7e
refroidir (tr)	cool down 8a
refuser (tr)	turn down 7a
réfuter (tr)	refute 7a
regarder (tr)	look at, watch 7a
regarder fixement (tr)	stare at, gaze at 7a
régler (tr)	settle 7e
régler sa note (tr)	check out, pay bill 7e
regretter (tr)	be sorry 7a
rejeter (tr)	reject 7c
rejoindre (tr)	rejoin 9o
rejoindre, se (ref)	link up 9o
réjouir, se (ref)	rejoice 8a
relâcher (tr)	loosen, slacken 7a
relayer (tr)	relay 7i
relever (tr)	lift, heighten 7d
remarquer (tr)	remark, notice 7a
rembobiner (tr)	rewind (cassette) 7a
rembourser (tr)	reimburse 7a
remercier (tr)	thank 7a
remettre à (tr)	hand over 9l

reprendre la forme (tr)	get fit 9q
représenter (tr)	represent, stand for 7a
réprimander (tr)	scold 7a
reprocher (tr)	reproach 7a
reproduire (tr)	reproduce 9d
réserver (tr)	reserve, book 7a
resister à (intr)	resist 7a
résonner (intr)	resonate, echo 7a
résoudre (tr)	resolve, work out 9r [M]
résoudre, se (ref)	decide, make up one's mind 9r
respecter (tr)	respect 7a
respirer (tr & intr)	breathe 7a
ressembler à (intr)	take after 7a
resserrer (tr)	tighten 7a
***ressortir** (intr)	stand out 8j
restaurer (tr)	restore 7a
***rester** (intr)	stay 7a
***rester à jeun** (intr)	fast 7a
***rester en arrière** (intr)	stop behind, drop back 7a
***rester là** (intr)	stand by 7a
résulter de (intr)	result from 7a
résumer (tr)	summarize 7a
retarder (tr & intr)	delay, be slow (clock) 7a
retenir (tr)	hold back, detain 8k
retentir (intr)	blare, echo 8a
retirer (tr)	draw out 7a
retirer, se (ref)	withdraw 7a
retourner (tr)	turn upside down 7a
***retourner** (intr)	return, go back 7a
retourner, se (ref)	turn round 7a
rétrécir (tr)	shrink 8a
rétrécir, se (ref)	narrow 8a
retrouver (tr)	find again, meet 7a
retrouver, se (ref)	meet each other (arranged) 7a
réunir (tr)	reunite, amalgamate 8a
réussir (intr)	succeed, take off (project) 8a
réussir à (intr)	succeed in, pass (exam) 8a
réussir à faire (tr)	manage to do, succeed in doing 8a
revaloir (tr)	pay back, get even 10i
rêvasser (intr)	daydream 7a
réveiller (tr)	wake (someone) 7a
réveiller, se (ref)	wake up 7a

savoir (tr)	know 10h [M]
savoir nager (intr)	know how, be able to swim 10h
savonner (tr)	soap 7a
savourer (tr)	savor 7a
sceller (tr)	seal 7a
sécher (tr)	dry 7e
sécher les cours (tr)	skip classes 7e
secouer (tr)	shake 7a
secourir (tr)	help, assist 8d
séduire (tr)	seduce 9d
séjourner (intr)	stay 7a
sélectionner (tr)	select 7a
seller (tr)	saddle 7a
sembler (intr)	look (seem) 7a
semer (tr)	sow 7d
sentir (tr & intr)	feel, sense, smell 8j [M]
sentir, se (ref)	feel 8j
séparer (tr)	separate 7a
séparer de (tr)	separate from 7a
séparer de, se (ref)	part (company) 7a
serrer (tr)	clamp 7a
servir (tr)	serve; bowl (sport) 8j
servir à boire (tr)	serve drinks 8j
servir à (+ infinitive) (intr)	serve to, be used for 8j
servir de, se (ref)	use 8j
servir de (intr)	put to use as 8j
shooter (intr)	shoot (soccer) 7a
shooter, se (ref)	inject oneself with drugs 7a
siffler (intr)	hiss, whistle 7a
signer (tr)	sign 7a
signer, se (ref)	cross oneself 7a
signifier (tr)	mean 7a
situer, se (ref)	be located 7a
soigner (tr)	care for 7a
solder (tr)	sell cheap 7a
solidifier (tr)	solidify 7a
songer (tr & intr)	dream, think 6b
sonner (intr)	sound 7a
sonner l'heure (tr)	chime 7a
sortir (tr)	bring out 8j
***sortir** (intr)	go out 8a
***sortir comme un ouragan** (intr)	storm out 8a
***sortir comme une flèche** (intr)	dart out 8j
***sortir de** (intr)	go out of 8j
soucier de, se (ref)	care about 7a

supporter (tr)	stand, bear 7a
supposer (intr)	suppose 7a
supprimer (tr)	cut out 7a
surgir (intr)	pop up 8a
surpasser (tr)	surpass 7a
surplomber (intr)	overhang 7a
surprendre (tr)	surprise 9q
sursauter (intr)	start 7a
surveiller (tr)	supervise 7a
survivre (intr)	survive 9v
survivre a qqn (intr)	outlive someone 9v
suspendre (tr)	suspend 9a
synthétiser (tr)	synthesize 7a

T

tabasser (tr)	beat someone up 7a
tacher (tr)	spot, dirty 7a
tailler (tr)	prune 7a
taire, se (ref)	be silent 9p
tambouriner (tr & intr)	drum 7a
tamiser (tr)	sieve 7a
taper (tr & intr)	hit, beat 7a
taper à la machine (tr)	type 7a
Il tape soixante mots par minute. (tr)	*He types sixty words per minute.*
taper du pied (intr)	stamp 7a
taper sur les nerfs de qqn (intr)	get on someone's nerves 7a
tapir, se (ref)	cower 8a
tapisser les murs (tr)	hang wallpaper 7a
tapoter (tr & intr)	tap 7a
taquiner (tr)	tease 7a
taxer (tr)	tax 7a
téléphoner (qch, à qqn) (tr)	telephone 7a
témoigner (intr)	witness, testify 7a
témoigner de qch (tr)	bear witness to 7a
tendre (tr)	stretch, hold out, offer 9a
tendre une embuscade (tr)	ambush 9a
tenir (tr & intr)	hold 8k M
Tiens! (intr)	*Really! Well!*
tenir bon (intr)	hold one's own 8k
tenir compte de (tr)	take into account, allow for 8k
tenir le coup (tr)	bear up 8k
tenir, se (ref)	stand 8k
tenter (tr)	tempt 7a

traverser (tr)	go across, cross 7a
trébucher (intr)	trip, stumble 7a
trembler (intr)	tremble 7a
tremper (tr)	soak, steep, dip 7a
tresser (tr)	twine, braid 7a
tricher (intr)	cheat 7a
tricoter (tr)	knit 7a
trier (tr)	sort 7a
tromper (tr)	mislead 7a
tromper, se (ref)	be mistaken 7a
trouver (tr)	find 7a
trouver, se (ref)	be found, be 7a
trouver à redire à (tr)	object to 7a
tuer (tr)	kill 7a
tutoyer (se) (tr & ref)	say "**tu**" (address informally) 7f
tyranniser (tr)	bully 7a

U

unir (tr)	unite 8a
unir, s' (ref)	bond 8a
uriner (intr)	urinate 7a
user (tr)	wear out 7a
user, s' (ref)	wear out, become worn out 7a
utiliser (tr)	use 7a

V

vaciller (intr)	flicker 7a
vaincre (tr)	overcome 9v ☐M
valoir (intr)	be worth 10i ☐M
vanter, se (ref)	boast, brag 7a
vaporiser (tr)	spray 7a
vaporiser, se (ref)	vaporize 7a
varier (tr)	vary 7a
vendre (tr)	sell 9a ☐M
vendre au détail (tr)	retail 9a
vénérer (tr)	worship, revere 7e
*****venir** (intr)	come 8k
venez vous asseoir auprés de nous	*come and join us, come sit with us*
*****venir à échéance** (intr)	fall due 8k
*****venir à l'esprit** (intr)	occur 8k
*****venir de Rome** (intr)	come from Rome 8k
*****venir de faire** (intr)	have just done 8k
*****venir voir** (tr)	come and see, come round 8k

Martin H. Manser has been a professional reference book editor since 1980. He has compiled or edited more than 150 reference books, particularly English language dictionaries, thesauruses, and Bible reference titles. He is also a language trainer and consultant with national companies and organisations. He and his wife live in Aylesbury and have a son and a daughter. Visit his website at www.martinmanser.com.

David Pickering is an experienced reference book compiler, free-lance since 1992. He has contributed (often as sole author or chief editor) to around 200 books in the fields of general reference, English language, the arts, history and popular interest. He has also broadcast many times on a variety of subjects on radio and television. He lives in Buckingham with his wife and two sons.

The Secret Life of the English Language

Buttering Parsnips, Twocking Chavs

MARTIN H. MANSER

Associate editor: David Pickering

PHOENIX

A PHOENIX PAPERBACK

First published in Great Britain in 2007
by Weidenfeld & Nicolson
as *Buttering Parsnips, Twocking Chavs:*
The Secret Life of the English Language
This paperback edition published in 2008
by Phoenix,
an imprint of Orion Books Ltd,
Orion House, 5 Upper St Martin's Lane,
London WC2H 9EA

An Hachette Livre UK company

3 5 7 9 10 8 6 4 2

A CIP catalogue record for this book
is available from the British Library.

ISBN 978-0-7538-2417-7

Printed and bound in Great Britain by CPI Mackays, Chatham, ME5 8TD

The Orion Publishing Group's policy is to use papers that
are natural, renewable and recyclable products and
made from wood grown in sustainable forests. The logging
and manufacturing processes are expected to conform to
the environmental regulations of the country of origin.
www.orionbooks.co.uk

Contents

Introduction

Welcome to the fascinating world of words – an exploration of the exciting 'nooks and crannies' of the vocabulary of the English language.

Can you think of words with five or six consecutive consonants? What is the origin of *chortle*, *cloud cuckoo land*, and the origin of many different kinds of slang?

Many of us have to listen to estate agents' sales patter: 'a *bijou* [crammed] kitchen', 'a mature [overgrown] garden'. We hear on the phone 'someone will be with you shortly' but are kept waiting for hours. We may read in foreign hotels 'Here speeching American', 'Please to bathe inside the tub'.

Here you will learn more about homophones (*right*, *rite*, and *write*) and spoonerisms (*a well-boiled icicle*), not forgetting famous last words ('either that wallpaper goes, or I do'). Then there are words in other languages that have no exact English equivalent, such as *puijilittatuq* (Inuktit, Canada) 'he does not know which way to turn because of the many seals he has seen come to the ice surface'.

So, word buffs – in a word – *enjoy*, be enraptured, gorge on this veritable cornucopia of surprising and delightful words!

Martin H. Manser   David Pickering

1 Baby talk

The building blocks of language

The English language is but one of thousands of languages that the inventive human mind has given birth to over the millennia. The vast majority are born, kicking and mewling, into a family of linked languages, which share a distinct ancestry and many key characteristics. Most have numerous brothers and sisters, with whom they may have remarkable similarities in terms of both grammar and vocabulary. Just like human babies, new languages are full of surprises. They are playful (gurgling with delight over words that might be 50 letters in length), unpredictable (finding three ways to pronounce what looks like the same word) and often difficult to control (defying all the rules to create irregular plurals or words with letters that are not even pronounced). They frequently infuriate by kicking their toys out of the cradle, only to redeem themselves by their irrepressible energy and inventiveness.

Every language rests upon its vocabulary, while the vocabulary rests ultimately upon its alphabet. The English alphabet of just 26 letters has provided the necessary building blocks for the creation of upwards of half a million words (perhaps five million, depending upon the definition of the term 'word').

In the beginning was the Word, and the Word
was with God, and the Word was God.

Bible. John 1:1

Family matters
Language families

There are thousands of languages in use throughout the world today, and to these must be added thousands more that have long since become extinct. The largest language families are listed here, though it should be noted that the division of languages into family groups is a contentious matter and the authenticity of some of these groupings is hotly disputed.

Language family	Number of languages
Niger-Congo	1514
Austronesian	1268
Trans-New Guinea	564
Indo-European [1]	449
Sino-Tibetan	403
Afro-Asiatic	375
Nilo-Saharan	204
Pama-Nyungan	178
Oto-Manguean	174
Austro-Asiatic	169
Sepik-Ramu	100
Tai-Kadai	76
Tupi	76
Dravidian	73
Mayan	69

1. the family to which English belongs

Keeping it within the family
Indo-European languages

The Indo-European family of languages to which English belongs may have evolved from an earlier Proto-Indo-European language that was first spoken in the region of the Ural Mountains around 5000 BC (though whether there was in reality such a language remains a matter of debate). The Indo-European family as we know it today includes most of the languages of modern Europe and several Asian languages, among them French, German, Portuguese, Russian, Spanish, Bengali and Hindi. It is now the largest language family in the world, with some three billion native speakers.

Subgroup	*First recorded*
Indo-Iranian [1]	*c.*2000 BC
Anatolian [2]	*c.*1800 BC
Greek	*c.*1400 BC
Italic [3]	*c.*1000 BC
Celtic	*c.*600 BC
Germanic [4]	*c.*100 AD
Armenian	*c.*400 AD
Tocharian [5]	*c.*500 AD
Balto-Slavic	*c.*1000 AD
Albanian	*c.*1400 AD

1. includes Sanskrit and Persian
2. spoken by the Hittites of Anatolia (modern Turkey); now extinct
3. includes Latin and the so-called 'Romance languages' (French, Italian, Spanish, Portuguese, etc.)
4. the subgroup to which English belongs
5. as spoken by an extinct civilization of NW China

Foreign legions
Languages by number of speakers

English currently ranks as the second most spoken language in the world, having long since established itself as the first language of commerce and technology. The following table lists languages with over 50 million speakers – as a native and as a second language:

Language	Number of speakers	Native speakers	As a second language
Mandarin Chinese	1051 million	873 million	178 million
English	510 million	340 million	170 million
Hindi	490 million	370 million	120 million
Spanish	420 million	350 million	70 million
Russian	255 million	145 million	110 million
Arabic	230 million	206 million	24 million
Bengali	215 million	196 million	19 million
Portuguese	213 million	203 million	10 million
Japanese	127 million	126 million	1 million
French	130 million	67 million	63 million
German	129 million	101 million	28 million
Urdu	104 million	61 million	43 million
Punjabi	88 million	60 million	28 million
Vietnamese	86 million	70 million	16 million
Tamil	77 million	68 million	9 million
Javanese	76 million	no data available	no data available
Telugu	75 million	70 million	5 million
Korean	71 million	no data available	no data available
Marathi	71 million	68 million	3 million
Italian	61 million	no data available	no data available

**I speak Spanish to God, Italian to women,
French to men, and German to my horse.**

Charles V, Holy Roman emperor

Alphabet soup
Alphabet facts

The spoken word existed long before the written word. The first essential step in the process of developing written languages was the introduction of written symbols resembling sounds, and in due course their organization into alphabets. For all its importance in the world today, English has neither the oldest alphabet nor the alphabet with the most vowels or consonants. It does, however, share with other alphabets of the world many features, such as the distinction of vowel from consonant and the convention of placing letters in a certain order when the alphabet is recited.

The word 'alphabet', incidentally, comes from the Greek words *alpha* and *beta* (the names of the first two words of the Greek alphabet).

Alphabet fact	*Language*
earliest written letters	Chinese, on pottery from Sian, Shensi, 5000–4000 BC
earliest written alphabet	Ugarit, Syria, *c.*1450 BC (32 letters) [1]
most letters	Cambodian (72 letters)
fewest letters	Rotokas in central Bougainville Island (12 letters)
most vowels	Sedang, Vietnam (55 vowels)
fewest vowels	Abkhazian (2 vowels)
most consonantal sounds	Ubykhs in the Caucasus (80–85 consonants)
fewest consonantal sounds	Rotokas in central Bougainville Island (6 consonants)

1. this may now have been overtaken by a Semitic alphabet discovered carved into a cliff on the western bank of the Nile in Egypt in 1999. It has been dated to between 1800 BC and 1900 BC

A to Z
Alphabet size

The number of letters in an alphabet varies considerably from language to language. The presence of unfamiliar characters in other languages makes them well nigh indecipherable to non-speakers, and this is without taking into account the various diacritic marks such as accents that many languages also employ. A basic comparison of the number of letters in a selection of languages illustrates the extent to which languages differ, even at this fundamental level:

Language	Number of letters	Language	Number of letters
Arabic	28	Italian	21
Armenian	38	Phoenician	22
Braille	63	Polish	32
Cambodian	72	Portuguese	23
Catalan	27	Punjabi	42
Danish	29	Roman	26
English	26	Rotokas	12
Etruscan	26	Russian	33
Finnish	21	Swedish	29
Georgian	33	Thai	59
Greek	24	Turkish	29
Hawaiian	18	Ukrainian	33
Hebrew	22	Uzbek	35

Therefore is the name of it called Babel; because the LORD did there confound the language of all the earth: and from thence did the LORD scatter them abroad upon the face of all the earth.

Bible, Genesis 11:9

Alpha to omega
The world's oldest living alphabet

The oldest alphabet still in use today is that devised by the ancient Greeks. According to legend, it was invented specifically as a way of ensuring that the *Odyssey* and other epic tales by the Greek poet Homer were passed down to posterity. At first glance the Greek alphabet, which much influenced the development of the English letter system, looks completely unrelated to the English alphabet. On closer examination, however, it becomes clear that most Greek characters correspond directly to English letters, though Greek lacks any equivalents for the English c, f, h, j, q, u, v or w:

Greek letter	English equivalent	Greek letter	English equivalent
A/α (alpha)	a	N/ν (nu)	n
B/β (beta)	b	Ξ/ξ (xi)	x
Γ/γ (gamma)	g	O/o (omicron)	o
Δ/δ (delta)	d	Π/π (pi)	p
E/ε (epsilon)	e	P/ρ (rho)	r
Z/ζ (zeta)	z	Σ/σς (sigma)	s
H/η (eta)	e	T/τ (tau)	t
Θ/θ (theta)	th	Y/ν (upsilon)	y[1]
I/ι (iota)	i	Φ/φ (phi)	ph
K/κ (kappa)	k	X/χ (chi)	kh
Λ/λ (lambda)	l	Ψ/ψ (psi)	ps
M/μ (mu)	m	Ω/ω (omega)	o

1. the letter 'y', incidentally, was supposedly invented by the mythological character Palamedes, a hero of the Trojan War

Lost letters
Old English letters

The oldest examples of written English consist of inscriptions written in the ancient runic alphabet, a writing system common to much of northern Europe from around the 3rd century AD and introduced to Britain by Anglo-Saxon invaders in the 5th century. It had disappeared from use by the 14th century. Each symbol (rune) had its own name and meaning, which was commonly a reference to a feature of everyday life or else to a sacred entity such as a god or animal with supposedly magical powers. The first six letters of the runic alphabet gave it the name by which it was once known, the 'futhorc'.

Rune	Name	Meaning	Modern equivalent
ᛉ	feoh	wealth	f
ᚾ	ür	aurochs [1]	u
ᛈ	þorn	thorn	th
ᛗ	ōs	mouth	o
ᚱ	räd	riding	r
ᚻ	cen	torch	c
ᚷ	gyfu	gift	g
ᛈ	wynn	joy	w
ᚺ	hægl	hail	h
ᛏ	nyd	need	n
ᛁ	ĭs	ice	i
ᛡ	ger	harvest	j
ᛍ	ēoh	yew	eo

Rune	Name	Meaning	Modern equivalent
ᛈ	peorþ	hearth	p
ᛉ	eolh	elksedge [2]	x
ᛋ	sigel	sun	s
ᛏ	tir	Tiw [3]	t
ᛒ	beorc	birch	b
ᛖ	eoh	horse	e
ᛗ	man	man	m
ᛚ	lagu	water	l
ᛝ	ing	Ing [4]	ng
ᛟ	eþel	homeland	oe
ᛞ	dæg	day	d
ᚪ	ac	oak	a
ᚫ	aesc	ash	æ
ᛦ	yr	bow	y
ᛠ	ear	earth	ea
ᚸ	gar	spear	g
ᛣ	calc	(unknown)	k

1. the old name for bison
2. a grasslike plant
3. Anglo-Saxon god (after whom Tuesday is named)
4. Anglo-Saxon hero

Lettering
English alphabet facts

The alphabet of modern English is close to that of Latin, as written down by the ancient Romans and introduced to Britain by Roman missionaries from the 6th century AD. The alphabet of the ancient Romans had its differences, however, with only 22 letters (no distinction being made between i and j or between u and v and there being no equivalent of w and y). The letters of the modern English alphabet all have distinct characteristics and histories. Some are remarkable for their age. Others are notable for the frequency with which they appear, or do not appear. More still have unique qualities of other kinds:

Alphabet fact	Letters
oldest letter	O [1]
newest letters	J and V (post-17th century)
most frequent letter	E
least frequent letters	Q and Z
most frequent digraph	TH
most frequent trigraph	THE
letters with no straight lines	C, O, S
letters with no curved lines	A, E, F, H, I, K, L, M, N, T, V, W, X, Y, Z
symmetrical letters	H, I, O, X

1. the letter 'O' made its first appearance (as a consonant) in the Semitic alphabet c.1300 BC and was later reinterpreted as a vowel by the Greeks and Romans before taking its place in the alphabet of Old English. Its shape has remained unchanged throughout its long history

A for 'orses
Cockney alphabet

There are many ways to remember the letters of the alphabet. One of the best-known, and more light-hearted, ways is the so-called 'Cockney alphabet', a series of puns and other comic tags designed some time early in the 20th century (possibly in the music hall and known in several variant forms) to make letters easier to remember:

Letter	Tag
A	for 'orses/for Gardner/for a disiac
B	for mutton
C	for yourself/for miles/for Seaforth Highlanders
D	for dumb/for 'ential/for mation/for rent/for dentures/for Mitty
E	for brick/for Peron/for Adam/for ning standard
F	for vescence/for been had
G	for crying out loud/for police/for get it
H	for retirement/for beauty/for consent
I	for lutin'/for the girls/for the engine/for an eye/for Novello
J	for oranges/for cakes
K	for teria/for restaurant
L	for leather
M	for sis
N	for lope/for a penny/for a dig
O	for the top/for a drink/for the wings of a dove/for the rainbow
P	for ming fleas/for a whistle/for urinalysis/for ming seals/for soup
Q	for everything/for a song/for flowers/for snooker/for the bus
R	for mo/for crown/for Askey/for Daley
S	for you/for Rantzen/for Williams/for midable
T	for two
U	for me/for instance/for mystic/for mism
V	for la différence/for la France
W	for quits/for a quid
X	for breakfast/for the spot
Y	for mistress/for crying out loud/for runts
Z	for breezes/for the doctor

Able to zebra
Phonetic alphabets

The need to identify letters clearly in radio messages led to the development (from World War I onwards) of large numbers of alternative phonetic alphabets, in which each letter of the alphabet is expanded into a full word or name, making confusion less likely. Three of the better-known phonetic alphabets are listed here:

Letter	Radio alphabet	NATO alphabet [1]	Names alphabet [2]
A	Able	Alpha	Andrew
B	Baker	Bravo	Benjamin
C	Charlie	Charlie	Charles
D	Dog	Delta	David
E	Easy	Echo	Edward
F	Fox	Foxtrot	Frederick
G	George	Golf	George
H	How	Hotel	Harry
I	Item	India	Isaac
J	Jig	Juliet	Jack
K	King	Kilo	King
L	Love	Lima	Lucy
M	Mike	Mike	Mary
N	Nan	November	Nellie
O	Oboe	Oscar	Oliver
P	Peter	Papa	Peter
Q	Queen	Quebec	Queenie
R	Roger	Romeo	Robert
S	Sugar	Sierra	Sugar
T	Tare	Tango	Tommy

Letter	Radio alphabet	NATO alphabet	Names alphabet
U	Uncle	Uniform	Uncle
V	Victor	Victor	Victor
W	William	Whisky	William
X	X-ray	X-ray	Xmas
Y	Yoke	Yankee	Yellow
Z	Zebra	Zulu	Zebra

1. adopted by the North Atlantic Treaty Organization around 1955

2. an example of many variant alphabets used in telephony internationally

Romeo foxtrot zebra

Weird words
English vocabulary facts

The English vocabulary is as rich as any in the world's many languages. Within that vocabulary there are many words that have unique
qualities not always immediately apparent. Consider the following
curiosities:

Vocabulary fact	*Word(s)*
longest one-syllable words	scraunched, screeched, strengths
longest run of consonants in a word	archchronicler, catchphrase, eschscholtzia, latchstring, lengthsman, postphthisic
longest word with letters in reverse alphabetical order	spoonfeed
longest word with letters lacking ascenders, descenders and dots in lower case	overnumerousnesses
longest word without a vowel	rhythm, syzygy
longest words with unrepeated letters	dermatoglyphics, misconjugatedly, uncopyrightable
longest word with each letter repeated at least twice	unprosperousness
longest word with each main vowel repeated twice	ultrarevolutionaries
only word ending in 'mt'	dreamt
only words beginning and ending in 'und'	underfund, underground

Vocabulary fact	*Word(s)*
only words ending in 'dous'	hazardous, horrendous, stupendous, tremendous
only words with a letter repeated six times	degenerescence, indivisibility, nonannouncement
only word comprising two letters used three times	deeded
only word with a triple letter	goddessship
only word with five consecutive vowels	queueing
only words with consecutive u's	continuum, muumuu, residuum, vacuum
only word with four back-to-back double letters	subbookkeeper/subbookkeeping
only word with two synonyms with opposite meanings	cleave (adhere and separate)
words with all the vowels in reverse order	duoliteral, neuroepithelial, subcontinental, uncomplimentary, unoriental
words with all the vowels in alphabetical order	abstemious, abstentious, acheilous, acleistous, affectious, anemious, arsenious, caesious, facetious, fracedinous, majestious, parecious
words with no rhyme	month, orange, purple, silver
word with the most definitions	set

Quick brown foxes
Pangrams

A pangram is a grammatical sentence containing every letter in the alphabet. The most admired pangrams are those that include all 26 letters of the alphabet in the shortest number of characters, although the elegance of the resulting sentence is also an important factor. Famous examples include the following:

Pangram	Number of characters
We promptly judged antique ivory buckles for the next prize	50
How piqued gymnasts can level six jumping razorback frogs	49
Crazy Fredericka bought many very exquisite opal jewels	48
Sixty zippers were quickly picked from the woven jute bag	48
Amazingly few discotheques provide jukeboxes	40
Jump by vow of quick, lazy strength in Oxford	36
Heavy boxes perform quick waltzes and jigs	36
The quick brown fox jumps over the lazy dog	35
Pack my box with five dozen liquor jugs	32
Jackdaws love my big sphinx of quartz	31
The five boxing wizards jump quickly	31
How quickly daft jumping zebras vex	30
Sphinx of black quartz, judge my vow	29
Quick zephyrs blow, vexing daft Jim	29
Waltz, bad nymph, for quick jigs vex	28

Talking common
Word frequency

Some words crop up frequently in everyday use, while others make appearances very rarely. Surveys of the most commonly used words in the English language often draw a distinction between spoken and written English and tend to vary somewhat in the order in which the words are placed, but the following list includes all the usual suspects:

Rank	Spoken English	Written English
1	the	the
2	and	of
3	I	to
4	to	in
5	of	and
6	a	a
7	you	for
8	that	was
9	in	is
10	it	that

Personally I like short words and vulgar fractions.

Winston Churchill

Sesquipedalianism
Longest words

For the purposes of the following list of longest words certain categories have been ignored. These include words that have never been used by anyone except their creator (for instance, James Joyce's 'mangongwheeltracktrolleyglarejuggernaut') and highly specialized technological terms, such as the 1185-letter word for a strain of the tobacco mosaic virus or the 3641-letter name of the protein bovine glutamate dehydrogenase. Longest of all 'words' could be said to be the systematic name for deoxyribonucleic acid of the human mitochondria, which is approximately 207,000 letters long.

The word 'sesquipedalianism', incidentally, comes from Horace and refers to words 'a foot and a half long'.

Word	Number of letters and meaning
sesquipedalianism	17 concerning long words
disproportionableness	21 capability for disproportion
incomprehensibilities	21 things not understood
interdenominationalism	22 between denominations
antitransubstantiationalist	27 doubting transubstantiation
honorificabilitudinitatibus	27 honourableness
antidisestablishmentarianism	28 defending state recognition of the church
floccinaucinihilipilification	29 estimating as worthless
hipomonsteresquipedalophobia	28 fear of long words
hippopotomontrosesquipedalianism	32 use of long words

Word	Number of letters and meaning
hyperpolysyllabicsesquipedalianist	**34** one who uses long words
hepaticocholangiocholecystenterostomies	**39** bladder operation
pneumonoultramicroscopicsilicovolcanokoniosis	**45** lung disease of miners
Chargoggagoggmanchauggagoggchaubunagungamaugg	**45** lake in Massachusetts
Taumatawhakatangihangakoauauotamateapokaiwhenuakitanatahu	**57** hill in New Zealand
Llanfairpwllgwyngyllgogerychwyrndrobwllllantysiliogogogoch[1]	**58** Welsh place name

1. the longest place name in Britain (created to attract 19th-century tourists), meaning 'the church of St Mary in a hollow of white hazel near a rapid whirlpool and near St Tysilio's church by the red cave'

I am a Bear of Very Little Brain, and long words Bother me.

Winnie-the-Pooh

Enough tough coughing
Spelling and pronunciation

The spelling of English is notoriously unpredictable and is made particularly problematic by the fact that there are often several different ways in which the same sound may be rendered on the page. Consequently, the pronunciation of apparently similar words may vary considerably (usually largely on etymological grounds). George Bernard Shaw once illustrated the problems presented by pronunciation in English by writing the word 'fish' as 'ghoti' ('gh' as in enough, 'o' as in women, and 'ti' as in nation). The problems are memorably summarized in the following well-known poem, by an anonymous hand:

> I take it you already know
> Of tough and bough and cough and dough?
> Others may stumble, but not you,
> On hiccough, thorough, lough and through?
> Well done! And now you wish, perhaps,
> To learn of less familiar traps?
>
> Beware of heard, a dreadful word
> That looks like beard and sounds like bird,
> And dead: it's said like bed, not bead –
> For goodness sake don't call it deed!
> Watch out for meat and great and threat,
> They rhyme with suite and straight and debt.
>
> A moth is not a moth in mother,
> Nor both in bother, broth in brother,
> And here is not a match for there
> Nor dear and fear for bear and pear;
> And then there's dose and rose and lose –
> Just look them up – and goose and choose,

And cork and work and card and ward,
And font and front and word and sword,
And do and go and thwart and cart –
Come, come, I've hardly made a start!
A dreadful language? Man alive!
I'd mastered it when I was five!

Though the tough cough and hiccough plough me through,
O'er life's dark lough my course I still pursue.
Anonymous

fork handles

Ghost letters
Silent letters

Spelling in English is further complicated by the presence in many words of silent, unpronounced letters. There are far more of these words in the English vocabulary than most people realize. It has been estimated, indeed, that around 60 per cent of words in English have silent letters. Old English was relatively free of them, but their number has proliferated chiefly through the absorption of thousands of words from other languages, which take a different approach to pronunciation. Unfortunately there are no rules that govern the behaviour of such silent letters or reliable ways of predicting their presence – the only option is to learn them all individually.

A   artistically, clinically, dramatically, logically, mortuary, musically, romantically, stoically

B   bomb, climb, comb, crumb, doubt, dumb, debt, lamb, limb, numb, plumb, subtle, thumb, tomb

C   indict, muscle, scene, scent, science, scissors, victual

D   badge, edge, handkerchief, handsome, hedge, wedge, Wednesday

E   bridge, careful, clue, corpse, eulogy, lonely, more, serve, stationery

F   halfpenny

G   align, benign, champagne, deign, design, diaphragm, feign, foreigner, gnarl, gnaw, gnome, high, light, might, nigh, night, paradigm, reign, resign, right, sign, taught, though

H   annihilate, exhaust, exhibition, exhort, ghost, height, heir, honest, hour, messiah, rhubarb, rhyme, rhythm, schism, vehement, vehicle, what, when, where, whether, which, while, white, why

I   business

J   fjord, marijuana

K   knack, knead, knee, knew, knickers, knife, knight, knitting, knob, knock, knot, know, knuckle

L   almost, calf, calm, chalk, folk, half, palm, psalm, salmon, talk, walk, yolk

M   mnemonic

N   autumn, column, condemn, damn, hymn, solemn

O   colonel, people

P   coup, pneumonia, psalm, pseudo, psychiatrist, psychology, receipt

Q   lacquer

R   myrrh

S   aisle, debris, fracas, island, isle, viscount

T   asthma, ballet, castle, Christmas, fasten, gourmet, listen, match, mortgage, often, ricochet, soften, thistle

U   building, catalogue, biscuit, guard, guess, guest, guide, guilty, guitar, rogue, tongue, vogue

V   revving

W   answer, sword, two, whole, whore, wrap, wreck, wren, wrestling, wriggle, wrinkle, wrist, writing, wrong, wrote

X   faux pas, Sioux

Y   they're

Z   chez, rendezvous

You can't be happy with a woman who pronounces both d's in Wednesday.

Peter de Vries

Accidentally sacrilegious
Common misspellings

Some words are misspelled more often than others. The worst offenders, such as *accommodate* and *separate*, are misspelled as frequently as they are spelled correctly. The following list includes many of the most frequently misspelled words, based on recent surveys of misspellings on the worldwide web:

Usual misspelling	*Correct spelling*
accidently	accidentally
accomodate	accommodate
brocolli	broccoli
calender	calendar
cemetary	cemetery
cooly	coolly
definately	definitely
dessicate	desiccate
desparate	desperate
ecstacy	ecstasy
embarassment	embarrassment
harrass	harass
innoculate	inoculate
insistant	insistent
irresistable	irresistible
liason	liaison
millenium	millennium
mischievious	mischievous
momento	memento
necesary	necessary
noticible	noticeable
occurence	occurrence

Usual misspelling	*Correct spelling*
pasttime	pastime
perseverence	perseverance
privelege	privilege
recieve	receive
sacreligious	sacrilegious
seperate	separate
supercede	supersede
transexual	transsexual

accidently mispellt

Of mice and men
Irregular plurals

Another problem area that leads to much spelling difficulty concerns plurals, which all too often involve something more than the simple addition of a final 's' to the singular form. An anonymous poem entitled 'Why English is so hard' details some of the more trouble-some plurals with which speakers of English must contend:

We'll begin with a box, and the plural is boxes;
But the plural of ox should be oxen, not oxes.
Then one fowl is goose, but two are called geese;
Yet the plural of moose should never be meese.
You may find a lone mouse or a whole lot of mice,
But the plural of house is houses, not hice.
If the plural of man is always called men,
Why shouldn't the plural of pan be called pen?
The cow in the plural may be cows or kine,
But the plural of vow is vows, not vine.
And I speak of a foot, and you show me your feet,
But I give you a boot – would a pair be called beet?
If one is a tooth and a whole set are teeth,
Why shouldn't the plural of booth be called beeth?
If the singular is this, and the plural is these,
Should the plural of kiss be nicknamed kese?
Then one may be that, and three may be those,
Yet the plural of hat would never be hose;
We speak of a brother, and also of brethren,
But though we say mother, we never say methren.
The masculine pronouns are he, his, and him,
But imagine the feminine she, shis, and shim!
So our English, I think you will all agree,
Is the trickiest language you ever did see.

2 Child's play

Word creation

The ultimate origins of many words in the English vocabulary are lost in the mists of time, having their roots in languages that were only spoken and are long extinct. The Germanic group of languages to which English belongs did not exist in isolation from the languages of other sub-groups, among them Latin, Norman French and Celtic. Many words from these equally old languages were absorbed into English at a very early date and have survived the various transformations the language has gone through since that time.

New words can arise through a number of different processes. As well as borrowings from other languages, sometimes with altered meanings, the standard vocabulary has been much enriched by the absorption of thousands of dialect terms, many of which are restricted to relatively small geographical areas. Other words owe their origination to mistakes or confusion with similar coinages. Many more have been created out of existing terms through the addition or removal of prefixes or suffixes, through the transformation of a word as a new part of speech or through the combination of two existing terms. Sometimes the invention of specific words can be credited to particular individuals, of whom few have equalled the contribution of William Shakespeare.

The intolerable wrestle with words and meanings.

T.S. Eliot

Dun crags

The oldest words in English

The oldest languages spoken by the native inhabitants of the British Isles were those of the Celtic peoples, who first settled the region around 2500 years ago. Relatively few Celtic words were retained in English, however, after the invading Romans pushed their communities into the remoter parts of western and northern Britain. The Romans in their turn brought the Latin language with them. The natives of Britain, however, proved less enthusiastic to learn the language than peoples of other conquered Roman territories and after the Romans left early in the 5th century only around 200 Latin words survived in the Anglo-Saxon vocabulary, a paltry tribute to nearly 500 years of Roman occupation.

Celtic word	Meaning	Celtic word	Meaning
Avon	river	dun	grey
boggart	ghost	Kent	(unknown)
bray	hill	London	(tribal name)
brock	badger	pen	top
crag	rocky outcrop	torr	peak
Dover	water		

Latin words

alibi, altar, angel, bishop, candle, canon, cell, chest, circus, clerk, community, contradiction, deacon, diocese, divine, education, elephant, equator, formal, grammar, history, hymn, index, interim, legal, lens, library, martyr, memorandum, minor, necessary, omnibus, oyster, priest, purple, rose, school, scripture, series, sock, solitary, temple, tunic, ulcer, vertigo, via.[1]

1. the number of Latin words in the English vocabulary was to increase greatly, however, at a much later date, as detailed later in this chapter

Olde English
Anglo-Saxon English

Anglo-Saxon (or Old English), the earliest form of the English language, dates back to a period that began with the departure of the Romans from Britain in the 5th century AD and ended around the start of the 12th century. Waves of migrating Jutes (from Jutland, in northern Denmark), Saxons (from Germany) and Angles (from southern Denmark) brought their Germanic languages with them and helped shape the vocabulary of Anglo-Saxon England and southern Scotland. Many of the words are short and blunt in nature.

Anglo-Saxon words
abbot, about, after, all, almighty, and, answer, any, arm, ash, ask, ass, at, back, bake, bath, be, beam, beat, bed, beer, belief, belt, bench, between, bird, black, bleak, blood, blossom, boar, body, bold, bond, bone, book, bosom, bridge, bright, bring, broad, broth, brother, burn, busy, can, cheese, chicken, church, cliff, cold, come, cook, crab, craft, dark, daughter, day, dead, death, deed, deep, dish, dive, do, door, down, drink, drive, dusky, ear, earl, earth, eat, edge, eel, eight, else, empty, end, evening, ever, fall, far, fast, fat, father, feather, fell, few, fight, find, finger, fish, five, float, floor, fly, foam, food, foot, for, ford, forth, four, free, friend, from, full, further, gate, ghost, gift, glass, go, God, gold, good, gospel, grim, grind, hail, hale, half, harm, havoc, he, head, heal, health, heat, heaven, help, hereafter, him, his, holy, home, horn, house, hunger, hunt, I, idle, in, joy, keen, kin, king, kiss, knee, ladder, land, lead, leap, learn, less, let, life, light, like, listen, little, lobster, love, lust, make, man, many, meet, mere, mew, midday, might, minster, mood, moor, murder, murky, nail, near, needle, never, new, night, no, offer, offspring, often, other, ox, pound, reach, read, reckless, red, rest, ride, rind, rise, rod, roof, sallow, say, sea, self, send, set, sheep, shellfish, ship, sing, sit, stand, swarthy, theft, then, thing, this, through, town, trap, wan, ward, was, water, wave, what, where, while, whistle, whole, wide, worth, write, yard

Mickle blather
Dialect words

Many of the oldest words in English may still be encountered today in the form of regional dialect terms. Some of these have their origins in the Old English of the Anglo-Saxon period (*c.*500 AD – *c.*1100), while others were purloined at a similar date from Old Norse, Old French and other contemporary languages, or have their origins in the Middle English, Middle Dutch, etc. spoken during the early medieval period (*c.*1100 – *c.*1450). Over the years some of these terms have escaped their regional associations to become considered part of the vocabulary of standard English. Others, however, remain linguistic curiosities rarely heard even in the places where they were formerly widely familiar.

Word	*Meaning*	*Origin* [1]
aboon	above	OE
addled	drunk, bad	OE
adlings	earnings	OE
afeared	frightened	OE
afore	before	OE
anenst	opposite to	OE
arran	spider	OF
arse	bottom	OE
ask	lizard	OE
ass	ask	OE
astead	instead	OE
attercop	spider	OE
atwixt	between	OE
awd	old	ME
aye	always, ever	OE
baht	except, without	OE

1. OE = Old English, OF = Old French, ON = Old Norse, ME = Middle English, MD = Middle Dutch

Word	Meaning	Origin
bairn	child	OE
ban	curse	ON
barf	hill	OE
barn	child	ON
beck	brook	ON
behunt	behind	OE
belk	belch	OE
belly-wark	stomach-ache	OE
besom	broom	OE
bide	endure	OE
bield	stable, stall	OE
blake	sallow	ON
blather/blether	chatter	ON
bocken	vomit	ME
bonny	attractive	OF
brass	money	OE
bray	beat, thrash	OF
breeks	trousers	OE
brek	break	OE
brock	badger	OE
byre	cowshed	OE
cack	excrement	ON
cam	bank, slope	ON
canny	careful, fine, cunning	ME
cap	surprise, surpass	OE
carr	marsh	ON
childer	children	ME
clarty	dirty	ME
clomp	tread heavily	MD
cloot	cloth	OE
clough	ravine	OE
coo	cow	OE
daft	stupid	OE
dale	valley	OE

Word	Meaning	Origin
dee	die	ON
delve	dig	OE
ding	hit	ON
doff	undress	ME
dollop	lump	ON
dowly	dismal, sad	ON
dree	wearisome	OE
ee	eye	OE
emmot	ant	OE
fain	glad	OE
fashion	bring oneself to	OF
fell	hill, slope	ON
fetch	give	OE
fettle	deal with	OE
flit	move house	ON
foisty	musty	OF
fond	foolish	ME
foss	waterfall	ON
gan	go	OE
gat	got	ON
gaum	commonsense	ON
gawk	fool	ON
gawp	gape	ON
gleg	glance	ON
gleyd	greedy	OE
gloppened	astounded	ON
gowk	cuckoo	ON
greet	cry	OE
happen	maybe	ON
hey up!	look out!	ME
hoss	horse	OE
keld	spring, well	ON
kelt	money, property	OE
ketty	unpleasant	ON

Word	Meaning	Origin
kist	chest, trunk	ON
kittle	tickle	ON
lad	boy	ME
laik	play	ON
lam	strike	ON
lang	long	OE
larn	learn	OE
lass	girl	ME
leet	light	OE
lief	willingly	OE
ling	heather	ON
lowp	leap	ON
maister	master	OF
mar	pond	OE
mawk	unfriendly person	ON
mickle	large, much	ON
midden	dungheap	ON
midgies	gnats	OE
moos	mouse	OE
moss	marsh	OE
mowdiwarp	mole	ME
muck	dirt	ON
mun	shall, will	ON
nawther	neither	OE
nay	no	ON
nebby	nosey	OE
neet	night	OE
nenst	beside	OE
nesh	squeamish	OE
ness	headland	ON
nobbut	only	OE
nowt	nothing	OE
oft	often	OE
ower	over	ME

Word	Meaning	Origin
owt	anything	OE
po	chamberpot	OF
poke	bag, pouch	ON
privy	outside lavatory	OF
rammy	smelly	ON
reckon	consider	OE
reek	smoke	OE
reet	right, very	OE
sackless	foolish	ON
sark	shirt	OE
scar	rocky outcrop	ON
sel	self	ME
sike	such	OE
skell up	overturn	ON
skitters	diarrhoea	ON
soft	weak, cowardly	OE
steeane	stone	OE
strang	strong	OE
tarn	lake	ON
thrang	crowded	OE
twa	two	OE
tyke	rough person, child	ON
ullot	owl	OE
urchin	hedgehog	OF
uzzle	blackbird	OE
wame	stomach	OE
wrang	wrong	OE
yammer	chatter	OE
yat	gate	ON
yon	those, that	OE
yonder	over there	OE

Norman conquests
The influence of Norman French

When the Normans invaded Britain in 1066 the language they spoke became that of the aristocracy and (alongside Latin) that of government and administration, although Anglo-Saxon continued as the basic tongue of the suppressed English populace, gradually evolving into what became known as Middle English (the variety of English spoken by most people living in England between the early 12th century and the middle of the 15th century). Norman French had inherited much of its vocabulary from Norse, as originally brought to Normandy by Scandinavian settlers. Many of these words in turn became embedded (often subtly changed) in the English language.

Norman French	English equivalent	Norman French	English equivalent
archier	archer	gardîn	garden
asaut	assault	getaison	jettison
bacun	bacon	lavender	lavender
cachi	catch	mahem	mayhem
canne	can	maquerel	mackerel
castel	castle	mogue	mug
cat	cat	parlement	parliament [1]
caundèle	candle	pie de grue	pedigree
court	court	pouque	pouch
craisse	grease	prison	prison
crime	crime	remedie	remedy
donjon	dungeon	repris	reprieve
eschequier	exchequer	surnom	surname
faichon	fashion	viquet	wicket
		wardein	warden

1. the degree to which Norman French became the language of the ruling classes is reflected today in the number of words of French origin that are used in the ranks of the senior aristocracy, among them *prince, duke, marquis, noble, countess* and *baron*

The Greeks had a word for it
Words from ancient Greek

The English vocabulary continued to develop during the later medieval period and beyond, moving from Middle English into what became known as Early Modern English (roughly spanning the years 1400 to 1800) and finally the Modern English that is spoken today. Among the most important influences on the vocabulary during this time was the introduction of a surprisingly large number of words that had their ultimate origins in ancient Greek, and can thus claim a history going back nearly 3000 years. Hundreds of such words were taken up with enthusiasm in the early 18th century, when fashionable society rediscovered the classical past and self-consciously took up many coinages of classical origin. Some of these words themselves had interesting origins and the following list comprises some colourful examples:

Word	Meaning	Origin
Adonis	a handsome young man	after Adonis, a beautiful youth whom the goddess of love Aphrodite fell for
barbarian	uncivilized, brutish	from the 'bar-bar-bar' sound of people who spoke Germanic dialects instead of Greek
crocodile	a large tropical reptile	from the Greek for 'pebble-worm', perhaps a reference to the animal's habit of spending much of its time basking on riverbanks
draconian	severe, harsh	after the authoritarian Athenian lawgiver Drakon, or Draco
eureka	'I have found it'	supposedly uttered by Archimedes in his bath when he worked out that the volume of an irregular solid could be calculated from the water it displaced
halcyon	peaceful, calm	from the Greek for 'kingfisher', which was said to nest at sea during the winter solstice after calming the waves by magic

Word	*Meaning*	*Origin*
laconic	terse	originally from the Greek name Laconian, by which they knew the Spartans, who were noted for their terseness of speech
marathon	a long or arduous task	a reference to the 20-mile run of the messenger who brought news of the victory at the Battle of Marathon to Athens in 490 BC
muse	a source of inspiration	after the Nine Muses, the sister goddesses of Greek mythology who provided inspiration in the arts and sciences
panic	uncontrollable fear	a reference to the frenzied rites associated with the Greek god Pan
parapher-nalia	bits and pieces	from the Greek for 'beside dowry', a reference to the personal possessions that came with a bride on marriage beside the official dowry
sardonic	ironic, mocking	originally from the Greek for 'of Sardinia' and a reference to the belief that Sardinians had rigid, unnatural grins as a result of eating a poisonous herb that grew on the island
solecism	a mistake, a violation of manners	after the Athenian colony of Cilicia, whose inhabitants spoke a corrupt version of Greek
treacle	a thick sugary liquid	originally from the Greek for 'antidote against the bite of a wild beast' and a reference to a medicinal compound believed to counter poison
zephyr	a soft breeze	from Zephyrus, the Greek god of the west wind

A Roman farrago
Words from Latin

A limited number of Latin words had been absorbed into English in the wake of the Roman occupation of Britain between the 1st and 5th centuries AD. The number of Latin words in English multiplied during the Renaissance period and into the 18th and 19th centuries as the admiration of scholars for classical civilization became a dominant factor in the nation's cultural life. Many Latin words were absorbed into the mainstream vocabulary and have remained there ever since. Some had colourful origins, as illustrated by the following selection:

Word	Meaning	Origin
aurora	dawn, light of dawn	after Aurora, Roman goddess of the dawn
caterpillar	larval form of butterflies etc.	from the late Latin words for 'cat' and 'hair' and thus meaning 'hairy cat', presumably inspired by the small hairs on certain caterpillars
dismal	causing gloom	from the medieval Latin for 'bad days', inspired by the belief that certain days of the year (24 in number) are particularly unlucky
farrago	jumble, confusion	from the Latin for 'mixed fodder'
fauna	animal life	after Faunus, Roman goddess of the groves
hiatus	interruption, break in continuity	from the Latin for 'opening' or 'gap', ultimately from *hiare*, meaning 'to yawn'
indigo	dark blue	from the Latin *indicus* (Indian) and thus a reference to the land where the blue dye originally came from
limbo	an indeterminate place or state of uncertainty, etc.	from the Latin meaning 'border' or 'edge'

Word	Meaning	Origin
mausoleum	tomb	a reference to the magnificent tomb of Mausolus of Caria at Halicarnassus
muscle	tissue capable of producing movement	from the Latin for 'little mouse' and a reference to the notion of mice moving about under the skin
posse	band of deputies	from the Latin *posse comitatus* (power of the country)
pyrrhic	at too great a cost	a reference to the costly victory achieved by Pyrrhus of Epirus against the Romans at Apulum in 279 BC
rota	roster of persons	from the Latin for 'wheel'
salary	earnings	from the *salarium* (salt-money) given to Roman legionaries to buy salt
video	relating to visual images	from the Latin meaning 'I see'

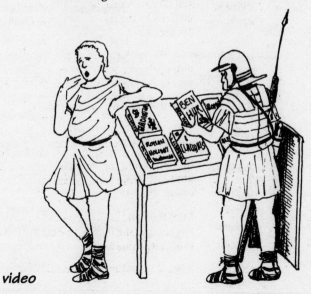

video

Old or ancient?
Anglo-Saxon versus Latin

The enthusiasm for all things classical that gripped educated society during the period that Early Modern English was taking hold inspired a new linguistic snobbishness. The simple, blunt terms of ancient Anglo-Saxon looked suddenly shabby beside their Latinate equivalents, which looked and sounded so much more sophisticated. It soon became possible to reach fundamental conclusions about a speaker's background, education and social standing purely from his or her choice of Latinate words in preference to their more pithy but often brutal Anglo-Saxon equivalents. One benefit of this phenomenon was an exponential increase in the size of the English vocabulary, with a bewildering (and often delightful) choice of alternative words meaning exactly the same thing.

Anglo-Saxon word	Latinate equivalent	Anglo-Saxon word	Latinate equivalent
anger	rage	god	deity
ask	inquire	guess	suppose
begin	commence	heed	attention
belly	abdomen	hound	canine
buy	purchase	home	residence
child	infant	leave	exit
come	arrive	match	correspond
deep	profound	mean	signify
fall	autumn	old	ancient
first	primary	see	perceive
flood	inundate	sleeping	dormant
forbid	prohibit	speak	converse
freedom	liberty	teach	educate
friendly	amicable	wage	salary
give	provide	wish	desire

In the beginning was the Word
Words from the Bible

For many people, the Authorized (King James) Version of the Bible (1611) represents an ideal of formal, well-written English. As well as presenting modern readers with a wealth of information about the words that were in use at the time, the King James Bible and other major English translations of the Bible around the same time contributed many memorable phrases to the language in their attempts to render the foreign tongues of older Bibles into the native language of English worshippers. We speak, often without realizing the biblical origins of the phrases we are using, of 'the salt of the earth', of 'the powers that be' or of 'the writing on the wall'.

Quotation	*Bible reference*
forbidden fruit is (or tastes) sweetest	Genesis 3:1–7
am I my brother's keeper?	Genesis 4:9
fire and brimstone	Genesis 19:24
the fat years and the lean years	Genesis 41:25–27
a stranger in a strange land	Exodus 2:22
a land flowing with milk and honey	Exodus 3:8
an eye for an eye, and a tooth for a tooth	Exodus 21:24
the apple of one's eye	Deuteronomy 32:10
a man after one's own heart	1 Samuel 13:14
gird up one's loins	1 Kings 18:46
a still, small voice	1 Kings 19:12
sackcloth and ashes	Esther 4:3
for such a time as this	Esther 4:14
escape by the skin of one's teeth	Job 19:20
out of the mouths of babes and sucklings	Psalm 8:2

Quotation	*Bible reference*
the valley of the shadow of death	Psalm 23:4
one's cup runneth over	Psalm 23:5
all the days of one's life	Psalm 23:6
go from strength to strength	Psalm 84:7
three score years and ten	Psalm 90:10
at death's door	Psalm 107:18 [1]
spare the rod and spoil the child	Proverbs 13:24
there is nothing new under the sun	Ecclesiastes 1:9
there's a time and place for everything	Ecclesiastes 3:1–8
eat, drink and be merry (for tomorrow we die)	Ecclesiastes 8:15
a fly in the ointment	Ecclesiastes 10:1
a drop in the ocean (or bucket)	Isaiah 40:15
a word in season	Isaiah 50:4
like a lamb (or sheep) to the slaughter	Isaiah 53:7
there is no peace for the wicked	Isaiah 57:21
holier-than-thou	Isaiah 65:5
the leopard cannot change his spots	Jeremiah 13:23
wheels within wheels	Ezekiel 1:16
feet of clay	Daniel 2:33
the writing on the wall	Daniel 5
weighed in the balances and found wanting	Daniel 5:27
the law of the Medes and the Persians	Daniel 6:8
sow the wind and reap the whirlwind	Hosea 8:7
do not despise the day of small things	Zechariah 4:10

1. from Miles Coverdale's translation of the Psalms, as found in the Book of Common Prayer (1662)

Quotation	*Bible reference*
a voice crying in the wilderness	Matthew 3:3
the salt of the earth	Matthew 5:13
hide one's light under a bushel	Matthew 5:15
a jot or tittle	Matthew 5:18
turn the other cheek	Matthew 5:39
go the second (or extra) mile	Matthew 5:41
one's left hand does not know what one's right hand is doing	Matthew 6:3
one's daily bread	Matthew 6:11
serve God and mammon	Matthew 6:24
judge not, that you not be judged	Matthew 7:1
the mote in someone else's eye and the beam in one's own eye	Matthew 7:3
cast pearls before swine	Matthew 7:6
a wolf in sheep's clothing	Matthew 7:15
say the word	Matthew 8:8
gnashing of teeth	Matthew 8:12
shake the dust off one's feet	Matthew 8:14
fall by the wayside	Matthew 13:4
a prophet is without honour in his own country	Matthew 14:57
the blind leading the blind	Matthew 15:14
at the eleventh hour	Matthew 20:1–16
the chosen few	Matthew 20:16
a den of thieves	Matthew 21:13
strain at a gnat and swallow a camel	Matthew 23:24
the spirit is willing but the flesh is weak	Matthew 26:41
wash one's hands of something	Matthew 27:24

Quotation	*Bible reference*
fall on stony ground	Mark 4:5–6
the labourer is worthy of his hire	Luke 10:7
the good Samaritan	Luke 10:30–37
pass by on the other side	Luke 10:31–32
the prodigal son	Luke 15:11–32
kill the fatted calf	Luke 15:23
born again	John 3:5–7
no respecter of persons	Acts 10:34
a law unto oneself	Romans 2:14
the powers that be	Romans 13:1
all things to all men	1 Corinthians 9:22
in the twinkling of an eye	1 Corinthians 15:51–52
the letter of the law	2 Corinthians 3:5–6
not suffer fools gladly	2 Corinthians 11:19
a thorn in the flesh (or side)	2 Corinthians 12:7
fall from grace	Galatians 5:4
like a thief in the night	1 Thessalonians 5:2
strong meat	Hebrews 5:12
cover a multitude of sins	1 Peter 4:8
alpha and omega	Revelation 1:8

The English Bible, a book which, if everything else in our language should perish, would alone suffice to show the whole extent of its beauty and power.

Lord Macaulay, British historian

Mimicking the majestic champion
Shakespearean words

Many individuals have contributed a handful of words to the language, but no one has ever matched the colossal linguistic achievement of the playwright William Shakespeare (1564–1616). It is often claimed that Shakespeare invented between 1700 and 2000 new words, though by no means all have survived into modern use. The words in the following list were all first recorded in the Bard's works and many were undoubtedly his own coinages:

abruption	buzzer	elbow
academe	cadent	eventful
accommodation	caked	excitement
accused	cater	exposure
addiction	champion	exsufflicate
advertising	circumstantial	eyeball
amazement	cold-blooded	fancy-free
appertainments	compromise	fashionable
arouse	conspectuities	fixture
assassination	countless	flawed
auspicious	courtship	frugal
backing	critic	generous
bandit	dauntless	gloomy
barefaced	dawn	gossip
bedroom	deafening	green-eyed
beached	discontent	gust
besmirched	disgraceful	hint
bet	dishearten	hobnob
birthplace	dislocate	hurried
blanket	drugged	impartial
bloodstained	dwindle	impede
blushing	epileptic	invulnerable
bump	equivocal	jaded

label	obsequiously	skim milk
lack-lustre	ode	soilure
laughable	Olympian	submerge
lonely	outbreak	summit
lower	panders	swagger
luggage	pedant	tortive
lustrous	persistive	torture
madcap	premeditated	tranquil
majestic	protractive	undress
marketable	puking	ungenitured
metamorphize	puppy-dog	unplausive
mimic	questrist	unreal
monumental	radiance	varied
moonbeam	rant	vastidity
mountaineer	remorseless	vaulting
negotiate	savagery	worthless
noiseless	scuffle	zany
obscene	secure	

lustrous champion

To be or not to be
Shakespeare's English

The influence of William Shakespeare was not confined to single words. Phrases from his plays and poems have become well-known idiomatic expressions and thus linguistic entities in their own rights, albeit sometimes with the meaning somewhat changed.

Idiom	Play
a dish fit for the gods	*Julius Caesar* (1599)
a foregone conclusion	*Othello* (1603–04)
all our yesterdays	*Macbeth* (1606)
a sea change	*The Tempest* (1611)
as good luck would have it	*The Merry Wives of Windsor* (1597–98)
a sorry sight	*Macbeth* (1606)
at one fell swoop	*Macbeth* (1606)
a tower of strength	*Richard III* (1592–93)
beggars all description	*Antony and Cleopatra* (1606)
caviare to the general	*Hamlet* (1600–01)
cold comfort	*King John* (1595–96)
dance attendance	*Henry VIII* (1613)
fair play	*The Tempest* (1611)
fancy free	*A Midsummer Night's Dream* (1595–96)
good men and true	*Much Ado About Nothing* (1598)
hoist with his own petard	*Hamlet* (1600–01)
hold the mirror up to nature	*Hamlet* (1600–01)
I must be cruel only to be kind	*Hamlet* (1600–01)

Idiom	Play
in my mind's eye	*Hamlet* (1600–01)
in stitches	*Twelfth Night* (1601)
it's Greek to me	*Julius Caesar* (1599)
lay it on with a trowel	*As You Like It* (1599–1600)
love is blind	*The Merchant of Venice* (1596–97)
make a virtue of necessity	*Pericles* (1607)
play fast and loose	*Antony and Cleopatra* (1606)
pound of flesh	*The Merchant of Venice* (1596–97)
primrose path	*Hamlet* (1600–01)
salad days	*Antony and Cleopatra* (1606)
star crossed lovers	*Romeo and Juliet* (1595)
the green-eyed monster	*Othello* (1603–04)
the truth will out	*The Merchant of Venice* (1596–97)
to be or not to be	*Hamlet* (1600–01)
to the manner born	*Hamlet* (1600–01)
what the dickens	*The Merry Wives of Windsor* (1597–98)
with bated breath	*The Merchant of Venice* (1596–97)

When I read Shakespeare I am struck with wonder
that such trivial people should muse and thunder
in such lovely language.

D.H. Lawrence

Chortling quarks
Literary coinages

Shakespeare was not the only author whose works helped transform the English vocabulary. Many words owe their birth to the imagination of individual authors and their origins can be traced back to a specific literary work. These literary creations typically travel far beyond their original contexts, which in many cases have been long forgotten by those who use them as part of their daily vocabulary.

Word	Meaning	Author
blatant	very obvious	Edmund Spenser, *Faerie Queene* (1590)
chortle	chuckle gleefully	Lewis Carroll, *Through the Looking-Glass* (1871)
doublethink	contradictory ideas	George Orwell, *Nineteen Eighty-Four* (1949)
gargantuan	immense	François Rabelais, *The History of Gargantua and Pantagruel* (1532)
heebie-jeebies	apprehension	W. De Beck, cartoon (1923)
knicker-bockers	loose breeches	Washington Irving, writing under the pseudonym Dietrich Knickerbocker
lothario	libertine	Nicholas Rowe, *The Fair Penitent* (1703)
malapropism	misapplication of words	Richard Brinsley Sheridan, *The Rivals* (1775)
mentor	experienced adviser	Homer, *The Odyssey* (8th century BC)
nerd	styleless bore	Dr Seuss, *If I Ran the Zoo* (1950)
pandemonium	uproar	John Milton, *Paradise Lost* (1667)

Word	Meaning	Author
pander	acquiesce	Giovanni Boccaccio, *Il Filostrato* (*c.*1350)
panjandrum	arrogant person	Samuel Foote, 'The Grand Panjandrum' (1755) [1]
quark	hypothetical particle	James Joyce, *Finnegans Wake* (1939)
quixotic	whimsical, romantic	Miguel de Cervantes, *Don Quixote* (1605)
Romeo	romantically-inclined man	William Shakespeare, *Romeo and Juliet* (1595)
robot	mechanical man	Karol Capek, *RUR* (1920)
runcible	three-pronged spoon	Edward Lear, 'How Pleasant to know Mr Lear' (1871)
Scrooge	miser	Charles Dickens, *A Christmas Carol* (1843)
Shangri-la	paradise	James Hilton, *Lost Horizon* (1933)
Shylock	miser, moneylender	William Shakespeare, *The Merchant of Venice* (1596–97)
Svengali	one who influences	George du Maurier, *Trilby* (1894)
syphilis	sexually transmitted disease	Girolamo Fracastoro, *Syphilis sive morbus Gallicus* (1530)
utopian	ideal	Thomas More, *Utopia* (1516)
wendy house	child's playhouse	J.M. Barrie, *Peter Pan* (1904)
yahoo	barbarian	Jonathan Swift, *Gulliver's Travels* (1726)

1. a passage of nonsense verse composed as a challenge to actor Charles Macklin's boast that he could remember anything perfectly after reading it just once (when he saw it Macklin was outraged and refused to attempt repeating it)

Odd origins
Curious etymologies

The origins of many words are not immediately obvious and some on closer examination are downright peculiar. The following selection of curious etymologies provides but a glimpse of the rich cultural and historical background that lies behind many a familiar term:

Word	Meaning	Origin and date
aftermath	after event	resulted from the combination of 'after' with 'math', which referred to the mowing of grass: the word thus refers to a second crop of grass *16th century*
bandy	exchange	originally from the French *bander*, which refers to hitting a ball back and forth and thus to tennis *16th century*
blarney	flattering talk	from the Blarney Stone at Blarney Castle in Ireland, said to confer on anyone who kisses it skill in flattery *19th century*
bunkum	empty talk	Buncombe county in North Carolina, where a Congressional representative once gave a particularly uninspired speech *19th century*
feisty	spirited	based on the Old English for 'farting dog' *19th century*
gamut	range	originally a musical term referring to the lowest note on a musical scale *15th century*
gossip	rumour-mongering, chatter	from the Old English for 'godparent' and a reference to the women who attended at childbirth and thus to their chattering *1st millenniumn AD*
maudlin	sentimental, tearful	after Mary Magdalene and her tears of repentance *17th century*

Word	Meaning	Origin and date
posh	smart, exclusive	popularly supposed to be an acronym of 'port out starboard home' (the preferred side of the ship on voyages between Britain and the East) but more likely from the slang 'posh', meaning 'dandy' *19th century*
punch	mixed, spiced fruit drink	probably from the Sanskrit *panca*, meaning 'five' (a reference to the fact that the drink was originally made with five ingredients) *17th century*
quiz	a series of questions	possibly arose as the result of a bet in which Irish theatre manager James Daly was wagered that he could not establish a new word in the language in the space of a single day: he accordingly wrote the word 'quiz' on walls all over Dublin, attracting everyone's attention to it, and won the bet *18th century*
shambles	a disordered mess	from the Old English *sceamel*, meaning stool or table (as used by butchers to display their meat, a messy business) *14th century*
sirloin	fine cut of beef	popularly supposed to have arisen after an English king knighted the excellent cut of meat that was presented to him, but more likely from the French *surlonge* (above loin) *16th century*
tabby	cat with striped markings	after the Baghdad suburb of Al Attabiya, formerly renowned for its production of striped cloth *17th century*
tawdry	cheap, gaudy	a reference to the St Audrey's Day fair held in Ely, at which cheap goods were bought and sold *16th century*

From adders to scapegoats
Words derived from mistakes

Some words are created as a result of errors concerning their etymologies or because of mistaken assumptions about their original form. The following represents a small selection of these:

Word	*Origin*
adder	prior to the medieval period the word was 'naddre' or 'nadder' until it was wrongly assumed that 'an' and 'adder' had been run together in error and the 'n' was mistakenly removed
apron	similarly changed from 'napron' in the mistaken belief that the 'n' had become wrongly attached from 'an'
kangaroo	folklore has it that when Captain Cook asked the aborigines what they called this unusual creature he is supposed to have got the reply 'kangaroo', meaning 'I don't understand what you are saying'
newt	originally 'ewt' until the letter 'n' was transposed from 'an'
nickname	changed from the original 'ekename' through the addition of 'n' from 'an'
orange	began life as the Sanskrit *naranga*, but had lost the initial 'n' by the time it reached England in the 14th century
scapegoat	from the words 'escape' and 'goat' and a coinage of William Tyndale when he translated the Bible from Hebrew in the 16th century, mistakenly thinking this an accurate translation of the Hebrew *azazel* (goat): in the ritual of Yom Kippur a goat was symbolically burdened with the sins of the Israelites and driven into the wilderness
umpire	mistakenly changed from the original 'noumpere' in the belief that the 'n' was an addition from 'an'

In-words
Prefixes

Many new words are created through the attachment of one or more letters to the front of an already-existing term. Such prefixes have a set meaning, which makes the understanding of such new coinages a relatively straightforward exercise. Prefixes used in English come from a variety of sources, as indicated by the selection below:

Prefix	Meaning	Example
a-	(Greek) not	atypical
anti-	(Greek) against, counter	antisocial
arch-	(Greek) chief	arch-villain
auto-	(Greek) self, same	autobiographical
bi-	(Latin) two	bifocal
co-	(Latin) joint, equal	coproducer
contra-	(Latin) against, opposite	contraflow
counter-	(Latin) against, opposite	countermeasure
de-	(Latin) remove, reverse	deforest
demi-	Latin) half, less than	demigod
di-	(Greek) two, double	dioxide
dis-	(Latin) remove, reverse	dismember
e-	(Modern English) electronic	e-bank
ex-	(Latin) out of, former	ex-wife
extra-	(Latin) beyond, outside	extracurricular
fore-	(Old English) before	foresight
Franken-	(English fiction) freakish	Frankenfood [1]
hyper-	(Greek) above, over	hyperactive
in-	(Latin) not	incomplete
inter-	(Latin) between	intermarry
intra-	(Latin) inside, within	intravenous
mal-	(Old French) bad, wrongly	maltreat

1. genetically modified food, a reference to the fictional character Frankenstein created by Mary Shelley in the novel (1818) of the same name

Prefix	Meaning	Example
mega-	(Greek) great, large	megaton
mini-	(Modern English) small	miniskirt
mis-	(Old French) not, wrong	misapprehend
mono-	(Greek) one	monorail
multi-	(Latin) many	multi-millionaire
neo-	(Greek) new, recent	neoclassical
non-	(Latin) not	non-entity
out-	(Modern English) exceed	outrun
over-	(Modern English) excessive, superior, beyond	overwhelm
palaeo-	(Greek) old, ancient	palaeolithic
pan-	(Greek) all, including	pan-African
poly-	(Greek) many, much	polychromatic
post-	(Latin) after	postwar
pre-	(Latin) before	prewar
pro-	(Latin) supporting, substitute	pro-abortion, proconsul
proto-	(Greek) first, primitive	prototype
pseudo-	(Greek) pretending	pseudo-intellectual
re-	(Latin) return, repeat	rejoin
semi-	(Latin) half, partly	semi-detached
spinach-	(Modern English) unappealing but beneficial	spinach-television
sub-	(Latin) under	submarine
super-	(Latin) above, greater	superabundant
sur-	(Old French) above, beyond, over	surcharge
tele-	(Greek) distant	telescope
trans-	(Latin) across, beyond	transplant
tri-	(Greek) three	tricycle
über-	(German) super	über-babe
ultra-	(Latin) beyond, extreme	ultraconservative
un-	(Old English) remove, reverse	unlikely
under-	(Old English) below, insufficient	underachieve
uni-	(Latin) one	unilateral
vice-	(Latin) deputy	vice-president

Wordrage
Suffixes

It is common practice to create new versions of existing words by adding one or more letters to the end of an already-existing term. Such suffixes variously alter the meaning of the existing word or serve to create a new part of speech, typically making verbs out of already-accepted nouns. Such words are often considered slang coinages that many people may avoid using.

Suffix	Meaning	Example
-athon	a long-lasting event	swimathon, telethon
-chic	fashion, style	gangster chic
-cide	murder	fratricide, regicide
-ee	recipient of an action	lessee
-er	one who performs an action	worker
-erati	belonging to a clique	glitterati
-eroo	and even more so	crackeroo
-ers	informal version of a term	champers, preggers, starkers
-ery	qualities or actions collectively	robbery
-ess	female of	lioness
-ette	small version of	kitchenette
-fest	indulgence in	boozefest, shagfest
-gate	denoting a scandal	Irangate
-ie	belonging to this category	oldie, quickie
-ies	pluralizing intensifier	the willies
-ism	of a state, condition or doctrine	ageism, elitism
-ista	an associate of a group	Sandinista, feminista
-less	without	endless, hopeless
-lite	low in	carb-lite, laughter-lite

Suffix	Meaning	Example
-ly	in the manner of	quietly, slowly
-o	belonging to this category	weirdo
-rage	aggression, hostility	air-rage, road-rage
-s	intensifier of affection	Moms, Gramps
-wash	changing the appearance of	greenwash[1]
-y/ie	intensifier of affection	auntie, baddy, daddy, goalie, telly

1. make environmentally friendly

insultathon

Backing up
Back formations

Some words are created through the process of back formation, in which new words are created out of existing terms by the removal of a prefix or suffix or a similar action. Another version of the process involves the adoption of an existing word as a new part of speech, for instance creating a verb out of an existing noun.

Original term	*Term created by back formation*
access (noun)	access (verb)
ask (verb)	ask (noun) [1]
baby-sitter	baby-sit
bag (noun)	bag (verb)
burglar	burgle
carpet (noun)	carpet (verb)
editor	edit
father (noun)	father (verb)
gift (noun)	gift (verb)
guest (noun)	guest (verb)
handbag (noun)	handbag (verb)
iron (noun)	iron (verb)
lazy	laze
message (noun)	message (verb)
orient	orientation
resurrection	resurrect
rubbish (noun)	rubbish (verb)
service (noun)	service (verb)
spend (verb)	spend (noun)
telephone (noun)	telephone (verb)
television	televise
text (noun)	text (verb)

1. as with many other words formed through back formation, the use of 'ask' as a noun is avoided by many speakers, who consider this slang

Slithy toves
Portmanteau words

Some new coinages come about through the combination of existing words. Lewis Carroll, creator of *slithy toves* (*slithy* being the result of the combination of *lithe* and *slimy*), as found in *Through the Looking-Glass, and What Alice Found There* (1871), ranks among the most well-known and prolific architects of such portmanteau words or 'blends', but he has had many successors. The following list represents just a selection of the results of their efforts:

Blend	*Words combined*
animatronics	animation + electronics
bit	binary + digit
blaxploitation	black + exploitation
blipvert	blip + advertisement (a brief television advert)
blog	web + log
blogcast	blog + broadcast
Bollywood	Bombay + Hollywood
breathalyzer	breath + analyzer
brunch	breakfast + lunch
bungaloft	bungalow + loft (a bungalow with a loft)
camcorder	camera + recorder
chocoholic	chocolate + alcoholic
cyborg	cybernetic + organism
docudrama	documentary + drama
dude[1]	duds + attitude
electrocute	electro + execute
Eurovision	European + television
fanzine	fan + magazine

1. an invention of Oscar Wilde and his friends

Blend	*Words combined*
flexative [2]	flexible + executive
ginormous	gigantic + enormous
glitterati	glitter + literati
guesstimate	guess + estimate
heliport	helicopter + airport
infomercial	information + commercial
motel	motor + hotel
Oxbridge	Oxford + Cambridge
palimony	pal + alimony
paratroops	parachute + troops
smog	smoke + fog
talkathon	talk + marathon
telethon	telephone + marathon
touron [3]	tourist + moron
transistor	transfer + resistor
WAPlash [4]	WAP + backlash
workaholic	work + alcoholic

2. a professional working flexible hours

3. a moronic tourist

4. a backlash against WAP-enabled mobile phones

Television? No good will come of this device.
The word is half Greek and half Latin.

C.P. Scott

Flamboyant blarney
Loanwords

The vocabulary of Modern English has been much enriched over the centuries by borrowings from foreign languages. In some cases the pronunciation is anglicized, although the original spelling is usually retained:

Source language	*Loanwords*
African languages	cola, guinea, raffia, safari, voodoo, zombie
Afrikaans	apartheid, commando, kraal, trek, veldt
Arabic	admiral, alchemy, algebra, assassin, cipher, cotton, harem, mattress, sofa, zero
Caribbean languages	barbecue, cannibal, canoe, hammock, hurricane, potato, tobacco
Chinese languages	kowtow, silk, tea, tycoon, typhoon
Czech	howitzer, pistol, robot
Dutch	cruise, dock, knapsack, landscape, sleigh, waffle
French	accuse, amorous, army, avalanche, baron, basin, beauty, camouflage, cathedral, cellar, challenge, chaplain, chocolate, continue, conversation, courage, dinner, elite, enemy, fete, flamboyant, garage, grotesque, guile, guarantee, lieutenant, majesty, medicine, parlour, poet, poison, precious, prison, rage, regard, sergeant, sugar, tax, tournament, vinegar, virtue, vision, vogue
German	blitz, gimmick, hamburger, kindergarten, lager, poltergeist, waltz
Hebrew	amen, behemoth, jubilee, rabbi
Hindi	bangle, bungalow, chutney, dinghy, juggernaut, pundit, samosa, shampoo, tikka
Hungarian	coach, goulash, hussar, sabre
Icelandic	geyser, saga
Inuit	anorak, igloo, kayak, parka

Source language	*Loanwords*
Irish Gaelic	banshee, blarney, brat, brogues, galore, smithereens
Italian	balcony, concerto, fiasco, giraffe, incognito, opera, parapet, studio, violin
Japanese	geisha, kamikaze, shogun, tycoon, yen
Malay	amok, bamboo, compound, gong, kapok, sarong
Maori	haka, kiwi
Nahuatl (Aztec)	avocado, chocolate, coyote, tomato
Native American languages	moccasin, powwow, squash, toboggan, totem
Native Australasian languages	boomerang, kangaroo, wombat
Norwegian	fjord, lemming, ski
Persian	bazaar, caravan, shawl, taffeta
Polish	horde, mazurka
Polynesian	taboo, tattoo
Portuguese	albatross, albino, caste, cobra, marmalade
Russian	commissar, glasnost, mammoth, sputnik, tsar
Scottish Gaelic	bairn, bonny, burn, cairn, ceilidh, clan, claymore, gillie, glen, ingle, loch, slogan, sporran, whisky
Serbo-Croat	cravat
South American languages	condor, jaguar, piranha, poncho, puma
Spanish	armadillo, barrack, bonanza, embargo, hammock, marmalade, mosquito, siesta, tornado
Swedish	ombudsman, tungsten, verve
Tamil	catamaran, cheroot, curry, pariah
Tibetan	shaman, yak, yeti
Turkish	coffee, divan, kebab, kiosk, yoghurt
Welsh	coracle, corgi, eisteddfod, flannel
Yiddish	chutzpah, kosher, schmaltz

Vive la différence
False friends

Certain words that are shared by English and other vocabularies do not necessarily mean the same thing and any similarity is misleading. In some cases they may share the same ultimate root but their meanings have grown apart over the years. In others any similarity may be no more than coincidence.

Language	Word	Foreign meaning
Czech	host	guest
Dutch	big	piglet
	brand	fire
	stout	naughty
Finnish	alas	down
	aura	plough
	home	mould
	manner	continent
French	actuel	current
	adept	follower
	ail	garlic
	appoint	contribution
	assister	attend
	blesser	injure
	chair	flesh
	chat	cat
	chef	chief
	coin	corner
	demander	ask for
	essence	petrol
	éventuel	possible
	front	forehead

Language	Word	Foreign meaning
French	lard	bacon
(*cont.*)	librairie	bookshop
	main	hand
	pain	bread
	petulant	playful
	phrase	sentence
	prune	plum
	queue	tail
	raisin	grape
	sympathique	pleasant
German	also	therefore
	arm	poor
	bad	bath
	bald	soon
	die	the
	gift	poison
	graben	dig
	handy	mobile phone
	hell	bright
	kind	child
	list	cunning
	rat	advice
	stark	strong
	tag	day
	tasten	feel
Greek	atomikòs	of the individual
	idiotikòs	private
Italian	caldo	hot
	contesto	context
	equivocare	misunderstand
	estate	summer
	fabbrica	factory

Language	Word	Foreign meaning
Italian (*cont.*)	fame	hunger
	male	evil
	morbido	soft
	pretendere	claim
Polish	karawan	funeral procession
	no	yes
	ten	this
Russian	angina	tonsillitis
	brat	brother
	kabinet	office
Spanish	campo	field
	desgracia	misfortune
	embarazada	pregnant
	exito	success
	genial	brilliant
	gracioso	funny
	moroso	in arrears
	pie	foot
	sensible	sensitive
Swedish	egg	edge
	far	father
	full	drunk
	glass	ice cream
	god	good
	hot	threat
	kreatur	cattle

Talk to the animals
Animal idioms

Many idioms have their origins in the animal world. These have remained in common use up to the present day despite the fact that the majority of English speakers no longer live in close communication with animals and the countryside.

Animal	Idiom	Meaning
bats	have bats in one's belfry	be mad
beavers	an eager beaver	an enthusiastic person
bees	busy as a bee	very busy
	make a beeline	go straight to
	the bee's knees	something very pleasing
birds	a cock and bull story [1]	an unbelievable story
	as the crow flies	in a direct line
	cloud cuckoo land [2]	an unreal, fantasy world
	lame duck [3]	someone or something that does not function properly
cats	let the cat out of the bag [4]	let a secret out
	no room to swing a cat [5]	in cramped surroundings
	raining cats and dogs [6]	raining heavily
crocodiles	shed crocodile tears [7]	pretend to be upset
dogs	a dog in a manger	one who selfishly denies others something he or she has no use for
	in the doghouse	in disgrace
donkeys	donkey's years [8]	a long time
geese	kill the goose that laid the golden egg [9]	destroy something from which one benefits

Animal	Idiom	Meaning
goats	get someone's goat	annoy someone
horses	a dark horse	a contender about whom little is known
	look a gift horse in the mouth	question an apparent benefit
pigs	buy a pig in a poke [10]	buy something without seeing it first
	go the whole hog	go the whole way
wolves	cry wolf [11]	cause alarm etc. without cause

1. probably from the *Fables* of Aesop, but possibly also linked to the tales exchanged by travellers changing coaches at the two coaching inns named respectively the Cock and the Bull in Stony Stratford, Buckinghamshire

2. a phrase from the comedy *The Birds* by Aristophanes, in which the birds build an imaginary city in the sky

3. a reference to the old hunting saying 'Never waste powder on a dead duck'

4. from the old ruse of putting a cat in a bag and selling it to someone by claiming it is a pig

5. probably a reference to the space required to wield a cat-o'-nine tails (a whip with nine strands used to flog sailors) on board ship

6. based on an ancient Norse association of cats and dogs with bad weather

7. from the notion that crocodiles make pathetic sounds to lure prey

8. probably originally 'donkey's ears' and a reference to their length

9. from one of Aesop's *Fables*

10. from the old trick of selling a cat in a bag (i.e. poke being a bag), pretending it is a pig (see above)

11. from one of Aesop's *Fables* about a boy who pretends to see a wolf when there isn't one and is then ignored when he really sees one

Black and white
Colour idioms

Some of the most familiar of idioms in common use have their origins in colours. In many cases the reasons for the association of a colour with a particular linguistic idea are obvious. In others, however, they require some explanation. The following list includes just a small selection of common idioms based on colour, with explanations where appropriate:

Colour	Idiom	Meaning
black	a black sheep	a disgrace to the family
	black and blue	bruised, beaten
blue	a bolt from the blue	an unexpected event
	blue in the face	exhausted
	once in a blue moon [1]	very rarely
	out of the blue	completely unexpected
	scream blue murder [2]	make an uproar
brown	browned off [3]	fed up
	brown study	introspection
green	green-eyed monster	jealousy
	green fingers	a talent for growing things
grey	grey matter	the brain
pink	in the pink [4]	in good health
	tickled pink	very pleased
purple	purple patch	run of success or good luck
red	catch redhanded [5]	catch in the act

Colour	Idiom	Meaning
red (*cont.*)	paint the town red [6]	go on a lively, drunken spree
	red-letter day [7]	special day
	red rag to a bull	something provoking anger
	red tape [8]	bureaucratic procedures
white	white elephant [9]	something costly but of no use
	white feather	accusation of cowardice
yellow	yellow streak	cowardice

1. very occasionally the moon takes on a bluish hue because of dust particles in the upper atmosphere

2. possibly a reference to the French oath *morbleu!* (literally meaning 'blue death!')

3. probably a reference to food that has been overcooked

4. short for 'in the pink of health' ('pink' here meaning the garden flower *Dianthus*)

5. as if literally with blood on the hands after a murder

6. possibly a reference to the entertainment to be had in 'red-light' districts

7. from church calendars, in which religious festivals are printed in red

8. from the red tape formerly used to secure batches of official documents

9. a reference to the practice by kings of Thailand of presenting honoured underlings with presents of (rare) white elephants, for which they would then have to pay the expensive upkeep

Number crunching
Number phrases

Numbers have contributed numerous phrases to the language, encompassing a rich variety of contexts and meanings, as illustrated by the following selection. The English vocabulary is luckier in this regard than some other languages. The Piraha tribe of the Amazon has just three words for numbers: one, two and many, and consequently much less scope for such number phrases.

Number	Phrase	Meaning
1	back to square one [1]	back to the start
	one-upmanship	the art of being 'one-up' on someone else
2	second best	not quite the best
	play second fiddle	play a subordinate role
	twopenny-ha'penny	cheap
3	three's a crowd	couples do not welcome a third person
	three sheets to the wind [2]	very drunk
	three strikes and you're out [3]	after three mistakes you will get no more chances
4	four corners of the earth [4]	the remotest parts of the world
5	bunch of fives	a fist, a punch with a fist
	five senses	hearing, sight, smell, taste and touch
6	at sixes and sevens [5]	confused, jumbled
	hit for six [6]	staggered, utterly defeated
7	seventh heaven [7]	complete delight, paradise
8	one over the eight [8]	drunk

Number	Phrase	Meaning
9	dressed to the nines [9]	smartly dressed
	nine days' wonder [10]	a shortlived phenomenon
10	number ten	10 Downing Street, office of the British prime minister
	ten to one	very likely to happen
11	at the eleventh hour	at the last minute
12	baker's dozen [11]	thirteen
13	number thirteen	teenage slang for marijuana
19	the nineteenth hole [12]	a golf club bar
20	twenty-twenty vision [13]	perfect vision

1. perhaps from early football match radio commentaries in which listeners could follow the action using a grid of numbered squares

2. a sheet being in nautical terms, a rope and a 'sheet in the wind' an unsecured sail that flaps uselessly in a breeze

3. originally from baseball, in which a batter has three chances to hit the ball

4. based on the ancient belief that the earth is flat

5. a reference to dice-throwing and players who risked everything on throwing unrealistically high numbers

6. the maximum number of runs to be scored by a batsman hitting a ball in cricket

7. the seventh heaven being the most blissful according to Islamic and Talmudic teaching

8. eight pints of beer being considered (in the days when beer tended to be less strong than it is today) the limit a person might drink without getting drunk

9. possibly through confusion with eyne, meaning 'eyes'

10. a reference to the fact that puppies are blind until their eyes open after nine days

11. from the tradition of bakers formerly adding an extra loaf to batches of twelve so that there was no risk of failing to meet standard weight regulations

12. golf courses having 18 holes

13. based on a system of gauging eyesight with a maximum score of 20 points

3 Yoof rap

The vocabulary of youth

The young have always been a driving force for new vocabulary, successive generations creating or embracing their own jargon and slang terms, many of which are subsequently accepted into the standard vocabulary. This process has been accelerated in recent years with the speed of technological change, and the young have responded with exceptional enthusiasm to the marvels of the computer, the mobile phone and the internet, while continuing to devise new terms in relation to more traditional preoccupations, not least that of inventing new insults with which to castigate opponents. While older generations may resist the introduction of fresh 'buzz words' that threaten to replace familiar existing terms, younger users of the language may prove much more adventurous.

New ways of coining words, or new meanings of existing words, are being invented all the time. One diverting example of recent times has been the introduction of 'predictive text' on mobile telephones, whereby the system tries (often mistakenly) to predict which words are meant. This has led to various oddities of vocabulary, such as the teen slang usage 'book' meaning 'cool' (in its sense of 'fine', 'excellent').

For last year's words belong to last year's language
And next year's words await another voice.

T.S. Eliot

Buzz words
New words

Of the thousands of new words and phrases that are introduced into the English language every year many quickly fade from view. A substantial proportion of them, however, survive and become permanent additions to the vocabulary. Consider the following selection of 10 new words introduced during each decade of the past century, all of which are still in regular use:

Decade	New words
1900s	cornflake, dashboard, dugout, egghead, gasket, hormone, newsflash, shock wave, speedometer, teddy bear
1910s	blues, celeb, cushy, floozy, gene, Jerry, legalese, tailspin, talkies, umpteen
1920s	demob, gimmick, hijack, kitsch, motel, pop, superstar, tearjerker, teenage, T-shirt
1930s	burger, demo, dumb down, ecosystem, evacuee, germ warfare, microwave, nightclubbing, oops, racism
1940s	apartheid, apparatchik, bikini, blitz, megabucks, mobile phone, pinup, radar, self-employed, snog
1950s	baby boomer, biopic, brainwashing, desegregation, discotheque, hi-fi, hippy, junk mail, psychedelic, tracksuit
1960s	byte, centrefold, cellulite, homophobia, laser, love-in, microchip, miniskirt, quark, trendy
1970s	chairperson, detox, fast food, flexitime, karaoke, palimony, put down, streaking, trainers, workaholic
1980s	Aids, biodiversity, glasnost, gobsmacked, infomercial, junk bonds, road rage, spin doctor, toy-boy, virtual reality
1990s	alcopop, blog, chat room, cybercafe, emoticon, ethnic cleansing, hot-desk, ladette, political correctness, sound byte
2000s	asbo, bluetooth, bouncebackability, happy slapping, locarb, metrosexual, muggle, podcast, shoe bomber, speed-dating

Hootin' and bangin'
Slang

Slang has always been a major contributor to the vocabulary and reveals language at its most robust and inventive. Most slang terms speak uniquely of their own era and the majority of them soon go out of fashion, serving only to identify the user as being behind the times. Others cling on and in due course are absorbed into the standard vocabulary. The following list gives just a taste of the slang of each decade over the past 100 years:

Decade	Slang terms
1910s	jellybean (fashionable young man), napoo (nothing, of no use)
1920s	hoot (something funny), oil can (unattractive woman), poontang (sex), porcupine (unattractive man), sheba (attractive woman), sheik (attractive man), wet (dull, feeble)
1930s	cheese it (run away), coffin nail (cigarette), hooray Henry (rowdy rich young man), payola (bribe), scream (something funny), sweater girl (girl with a generous bust)
1940s	angel cake (attractive woman), drip (spineless person), full monty (nothing left out), hip (fashionable), prang (crash), snazzy (fashionable), spiv (fashionable young man), square (unfashionable person)
1950s	ankle-biter (child), bash (party), blast (good time), cool (fashionable), dig (approve), eyeball (look around), flick (film), go ape (get angry), no sweat (no problem), party pooper (someone who is no fun), put down (criticize), rightho (very well), split (leave), wig out (go crazy)
1960s	bad (good), chick (girl), crash (go to bed), drag (something boring or tiresome), fab (great), funky (fashionable, pleasing), go steady (date one person), groovy (fashionable, exciting), heavy (deep, serious), knocked up (pregnant), nifty (good, impressive), pad (apartment, house), sad (unfashionable), shades (sunglasses), solid (satisfactory), zit (spot)

Decade	Slang terms
1970s	awesome (good, great), boob tube (television), chill (relax), couch potato (television-watching slob), far out (impressive), fuzz (police), rip off (cheat, steal), shag (have sex), skanky (second-rate), totally (definitely), wimp (weak-willed person)
1980s	def (good), ditzy (scatterbrained), fake bake (artificial suntan), gnarly (amazing, bizarre), loadsamoney (person who flaunts their wealth), preppy (stylish), rad (extreme, excellent), wannabe (a person who imitates someone else), wicked (good), yoof (youth)
1990s	bangin' (going well), bootylicious (attractive), cha-ching! (expensive), double whammy (twofold blow), naff (shoddy), oogly (very ugly), pants (rubbish), spin (to give a news story a particular slant), suit (someone in authority), well (very)
2000s	babylicious (attractive), bessie (best friend), bling (flashy), chav (person ostentatiously wearing designer-labelled clothing), do one (go away), fly (cool, attractive), homies (mates), large it (enjoy oneself), lashed (drunk), monged out (drunk, on drugs), newzak (trivial news), noisy (talked about), random (weird), rude (attractive), safe (cool), sex up (enhance), trolleyed (drunk), trev (wearer of designer clothes), wagon (ugly woman), wagon train (group of ugly women), weapons-grade (extreme), whacked (out of control), willy-waving (macho behaviour)

Slang is a language that rolls up its sleeves, spits on its hands and goes to work.

Carl Sandburg

A Couple of Britney Spears down the rub-a-dub-dub
Cockney rhyming slang

Perhaps the best-known variant of regional slang is the Cockney rhyming slang associated with the East End of London. Though Victorian or earlier in origin, it continues to be widely used and added to into the 21st century, as evidenced by some of the more recent coinages among those listed below:

Slang term	Meaning	Date
Adam and Eve	believe	1910s+
Alan Whickers	knickers	1960s+
almond rocks	socks	1970s
Al Pacino	cappuccino	1990s
apples and pears	stairs	mid-19C+
April showers	flowers	20C+
Aristotle	bottle	late 19C+
artful dodger	lodger	mid-19C+
Ascot races	braces	20C+
baked bean	queen	1990s+
baker's dozen	cousin	20C+
ball and chalk	walk	20C+
Barnaby Rudge	judge	20C+
Barnet Fair [1]	hair	mid-19C+
Basil Fawlty	balti	1990s
battlecruiser	boozer	1930s+
Billy Ocean	suntan lotion	1980s
boat race	face	1940s+
Bob Hope	soap	1960s+
boracic lint	skint	1940s+

1. formerly the country's most important horse fair

Slang term	Meaning	Date
bottle and glass	arse	1910s+
Brad Pitt	shit	1990s+
Brahms and Liszt	pissed	1920s+
brass tacks	facts	late 19C+
bread and honey	money	1950s+
bricks and mortar	daughter	20C+
Bristol City	titty	20C+
Britney Spears	beers	2000s
brown bread	dead	1960s+
bubble and squeak	Greek	1950s
butcher's hook	look	1910s+
Cain and Abel	table	mid-19C+
Chalfont St Giles	piles	1970s+
Chalk Farm	arm	mid-19C+
china plate	mate	late 19C+
cobbler's awls	balls	1930s+
cock and hen	ten	1910s+
currant bun	sun	1930s+
daisy roots	boots	mid-19C+
dicky bird	word	1930s+
dicky dirt	shirt	late 19C+
dog and bone	telephone	1940s+
Duke of Kent	rent	1930s+
dustbin lid	kid	20C+
flowery dell	cell	20C+
frog and toad	road	mid-19C+
George Raft	daft	1930s+
Gregory Peck	cheque	1950s+
gypsy's kiss	piss	1970s+
half-inch	pinch	20C+
Hampton Wick	prick	20C+

Slang term	Meaning	Date
Hampstead Heath	teeth	late 19C+
Hank Marvin	starving	2000s
hey-diddle-diddle	fiddle	1950s+
I suppose	nose	mid-19C+
jam jar	car	1910s+
Jerry Springer	minger	2000s
Jimmy Riddle	piddle	1930s+
Joanna	piano	late 19C+
Khyber Pass	arse	20C+
Lady Godiva	fiver	20C+
lean and lurch	church	mid-19C+
Lionel Blairs	flares	1970s+
loaf of bread	head	1910s+
Mae West	breast	1930s+
mince pies	eyes	mid-19C+
Mutt and Jeff [2]	deaf	1930s+
north and south	mouth	mid-19C+
oily rag	fag	1930s+
Pavarotti (tenor)	ten-pound note (tenner)	1990s
Peckham Rye	tie	1910s–80s
pen and ink	stink	mid-19C+
Pete Tong	wrong	1980s+
plates of meat	feet	mid-19C+
pony and trap	crap	1930s+
porky pies	lies	1940s+
pot of honey	money	late 19C+
Raquel Welch	belch	1960s+
read and write	fight	mid-19C+
Richard the Third	turd	late 19C+
rip and tear	swear	mid-19C
Rosie Lee	tea	1910s+

Slang term	Meaning	Date
round the houses	trousers	mid-19C+
rub-a-dub-dub	pub	late 19C+
Ruby Murray [3]	curry	1980s+
Russell Crowe	go	2000s
salmon and trout	snout	mid-19C+
sausage and mash	cash	late 19C+
sherbet dab	cab	1990s+
shiver and shake	cake	1940s
skin and blister	sister	1910s+
sky rocket	pocket	late 19C+
strike me dead	bread	late 19C+
Sweeney Todd	Flying Squad	1930s+
syrup of figs	wig	1970s+
tea leaf	thief	late 19C+
tit for tat	hat	1910s+
Tod Sloan [4]	alone	20C+
Tom and Dick	sick	1970s+
tomfoolery	jewellery	20C+
Tommy Trinder	window	1990s+
Tony Blair	hair	1990s+
trouble and strife	wife	20C+
Vera Lynn	gin	1940s+
whistle and flute	suit	1910s+

2. after the US cartoon characters Mutt and Jeff, introduced in 1907

3. after the Irish-born popular singer Ruby Murray (1935–96)

4. after the US jockey Tod Sloan (1874–1933)

Strine
Australian slang

The undisputed kings of slang in the English-speaking world are the Australians, who have long been known and admired for their inventive approach to informal English. No other region of the world has been able to match the vividness and colour of Australian slang, as evidenced by the following selection:

Slang term	*Meaning*
amber fluid	beer
arvo	afternoon
Aussie	Australian
banana bender [1]	person from Queensland
beaut	something great
bingle	car crash
bitzer [2]	mongrel
bludger	layabout
blue	fight
bog in	start eating
bonzer [3]	great
brumby	wild horse
budgie smugglers	men's bathing trunks
bush telly	campfire
cactus	dead
chuck a sickie	take a day off work feigning ill health
chunder [4]	vomit
cobber	friend
crook	sick, broken
come the raw prawn	deceive someone
dag	nerd
dead horse	tomato sauce
dero	tramp (a 'derelict')
digger [5]	soldier

Slang term	Meaning
dingo's breakfast	a yawn, a piss and a look round
dinkum [6]	good, true
dob	inform on
Down Under	Australasia
drongo [7]	idiot
dunny	outside lavatory
feral	hippie
fossick [8]	search
franger	condom
furphy [9]	unreliable rumour
galah [10]	idiot
gone walkabout	lost
grundies [11]	underwear
Jackaroo	male farm worker
Jilleroo	female farm worker
larrikin	party-loving prankster
liquid laugh	vomit
Matilda	sleeping bag

1. bananas are Queensland's main crop

2. because it is 'bits of' different breeds

3. a mixture of 'bonanza' and 'bontoger' (Aussie version of the French bons toujours, meaning 'good all the time')

4. supposedly from the nautical shout of warning 'watch under!'

5. originally a form of address among Australian miners

6. usually in the phrase 'fair dinkum'

7. supposedly from the name of a racehorse that did spectacularly badly in races of the 1920s

8. originally applied to people who searched for gold on the surface of the ground

9. after John Furphy, whose sanitary carts were used by Australian forces in World War I

10. also the name of an Australian cockatoo noted for its 'chattering'

11. after Australian media executive Reg Grundy (b.1923)

Slang term	*Meaning*
mozzie	mosquito
ocker [12]	lout
Oz	Australia
pom [13]	Englishman
rack off	go away
reffo	refugee
rip snorter	great
ripper	fantastic
shark biscuit	novice surfer
sheila [14]	woman
slab	carton of beer bottles or cans
stoked	delighted
'strewth! [15]	crikey! (a mild exclamation)
strine	Australian slang
stubby	375-ml beer bottle
sunnies	sunglasses
swag	bedding
technicolour yawn	vomit
tinny	can of beer
troppo	mad, feverish
tucker	food
white pointer [16]	topless female sunbather
wombat	person who eats, roots and leaves
yakka	work

12. after a character in *The Mavis Bramston Show* (1965–68)

13. either an abbreviation of 'pomegranate', rhyming slang for 'immigrant', or inspired by the English exclamation "pon my word!"

14. ultimately from the Irish *caille*, meaning 'young girl'

15. abbreviation of 'God's truth!'

16. after the shark of the name

Dolly cackle
Polari

Polari was a specialized form of slang that was introduced in the 1950s in theatrical and homosexual circles in London. Absorbing elements of Romany, Yiddish, Italian and other forms of slang, it became well known through the characters Julian and Sandy (Kenneth Williams and Hugh Paddick) in the BBC radio comedy programme *Round the Horne* in the 1960s. Several polari inventions have long since entered the language, albeit as informal terms.

Polari term	Meaning
baloney [1]	rubbish
bijou	small
blag	pick up
bod	body
bona	good
butch [2]	masculine
buvare	a drink
cackle	gossip
camp	effeminate
charpering omi [3]	policeman
cod	naff
cottage	public lavatory
dizzy	scatterbrained
dolly	pleasant
dona	woman
drag	clothes

1. probably from the Romany *peloné* (testicles)
2. from 'butcher'
3. ultimately from Italian *cercare* (to seek) and *uomo* (man)

Polari term	Meaning
ecaf	face
fantabulosa	wonderful
fruit	queen
khazi [4]	lavatory
mangarie	food
meshigener	crazy
mince	walk (in an effeminate manner)
naff [5]	drab
nanti	no, not
oglefakes	glasses
ogles	eyes
omi-polone [6]	homosexual
orbs	eyes
palare pipe	telephone
polari	chat
riah	hair
scarper	run away
slap	make-up
vada	see

4. from Italian *casa* (house)

5. possibly from Romany *naflo* (no good)

6. from Italian *uomo* (man) and *polone* (woman)

**One's vocabulary needs constant fertilizing
or it will die.**

Evelyn Waugh

Flowin' with da rap
Rap slang

In recent years slang has been much enriched by the influence of rap music, mostly of US origin, which has generated hundreds of new coinages. The following list includes just a small selection:

Street term	*Meaning*
baby mama	the mother of an unmarried man's baby
bail	leave
ballin'	doing well
B.G. (baby gangsta)	young gangster
biscuit	gun
bitch	girl
bling-bling	showy jewellery, ostentation generally
blunted	intoxicated
bodacious [1]	impressive
bounce	leave
bugged out	upset, behaving strangely
bumpin'	cool, pleasurable
busted	ugly
chill	relax
cold	good, mean
crunk [2]	having a good time
da	the
def	cool, pleasing
dip	leave
diss	criticize, disrespect
dog	friend
dope	cool, pleasing

1. *a combination of 'bold' and 'audacious'*

2. *a combination of 'crazy' and 'drunk'*

Street term	Meaning
down	willing, ready
fat	cool, appealing
flow	be in rhythm with the beat
fly	cool, pleasing
gangsta	street gang member
gank	steal
ghost	leave quietly
happenin'	exciting
homeboy, homie	friend
hood	neighbourhood
ill	cool, pleasing
kickin'	cool, pleasing
lamp	relax
piece	gun
pig	police officer
playa	one who influences matters
pussy	coward
rap	street-talk
scratch	money
straight	fine, okay
tight	cool, pleasing
trippin'	intoxicated with drugs, out of control
wazzup?	what's up?
yo	hi

Grant me some wild expressions, heavens, or I shall burst ...

Words, words or I shall burst.

George Farquhar

Chasing the dragon
Drug slang

Street slang is nowhere more colourful than it is when referring to drugs. The need for secrecy among drug-users, combined with the urban chic element in drug-taking, has inspired the invention of countless slang names for popular drugs, which vary considerably from place to place. The following list represents just a small selection of the more commonly heard names:

Drug	*Slang names*
amphetamines	aimies, amp, beans, bennies, benzedrine, biphetamine, black beauties, black bombers, bumblebees, cartwheels, Christmas tree, co-pilots, crank, dexedrine, footballs, hearts, ice, pep pills, speed, star, uppers, ups
amyl nitrate	poppers, snappers
barbiturates	amytal, barbs, blue devils, downers, Nembutal, red devils, reds, yellow jackets, Seconal, Tuinals, yellows
butyl nitrate	bolt, bullet, climax, locker room, rush
cocaine	all-American, Angie, Aunt Nora, base, bazooka, beam, Bernie, big C, black rock, blanca, blast, blizzard, blow, bobo, Bolivian marching powder, booth, California cornflakes, candy, Cecil, coke, cola, divits, dust, foo foo, happy dust, happy trails, heaven, hooter, ice, icing, ivory flakes, king, lady, lines, nose candy, pearl, powder, railers, ringer, rocks, sleigh ride, sneeze, snort, snow, snow bird, snowcones, snow white, soda, toot, white, white dust, yahoo, yale, yam, yao, yay, yayoo, yeaho, zipblanca
crack cocaine	apple jacks, ball, baby T, baseball, B.J.s, bolo, cloud, cookie, crack, dip, freebase, glow, hardline, paste, rock, yimyom

Drug	Slang names
hashish	black hash, chocolate, finger, gram, hash, kif, Lebanese, Mister Brownstone, oil, platters, quarter moon, soles, temple balls, thai sticks
heroin	antifreeze, Aries, Aunt Hazel, bad seed, ballot, big H, Bin Laden, black pearl, black tar, blanco, brown sugar, china white, crank, dirt, dope, dust, fix, H, harry, horse, horsebite, junk, mother pearl, mud, smack, snow, whack
LSD	A, acid, animal, back breakers, barrels, battery acid, big D, black acid, black star, black tabs, blaze, blotter, blotter acid, blotter cube, boomers, blue acid, blue chairs, blue cheers, blue heaven, blue microdot, blue mist, blue moons, candy flip, cheers, Cid, doses, dots, frogs, fry, gel pyramid, L, microdots, mind blow, moons, pane, paper, paper acid, purple haze, snowmen, sugar, sugar cubes, tabs, trips, window glass, white lightning, window panes, yellow, yellow dimples, yellow sunshine, Zenacid
marijuana	African, airplane, ashes, Aunt Mary, baby, babysitter, bale, bamba, bash, blaze, bo, boom, broccoli, cannabis, charge, chunky, dope, ganja, giggle smoke, grass, jive stick, locoweed, Mary Jane, mother, pot, reefer, weed, sinsemilla, urb
MDMA[1]	Adam, baby slits, beans, biscuits, candy, candy flip, double stack, E, E-bombs, ecstasy, Eve, herbal bliss, illies, XTC
mescaline	big chief, buttons, cactus, mesc, mess
methampheta- mines	bam, biker's coffee, blue belly, chicken powder, Christina, crank, crystal meth, crystal methadrine, speed
opium	Auntie, Auntie Emma, big O, black, black hash, black pill, black Russian

1. methylenedioxymethamphetamine, usually called ecstasy

Drug	Slang names
phencyclidine	amoeba, angel, angel dust, angel hair, angel mist, animal, animal trank, animal tranquillizer, aurora borealis, black whack, boat, crystal, dummy dust, dust, elephant, elephant flipping, embalming fluid, fry, high, hog, illy, juice, killer joints, kools, loveboat, lovely, ozone, PCP, peace, rocket fuel, sherms, supergrass, wack, wet daddies, yellow fever, zombie
psilocybin mushrooms	magic mushrooms, shrooms
rohypnol	circles, forget-me pills, mexican valium, rib, roaches, roche, roofies, roopies, rope, rophies, ropies, ruffies

---

Words are, of course, the most powerful drug used by mankind.

Rudyard Kipling, speech.

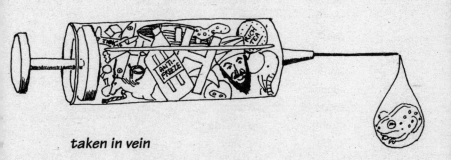

taken in vein

English as she is spoke
Written speech

The rendering of the slangy dialogue of the street so as to make it look natural on the page is an old and continuing challenge for novelists, playwrights, screenwriters, advertisers and other writers. One solution is to respell or contract words so that they resemble more closely the sounds they represent. The trick has always been to match colloquialism to context: in the wrong circumstance, such as a formal piece of writing, the use of such colloquial contraction or respelling risks accusations of 'bad' English. Some of the contractions in the following list of examples (such as *can't, don't, isn't, wouldn't*) are used increasingly, though by no means universally, in relatively formal contexts, while others (such as *ain't, geddit?, outta, wanna*) are unambiguously colloquial.

Colloquial form	Standard form
ain't	is not
aintcha	aren't you
bin	been
can't	cannot
c'mon	come on
couldn't	could not
cuppa	cup of
don't	do not
dunno	do not know
d'you	do you
'em	them
fella	fellow
fer	for
geddit?	get it?
gimme	give me
gonna	going to

Colloquial form	Standard form
gotcha	got you
gotta	got to
howzat?	how is that?
innit?	isn't it?
isn't	is not
-ite	-ight
kinda	kind of
luv	love
me	my
mightn't	might not
'n'	and
orf	off
outta	out of
sorta/sort've	sort of
s'pose	suppose
ter	to
wanna	want to
whaddyacallit	what do you call it?
won't	will not
wot	what
wotcha!	what cheer!
wouldn't	would not
woz/wuz	was
yer	your
y'know	you know

It is a damn poor mind that can think of only one way to spell a word.

Andrew Jackson

Cyberspeak
Computer jargon

Today's younger generations have grown up with the computer and much of their work and leisure time depends upon electronic communication of one kind or another. This has led to the development of a whole sub-language relating to the computer, the internet, the iPod and the mobile phone, some of it the work of information technology specialists and marketing teams and some of it contributions from users themselves. The following list includes a range of terms, most of which will be familiar to any self-respecting teenaged computer geek, and many more besides. Most date from no earlier than the 1990s, although a few (such as *hacker*) go back to the 1960s:

Term	*Meaning*
black-hat hacking	breaking into a website without permission
bleeding edge	the very latest in technological thinking
blog [1]	online journal
blogosphere	online journals collectively
blogroll	links to other blogs on a blog site
chatiquette	chat room etiquette
cluebie	new member of an internet forum who seems to know what he or she is doing
cracker	person who breaks a system's security
crash	cease operating
dark-side hacking	breaking into a website without permission
egosurf	to look up one's own name on the internet
escribitionist [2]	writer of a personal blog
FAQ	frequently asked questions
flame bait	posting to a discussion board intending to provoke hostile responses
flamer	person who posts hostile messages in a chat room
gamer	person who plays computer and video games
hacker	person who breaks into other computer systems

Term	Meaning
IRL	in real life
keypal	person one knows only through the internet
lamer	immature or dimwitted user of online bulletin boards
LAN party	local area network party (of online live action role-players)
larper	live action role-player (computer games player)
leet [3]	regular user of a chat room
leetspeak	cyberslang using abbreviations
liveblogging	blog sent from a live event
lurker	internet user who logs onto chat rooms or news groups but does not participate
luser	a 'lame user' of computers
MMORPG	massive multi-player online role-playing game
moblogging	uploading a blog from a mobile phone
MUCK	multi-user chat kingdom (gaming involving player interaction)
MUD	multi-user dungeon game (roleplay gaming)
Muggle [4]	person who is computer-illiterate
MUSH	multi-user shared hallucination (roleplay gaming for multiple users)
netfriend	person one knows only through the internet
newbie/newbee	newcomer to a chat room
nick	nickname used in a chat room
ohnosecond	instant of regret on realizing one has pressed the wrong computer key
phishing	fraudulently obtaining a person's credit card details via a fake website
phreak	person who illegally interferes with telephone systems

1. an abbreviation of 'weblog'

2. from the combination of English 'exhibitionist' and Spanish *escribir* (writer)

3. from 'elite'

4. a reference to the non-wizard humans in the *Harry Potter* books of J.K. Rowling

Term	Meaning
podcast	an audio or video broadcast downloaded from the internet to a personal computer, iPod, etc.
poddie	user of an iPod digital music player
reg	regular user of a chat room
RTBM	read the bloody manual
screenager	young internet user
script kiddie	person who unknowingly downloads script sent by a hacker
serial adder	person who befriends a lot of blog users at the same time
sha-mail [5]	the taking and sending of pictures using mobile phone cameras
silver surfer	elderly internet user
SLM	see last mail
SMS	short message system
snert	snot-nosed egotistical rude twit/teenager
spod	one who plays simplified role-playing games
talker	virtual role-playing game with simplified commands
TPTB	the powers that be
troll	person who insults the users of an internet forum
TSR	totally stupid rules
unfriending	removing oneself from a list of internet friends
URL [6]	internet address
vlog	blog containing video footage
wardriving	moving about with a mobile computer in search of an open wireless network to hack into
whitelist	a list of approved email addresses from which messages may be received on a computer
wiki	website to which anyone can contribute
wiLDing	moving about with a mobile computer in search of an open wireless network to hack into
worm	programme that infects other computer programmes

5. from the Japanese *shashin* (photograph) plus 'mail'

6. Uniform Resource Locater

C%L txt
Text messaging

The advent of the mobile phone and the chat room has led to much elaboration of the stock of previously existing abbreviations, which are now increasingly being employed in emails as well as more generally. Typically, words are rendered shorter through the reduction of words to their initial letters or through the replacement of certain letters with numbers or symbols. The following list includes some of the more widely recognized examples:

Abbreviation	Meaning
AAMOF	as a matter of fact
AFAIK	as far as I know
AFK	away from keyboard
AISI	as I see it
AND	any day now
B4	before
BBL	be back later
BCNU	be seeing you
BCOS	because
BF	boyfriend
BFN	bye for now
BION	believe it or not
BOT	back on topic
BRB	be right back
BTU	back to you
BTW	by the way
C%L	cool
C2C	cheek to cheek

Abbreviation	Meaning
CRBT	crying real big tears
CUL8R	see you later
CUS	see you soon
CWOT	complete waste of time
CYA	see ya
DIYU?	do I know you?
F2F	face to face
FITB	fill in the blanks
FWIW	for what it's worth
FYI	for your information
GAL	get a life
GF	girlfriend
GL	good luck
GR&D	grinning, running and ducking
GR8	great
H&K	hugs and kisses
HAGN	have a good night
HAND	have a nice day
HB	hurry back
HHIS	head hanging in shame
HSIK	how should I know?
HTH	hope this helps
IANAL	I am not a lawyer
IC	I see
ILY	I love you
IRL	in real life
IMO	in my opinion
IOW	in other words

Abbreviation	Meaning
IRL	in real life
ITA	I totally agree
IYKWIM	if you know what I mean
J2LUK	just to let you know
JAM	just a minute
JK	just kidding
KISS	keep it simple, stupid
KIT	keep in touch
KOL	kiss on lips
KOTC	kiss on the cheek
L8R G8R	later 'gator
LMAO	laughing my ass off
LOL	laughing out loud/lots of luck/lots of love
LY4E	love you forever
MUSM	miss you so much
MYOB	mind your own business
NBD	no big deal
NE	any
NE1	anyone
NHOH	never heard of him/her
NME	enemy
NP	no problem
OIC	oh I see
OTOH	on the other hand
OTL	out to lunch
P2P	person to person
PCM	please call me
PLS	please

Abbreviation	Meaning
PMBI	pardon my butting in
POAHF	put on a happy face
POS	parent over shoulder
POV	point of view
RME	rolling my eyes
ROTFL	rolling on the floor laughing
RUOK?	are you OK?
SIG2R	sorry, I got to run
SO	significant other
STR8	straight
SUP	what's up?
SWIM	see what I mean?
SYT	sweet young thing
TANSTAAFL	there ain't no such thing as a free lunch
TLK2UL8R	talk to you later
TOY	thinking of you
TTFN	ta-ta for now
TTYL	talk to you later
TXT MSG	text message
TY	thank you
U@	where are you?
WAN2TLK	want to talk?
WB	welcome back
XLNT	excellent
XOXOX	hugs and kisses
Y	why
YW	you're welcome
YYSW	yeah, yeah, sure, whatever
Z	said

Where it's @
The @ sign

One of the most useful symbols in the new 'languages' of the emoticon, the mobile phone and the chat room is the humble @ sign (in English usually called the 'at-sign' or 'cabbage'). As an essential component of electronic addresses, it has become one of the most important of all the keyboard symbols in use today. Its seemingly universal acceptance is reflected in the many names by which it is known around the world, of which the following are a selection:

Country	Name	Meaning
China	*siu lo tsu / xiao lao shu*	little mouse
Czech Republic	*zavinac*	rollmop
Denmark	*snabel*	elephant's trunk
Finland	*apinanhäntä*	monkey tail
	kissanhäntä	cat's tail
	miukumauku	the sign of the meow
France	*petit escargot*	small snail
Germany	*Klammeraffe*	monkey tail
Hungary	*kukac*	maggot/worm
Israel	*shablul*	snail
	strudel	roll-shaped bun
Italy	*chiocciola*	small snail
Korea	*dalphaengi*	snail
Netherlands	*apestaartje*	monkey tail
Norway	*grisehale*	pig's tail
	krullalpha	curly alpha
Poland	*malpa*	monkey tail
Portugal	*arroba*	(unit of measure)
Russia	*sobachka*	little dog
South Africa	*aapstert*	monkey tail
Spain	*arroba*	(unit of measure)
	ensaimada	spiral-shaped bagel
Sweden	*kanelbulle*	cinnamon roll
Turkey	*gul*	rose

Smiley and friends
Emoticons

The potential of the computer keyboard has been thoroughly explored with the introduction of email and the internet chat room. This is nowhere more evident than in the inventive use of standard keyboard symbols in the emoticon, a pictorial entity with its own particular meaning. The following list includes some of the more frequently used emoticons:

Symbol	Meaning	Symbol	Meaning
:-)	happy/smiling	X=	fingers crossed
:-))	very happy	b	winking
:-D	laughing	;-)	winking
:-(	sad	:-,	smirking
:'-(	sad/crying	:v	wicked grin
[:-(	frowning	:-L~~	drooling
:/	frustrated	:-*	kiss
:-|	angry	{}	kissing
:-V	shouting	@}-`-,-	a rose
:-@	screaming	8:)3)=	happy girl
:->	sarcastic	O:-)	angel
:-I	indifferent	}:>	devil
:-Q	I don't understand	>:->	devilish
%-)	confused	:-Y	aside comment
:-/	sceptical	:-o	shock/surprise
:-"	pursing lips	:*	greedy
:-X	my lips are sealed	:*)	drunk
X-)	I see nothing	:=)	little Hitler
:-P	I'm sticking my tongue out		

Love letters
Postal acronyms

In the days when lovers communicated chiefly by mail, long before the advent of the mobile phone, many a lovestruck young man or woman scrawled a 'secret' final message on the envelope before rushing for the post. These fondly remembered one-word acronyms date mostly from World War II, when many love affairs were interrupted by the man being called up and sent far from home in the armed services. Some of these coinages are still familiar to many people today:

Acronym	Meaning
BITS	be in touch soon
BOLTOP	better on lips than on paper
BURMA	be upstairs/undressed and ready my angel
CHINA	come home, I need affection
CHIP	come home, I'm pregnant
EGYPT	'e got you pregnant then!
FISH	forget it, I'm staying here
HOLLAND	hope our love lasts/lives and never dies
ILYA	I love you always
ITALY	I trust and love you/I truly always love you
MALAYA	my ardent lips await your arrival
MEXICO CITY	may every kiss I can offer carry itself to you
NORWICH	(k)nickers off ready when I come home
SAG	Saint Anthony guide[1]
SIAM	sexual intercourse at midnight
SIDCUP	sexual intercourse definitely causes unwanted pregnancies
STARDUST	still thinking and remembering, darling, unforgettable seconds together
SWALK	sealed with a loving kiss
WALES	with a love eternal, sweetheart

1. Saint Anthony, as the patron saint of lost things, was thus requested to see the letter safely to its destination

Bozo to baphead
Insults

The origins of some insults bandied about on a daily basis today are lost in the mists of time; others, however, can be dated fairly accurately. Some speak uniquely of their own time, but there are others still in common use, like *wally* or *wimp*, that are much older than might at first be suspected, as revealed in the following selection:

Decade	Insults
1910s	bozo, cocksucker, freak, lamebrain, melonhead, nitwit, pansy, pipsqueak, twat, twerp
1920s	bum, creep, dimwit, git, moron, palooka, prick, shitbag, twit, wally, wimp, yobbo
1930s	arse, arsehole, berk, drip, dumbo, fart-face, jack-off, jerk, knobhead, knucklehead, schmuck, screwball
1940s	birdbrain, cluckhead, cretin, deadhead, dill, jarhead, shit head, tit, tosspot, wanker
1950s	bubblehead, doofus [1], flake, headcase, klutz, mother, nerd, nutcase, weirdo
1960s	chickenhead, dickhead, dipshit, dork, dweeb, gonk, nana, nutcake, pillock, prat, retard, scally, tight-arse
1970s	airhead, div, grunt, tosser, wuss
1980s	bimbo, butthead, dipstick, fruit loop [2], goonhead, pisshead, plonker
1990s	fart-knocker, fugly [3], mofo [4], muppet [5], pondlife, toss-bag, wazzock
2000s	baphead, blonde, cheese-eating surrender monkeys (the French), minger, twathead

1. from the German *doof* (stupid)

2. from the name of a popular US breakfast cereal

3. from the combination of 'fucking' and 'ugly'

4. abbreviation of 'mother-fucker'

5. after Jim Henson's *Muppet Show*

4 All growed up

Words at work

By the time a young man or woman enters the world of work they may reasonably expect to be a master (or mistress) of their language, as well as being well schooled in jargon, slang, and circumlocution. To the language of the home, the school and (perhaps) university comes now the vocabulary of money, of the workplace, the media and politics, of war and crime, of newspapers, and the world of sport and entertainment.

Deciphering what it all means can be a challenging task: the very obscurity of much of the modern vocabulary is often the whole point of it (as is the case, for instance, with the codenames of the military establishment or the slang of the criminal underworld). The language becomes subdivided into exclusive strata that can be seen as modern equivalents of regional dialects, decipherable only to the initiated. In using these specialized sub-vocabularies the speaker flaunts his or her familiarity with and perhaps authority within the relevant group. At its extreme, the use of complicated and obscure jargon in the world of the workplace may serve to conceal the fact that the speaker really has nothing to say at all ...

This chapter, then, steps boldly into the language of the adult world, exploring just some of its many branches.

What is an adult? A child blown up by age.

Simone de Beauvoir

Bobs and bits
Slang terms for money

Money occupies an important role in everyone's lives and it is hardly surprising then that the topic should have been long familiarized through the use of a host of nicknames, many of them slang. Most, like 'copper' and 'bob', are centuries old and date back to before the introduction of the present decimal coinage in 1971. A few of these, like 'quid' and 'tenner', have survived into modern times, alongside such recent additions to the canon as 'archer' and 'pavarotti'.

Amount	Slang name	Origin
PRE-DECIMAL		
1d[1]	copper	the colour of the coin
3d/4d	joey	radical politician Joseph Hume, who introduced the threepence (pronounced 'thruppence') or threepenny (pronounced 'thrupunny') bit in the 19th century
1s[2]	bob	short for 'bobstick' (etymology otherwise unknown)
2s 6d	half a dollar	a nickname dating from the middle of the 20th century when the exchange rate was US$4 to £1 sterling (20 shillings)
	two and a kick	'kick' being loose rhyming slang for 'six'
5s	cartwheel	similarity in shape
	dollar	a nickname dating from the middle of the 20th century when the exchange rate was US$4 to £1 sterling (20 shillings)
£1	dollar	from German taler, abbreviated from Joachimsthaler, a coin made with metal mined in the Czech town of Joachim-sthaler Jachymov
	foal	play on 'pony' (see below)

Amount	Slang name	Origin
£1 *(cont.)*	quid	possibly from the Latin *quid*, what (one needs)
	smacker	possibly from the noise a £1 note made when 'smacked' down on a table
	sov	abbreviated from 'sovereign'
sovereign[3]	Jemmy O'Goblin	rhyming slang
£5	blue	its (original) colour
	fiver	the number five
	godiva	rhyming slang
	jack	abbreviated from 'Jack's alive' (rhyming slang for five)
£10	cock	abbreviation of 'cock and hen' (rhyming slang for 10)
	tenner	the number ten
£20	score	standard slang for the number 20 (relating to the days when sheep were counted in 20s, each 20 being recorded by scoring a notch on a stick)
£25	macaroni	rhyming slang for 'pony' (see below)
	pony	possibly a reference to the placing of a relatively small bet (ponies being relatively small) on a horse in a race
£50	bull's eye	a bull's eye in darts (worth 50 points)
	half-a-ton	half of £100 (see below)
£100	century	a 'century' being 100 of anything

1. the 'd' here representing 'penny' was an abbreviation of the Latin *denarius*, the basic component of Roman coinage. The predecimal coinage was commonly referred to as 'LSD', which was short for the Latin *librae, solidi, denarii* (meaning 'pounds, shillings and pence')

2. the 's' here represents 'shilling', equivalent to 12 pence

3. the sovereign was a gold coin worth £1 sterling

Amount	Slang name	Origin
£100 (*cont.*)	ton	the standard 'ton' (100 cubic feet), seen as a large amount of something
£500	monkey	etymology unknown
£1000	cow	etymology unknown
	gorilla	a gorilla being twice the size of a monkey (see above)
	grand	standard adjective 'grand' for anything large or impressive

DECIMAL

Amount	Slang name	Origin
£10	pavarotti	Luciano Pavarotti, the Italian tenor (and thus a pun for 'tenner')
£2000	archer	a disputed payment of £2000 in a 1987 libel case between the *Daily Star* newspaper and writer and politician Jeffrey Archer

US

Amount	Slang name	Origin
1c	penny	Old English *penig* or *pening*
	red Indian	the appearance of the head of a native American chief on one-cent coins at the end of the 19th century
5c	nickel	the metal nickel
10c	dime	Old French *disme*, meaning 'tenth'
25c	quarter	a 'quarter' of a dollar
	two bits	'bit' as a small amount of anything
50c	four bits	'bit' as a small amount of anything
$1	buck	abbreviated from 'buckskin', which was used in bartering in the USA in the 19th century
	cartwheel	similarity in shape

Amount	Slang name	Origin
$1 (*cont.*)	smacker	possibly from the noise it makes when 'smacked' down on a table
$10	sawbuck	the cross-shaped sawhorse, the cross shape being reminiscent of the Roman numeral for 10
$100	century	a 'century' being 100 of anything
$500	monkey	etymology unknown
$1000	G, grand	standard adjective 'grand' for anything large or impressive

three tenors

Offlish
Business words

Modern business has developed its own private vocabulary, or 'Offlish' (office English), which in many cases is entirely incomprehensible to uninitiated outsiders. Some of these terms are used and understood throughout industry and commerce and have even entered everyday language, while others are unique to a particular sector, such as the stock exchange. Such business- or management-speak can be very colourful, as evidenced by the following selection of such terms.

Jargon term	*Meaning*
B2B	business to business
bangalore	outsource business activity to India [1]
banjo	bang another nuisance job out
blamestorming	meeting to assign blame for something [2]
blue-sky thinking	imaginative thinking [3]
bogof	buy one get one free [4]
boiled frog syndrome	inability or unwillingness to react to change
boomerang worker	former employee who continues to work for his or her old company
bottom feeder	one who buys shares when they are worth least
cockroach problem	problem that appears worse than it actually is
cybersquatting	registering potentially lucrative internet domain names to sell for a profit later
dead-cat bounce	temporary recovery in share prices after a big fall
decruit	make redundant
dot-bomb	unsuccessful dot-com company
dot-com	internet-based company
double-hatting	being responsible for more than one job
downsize	make redundant

Jargon term	*Meaning*
drop one's pants	lower the price of a product
duvet day	day off because of tiredness
empty suit	executive with no real influence
entreprenerd	computer company entrepreneur
ford	found on roadside, dead
get one's ducks in a row	put things in order
glass ceiling	level beyond which women or other groups of employees are not promoted
golden bungee	financial lure to persuade an executive to leave a company
golden handcuffs	financial rewards paid to an employee to keep their services
golden handshake	financial reward paid as compensation for dismissal or retirement
golden hello	financial bonus paid to a new employee
golden parachute	clause assuring an executive of compensation if dismissed after a takeover
halve the footprint	make half the workforce redundant
head up	provide leadership
ideas hamster	entrepreneur who is full of ideas
interface	communicate
JFDI	just fucking do it
joy-to-stuff ratio	work/life balance
Lady Macbeth strategy	takeover bid by a third party secretly in league with another bidder [5]
lifestyle office	office equipped with gym, bar, etc.
low-hanging fruit	easily attained targets

1. in order to take advantage of the relatively cheap labour there

2. a pun on 'brainstorming'

3. the verb 'blue sky', meaning 'day-dream', actually goes back to the 1950s

4. particularly associated with supermarket offers

5. specifically a reference to Lady Macbeth's encouragement to her husband to murder King Duncan

Jargon term	Meaning
make it happen	do it, or else
moose on the table	obvious solution that no one wants to take up
mundane	person who is not employed in the computer industry
networking	mixing with colleagues (to one's own advantage)
New York minute	a very short time
no pressure	pressure if it does not happen
not rocket science	fairly easy
open collar worker	person who works from home
out-of-the-box	lateral thinking
paradigm shift	big change in approach or thinking
PDQ	pretty damn quick
POETS	piss off early, tomorrow's Saturday
prairie-dog	person who spies on fellow-workers over the wall of an office cubicle
prawn-sandwich man	corporate freeloader
pull up the manhole cover	look into in depth
push the peanut forward	make progress
put skin in the game	make a financial commitment to a company
rate tart	one who switches credit cards to get a better interest rate
re-engineer	restructure
rightsize	make redundant
road warrior	businessman who travels a lot
suit	high-ranking executive
TGIF	thank God it's Friday
upshift	embrace a high-pressure lifestyle
vulture fund	company that takes over other failing companies
with all due respect …	I disagree entirely …
wysiwyg	what you see is what you get [6]

6. originally a computer acronym, but now used more widely

Glam yappies
Business acronyms

In business it is important to identify one's potential clients. In recent years many business people have sought to categorize their customers by means of handy acronymic labels (or 'socionyms') that say much about the target's disposable income and their priorities in life. Many of these were originally coined by US marketing experts in the 1980s. Some were devised as means of communicating useful information about possible customers in as succinct a manner as possible; others are clearly more facetious in origin. The following list includes some of the more widely used such acronyms:

Acronym	*Meaning*
buppie	black upwardly mobile professional person
dinky	dual/double income, no kids yet
dump	destitute unemployed mature professional
glam	greying, leisured, affluent and married
guppie	gay/green upwardly mobile professional person
hopeful	hard-up old person expecting full useful life
lombard	lots of money but a right dickhead
nipplie	new Irish patriot permanently living in exile
nony	not old, not young
oink	one income, no kids
pippie	person inheriting parents' property
posslq	person of the opposite sex sharing living quarters
puppie	poncy upwardly-mobile professional person
rubbie	rich urban biker
scum	self-centred urban male
silky	single income, loads of kids

Acronym	Meaning
Sinbad	single income, no boyfriend, absolutely desperate
sink	single, independent, no kids
sitcom	single income, two children, oppressive/ outrageous mortgage
woopie	well-off older person
wow	women organizing the world
yappie	young affluent parent
yettie	young entrepreneurial technocrat (one who earns money on the net)
yuppie	young upwardly mobile professional person

yettie

Bites, blurbs and by-lines
Media words

People who work in the media use a host of technical terms and jargon, some of which are understandable only to themselves. Some are fairly simple terms relating to the physical communication of news; others, like 'blurb' and 'puff', are more fanciful comments upon the nature of the media and the way it works. The following list includes a selection of some of the better-known terms:

Term	Meaning
actuality	an audio recording of natural sound
beat	a reporter's particular field
beat up	write an extravagantly exaggerated story
bite	brief section of an interview, usually just seconds long, suitable for extracting for headlines etc.
blurb [1]	promotional material on the back of a book etc.
break	make the first announcement of a new story
by-line	the crediting of an author as the writer of a story
classified	an advertisement in a newspaper or magazine
copy	the text of a story
cut	the removal of material from a story
cutaway	extra material shot after an interview has been filmed, to be inserted later
editorial	the main opinion column of a newspaper or other publication
embargo	a time before which a story may not be published or broadcast

1. coined in 1907 by US humorist Gelett Burgess, who identified the attractive woman commonly depicted on the front cover of comic books as 'Miss Belinda Blurb'

Term	Meaning
file	to submit a story for publication
filler	a short story to fill space in a newspaper or news programme
grab	a brief section of an interview that can be extracted for use in an edited version
leader	the opinion column of a newspaper or other publication
noddies	in television interviews, reverse shots of the interviewer nodding as the interviewee talks (usually filmed after the interview has been completed)
off the record	material released to a journalist on the understanding that it will not be published
puff	promotional material
round	the field of activity in which a journalist specializes
run	to publish a story
scoop	to publish a story before anyone else
sub	to edit a story
teaser	a fact or other material released to attract attention to a longer story
throw	to transfer from a reporter in the field to a presenter in the studio, and other transitions
wild sound	an audio recording of natural sound

Language is not an abstract construction of the learned, or of dictionary-makers, but is something arising out of the work, needs, ties, joys, affections, tastes, of long generations of humanity, and has its bases broad and low, close to the ground.

Walt Whitman

Sales patter
The language of marketing

Successful salespersons know the importance of language in securing sales. In the marketplace the vocabulary is commonly manipulated to conceal as well as reveal essential features of a proposed deal. Few salespersons are more notorious for such sleights of hand as car dealers and estate agents, although similar euphemistic language may be encountered throughout the commercial world. The following list largely comprises jocular examples of attempts to decipher the obfuscatory jargon of marketing:

Business	*Patter*	*Meaning*
car dealers	bargain	on its last legs
	certified	used
	compact	tiny
	experienced	secondhand
	fair condition	tatty
	family runabout	will not manage long journeys
	nearly new	secondhand
	offer valid at participating dealers	but not the one you are in
	pre-driven	secondhand
	pre-enjoyed	used
	previously cared-for	secondhand
	used	worn-out
estate agents	bijou	cramped
	character	unfashionable
	cosy	cramped

Business	Patter	Meaning
estate agents (*cont.*)	cottage	anything old and small
	handy for public transport	next to a noisy bus-stop
	ideal for modernization	derelict
	interesting	unsaleable
	mature garden	overgrown garden
	original features	unreliable wiring and plumbing
	realistically priced	outrageously expensive
	requiring attention	ruinous
	retro	unfashionable
	secluded	no local facilities at all
	starter home	not one to stay in long
	studio apartment	one-room apartment
	suitable for conversion	in need of repair
	town house	front entrance through garage
high street sales	can I help you?	I have a sales target to meet
	card declined	aren't you ashamed you are so poor?
	customer service representative	shop assistant
	loss prevention	store security
	sales associate	shop assistant
postal sales	as one of our best customers	your address is on our list
	certain restrictions may apply	this deal is not as good as you think it is

Business	Patter	Meaning
postal sales (*cont.*)	each sold separately	because that way we can charge you more
	fine print	things we do not want you to notice
	not available in all stores	almost certainly not in the store you go to
	price adjustment	price increase
	sorry, you're not a winner	we're not sorry at all because now you will buy another
	valued customer	anyone
telesales	someone will be with you shortly	we may keep you waiting for hours
	telemarketing representative	telephone operator
	this call may be monitored	don't swear or threaten us
	your call is important to us	we want your money

You can stroke people with words.

F. Scott Fitzgerald, **The Crack-Up**

What it says on the tin
Slogans

Few words work harder for their money than slogans, whether in the service of commerce or other public campaigns. The best slogans arrest the attention, combining originality, humour and style. Others, however, seem less likely to impress (one may question, for instance, the wisdom of the slogan for Electrolux vacuum cleaners, 'nothing sucks like an Electrolux' or, for IKEA's self-build furniture, 'screw yourself').

Slogan	*Source and date*
A diamond is forever [1]	De Beers Consolidated Mines 1939
A Mars a day helps you work, rest and play	Mars bar *c.*1960
Access, your flexible friend	Access credit card 1970s
All the news that's fit to print	*New York Times* 1896
All the way with LBJ	Lyndon Baines Johnson presidential campaign 1967
And all because the lady loves Milk Tray	Cadbury's Milk Tray chocolates 1968
Any time, any place, anywhere	Martini 1970s
Australians wouldn't give a XXXX for anything else	Castlemaine lager 1986
Ban the bomb	anti-nuclear weapons campaign *c.*1960
Be all that you can be	US army recruitment campaign 1981
Beanz Meanz Heinz	Heinz baked beans *c.*1967
Black is beautiful	anti-racism campaign 1966
Blow some my way	Chesterfield cigarettes 1926
Burn your bra!	pro-feminism campaign 1960s

Slogan	*Source and date*
Buy British	pro-British goods campaign 1968
Careless talk costs lives	World War II campaign 1941
Central heating for kids	Ready Brek cereal 1970s
Clunk click every trip	seat belt campaign 1970s
Cool as a mountain stream	Consulate cigarettes early 1960s
Don't die of ignorance	Aids awareness campaign 1980s
Drinka pinta milka day	Milk Marketing Board campaign 1958
'Ello, Tosh, got a Toshiba?	Toshiba cars 1984
Even your closest friends won't tell you	Listerine mouthwash *c.*1923
For mash get Smash	Cadbury's Smash instant mashed potato 1967
Good to the last drop	Maxwell House coffee 1907
Go to work on an egg [2]	British Egg Marketing Board 1960s
Guinness is good for you	Guinness beer 1929
Happiness is a cigar called Hamlet	Hamlet cigars 1960s
Heineken reaches the parts other beers cannot reach	Heineken lager 1975
Hello boys	Playtex Wonderbra 1994
I bet he drinks Carling Black Label	Carling Black Label 1990
I'd walk a mile for a Camel	Camel cigarettes 1921
I liked it so much, I bought the company	Remington Shavers 1985
I'm backing Britain	pro-British goods campaign 1960s
It beats as it sweeps as it cleans	Hoover vacuum cleaners 1926
It does exactly what it says on the tin	Ronseal wood varnish late 1980s
It's fingerlickin' good	Kentucky Fried Chicken 1952
It's good to talk	BT 1990s

1. also well known as the basis of the title of the James Bond novel (1956) and film (1971) *Diamonds are Forever*

2. often credited to writer Fay Weldon or, sometimes, to playwright Anthony Shaffer

Slogan	Source and date
It's the real thing	Coca-Cola 1970
Just do it	Nike 1998
Make love, not war	anti-war campaign 1960s
Naughty but nice	Dairy Council 1981
Nice one, Cyril!	Wonderloaf 1972
Put a tiger in your tank	Esso petrol 1964
Reassuringly expensive	Stella Artois beer 1981
Say it with flowers	Society of American Florists 1917
Schhh … you know who	Schweppes mineral drinks 1960s
That will do nicely	American Express credit card 1970s
The best a man can get	Gillette razors 1970s
The future's bright, the future's Orange	Orange mobile phones 1996
Think outside the box	Apple computers 1990s
Vorsprung durch Technik [3]	Audi cars 1982
What's in *your* wallet?	Capital One credit cards 2005
Where do you want to go today?	Microsoft computers 1990s
Where's the beef?	Wendy's fast-food chain 1984
You can be sure of Shell	Shell petrol *c.* 1931
Your country needs you!	World War I recruiting poster 1914
You're never alone with a Strand [4]	Strand cigarettes 1960

3. translates as 'progress through technology'

4. an infamous example of a slogan that backfired: nobody wanted to be lonely, so they stopped smoking Strand cigarettes

---

Words may be false and full of art.

Thomas Shadwell

Spinning and sexing up
Political words

Politicians have always relied upon language to communicate both
their policies and their personalities. It is not surprising, then, that
they should prove particularly inventive in coming up with new terms
and new meanings of existing words, particularly since the advent
of 'spin' in the late 1990s and the growing awareness that euphemism
and obfuscation are powerful (if highly controversial) political tools.
The following selection of examples associated with both past and
present generations of political leaders illustrates the imaginative-
ness with which they have approached the vocabulary.

Term	*Meaning*
axis of evil [1]	(in US eyes) countries accused of endangering world security
behindology	what lies behind the spin
big bang	enlargement of the European Union in 2004
big tent	acceptance of a range of political views within a party
bleeding heart	a liberal politician who supports government spending on social programmes
chardonnay socialist [2]	new version of the old 'champagne socialist', who expresses working-class ideals while adopting an (almost) upper-class lifestyle
dodgy dossier [3]	dubious briefings etc. released in support of a contentious policy

1. particularly associated with US President George W. Bush; the original 2002
reference was to Iran, Iraq and North Korea

2. the new term relates to a somewhat different type of person, namely the
fashionable middle-class urban socialites of the 1990s and 2000s whose
favourite tipple is supposedly chardonnay wine

3. the term originally referred specifically to a notorious dossier relating to the
Iraq War presented by Alistair Campbell in 2003

Term	Meaning
doublespeak [4]	evasion of the truth by politicians
economical with the truth [5]	lying
economic migrant	immigrant who arrives in search of a better standard of living
eurocreep	the halting acceptance of the euro by countries of the European Union
fiscal underachiever	pauper
fishing expedition	an inquiry made with no other purpose than seeking to damage an opponent
full and frank discussion [6]	argument
hearts and minds	popular support
joined-up government	government branches that act in synchronization
negative patient care outcome	death in hospital
nimby [7]	not in my back yard
pollutician	politician who fails to oppose policies that will damage the environment
prebuttal	refutation of a hostile argument before it has even been voiced
regime change	the toppling of a hostile government
revenue enhancement	tax increase
road map [8]	future plan
rubber chicken circuit	the numerous public lunches and dinners at which politician-guests are often served reheated chicken
smoked-filled room	a place where political wheeling and dealing goes on behind the scenes
spin	biased information
sex up	make more appealing or acceptable
terminological inexactitude [9]	lie
wiggle room	room for political manoeuvring

4. the term probably has its origins in the 'doublethink' and 'newspeak' introduced by George Orwell in his novel *Nineteen Eighty-Four* (1949)

5. the phrase was first heard during the 1986 *Spycatcher* trial, when it was spoken by British Cabinet Secretary Sir Robert Armstrong

6. for years a well-known journalistic cliché

7. the acronym dates from 1986, when it was coined to describe protesters against the building of nuclear power stations near their homes

8. first used in a political context in 2003 in discussions of Israeli-Palestinian affairs

9. first so used in a 1906 speech about labour contracts by Winston Churchill

---

Words – so innocent and powerless as they are, as standing in a dictionary, how potent for good and evil they become, in the hands of one who knows how to combine them!

Nathaniel Hawthorne

full and frank discussion

War of the words
Military words

War has always been a rich source of new vocabulary, often inspired by new developments in weapons and tactics. Many, inevitably, are euphemisms intended to disguise the horrific nature of warfare. It is noticeable how such euphemistic coinages have proliferated in relatively recent times, presumably in response to various governments realizing the influence of public opinion upon their plans and hence the need to control that opinion. Some coinages, like *blitz* or *fallout*, have proved so useful they have been absorbed into general use, often far removed from the business of war; others, like *yomp* or *shock and awe* remain closely associated with the conflict with which they originated. The following list includes just a few of the more significant military words to emerge over the past 100 years or so:

Term	*Meaning*
SECOND BOER WAR (1899–1902)	
commando [1]	amphibious military raiding force
concentration camp	prison for political prisoners or minority groups, where they are held without trial
WORLD WAR I (1914–18)	
no man's land	area between the front lines
shellshocked	affected by post-traumatic stress
slacker	person who evades work
WORLD WAR II (1939–45)	
blitz(krieg)	a sudden, overwhelming attack
ersatz [2]	artificial
firestorm	fires resulting from heavy bombing

Term	*Meaning*

WORLD WAR II (1939–45) (*cont.*)

flak [3]	anti-aircraft fire
ground zero	the site of a large (nuclear) explosion
Jeep	general purpose vehicle
nose dive	(of an aircraft) plunge towards the ground
snafu	situation normal, all fouled/fucked up
storm trooper	member of a force of shock troops

COLD WAR (1940s–80s)

blue-on-blue [4]	accidental killing of one's own troops
fallout	radioactive material released by an atomic explosion
Iron Curtain [5]	the division between the capitalist West and the Communist East
Red Menace	Communism

KOREAN WAR (1950–53)

brainwash [6]	alteration of someone's thoughts

1. from the Afrikaans *commando*, itself from the Dutch *commando* (command)

2. from the German *ersetzen* (to substitute)

3. from the German *Flugabwehrkanone* or *Fliegerabwehrkanone* (German names for anti-aircraft guns)

4. a reference to NATO war games, in which friendly forces were represented in blue and enemy forces in red

5. though particularly associated with the Cold War after being employed by Winston Churchill in a 1946 speech, the phrase was used at an earlier date by Josef Goebbels and even as far back as 1819, when it appeared in the journal of the Earl of Munster

6. notion that the only way to explain the breakdown of US soldiers during the war was through the use of 'mind-altering' weapons by the enemy

Term	*Meaning*
VIETNAM WAR (1964–75)	
air support	bombing
body bag	bag in which the body of a dead soldier is brought home
body count	number of casualties
carpet bombing	concentrated bombing
collateral damage	accidental damage to civilian targets
fragging	deliberately killing a superior officer with a fragmentation grenade
friendly fire	fire directed at soldiers on the same side
grunt [7]	ordinary soldier
incursion	invasion
police action	war
smoke	kill
waste	kill
FALKLANDS WAR (1982)	
yomp	march over difficult terrain
GULF WAR (1990–91)	
smart bomb	electronically-controlled missile
surgical strike	a precision attack on a specific target, avoiding collateral damage
BOSNIAN CIVIL WAR (1991–95)	
ethnic cleansing	elimination of a population on ethnic grounds
IRAQ WAR (2003)	
decapitation exercise	warfare with the aim of removing an enemy's leadership

Term	*Meaning*
IRAQ WAR (2003) *(cont.)*	
embedded [8]	attached to a military unit
kill box	square on an electronic grid into which a laser-guided bomb is then fired
mission creep	the tendency for a mission to go beyond its initial purpose
operating in a target-rich environment	outnumbered
shock and awe	the use of large numbers of precision weapons to overwhelm an enemy
unselected rollback to idle	aeroplane engine failure
vertically deployed anti-personnel device	bomb
weapon of mass destruction (WMD) [9]	any weapon that will kill large numbers

7. inspired by the endless complaining of the common soldier

8. usually relating to journalists

9. actually first heard in the run-up to the Iraq War when suspicion that Iraq had such weapons was quoted as a reason for invading

Rolling Thunder, Desert Storm
Military campaign names

The codenames given to military operations are often deliberately obscure and irrelevant to the plans in question. Others, like Barbarossa, contain a historical reference and reflect the grandiosity of an aggressor's ambitions (it was named after Emperor Frederick I (1123–90), whose nickname Barbarossa meant 'redbeard'). Some, like Overlord or Desert Storm, become so well known that no explanation may be required to identify the campaign being referred to. Consider the following selection of famous military codenames:

Name	*Campaign*
Avalanche	Allied invasion of Italy (1943)
Barbarossa	German invasion of USSR (1941)
Baytown	British invasion of the Italian mainland (1943)
Big Switch	US Korean War campaign (1950)
Buffalo	Allied breakout from Anzio, southern Italy (1943)
Chromite	US landing at Inchon, Korea (1950)
Cobra	US breakout after D-Day (1944)
Crossbow	RAF attacks on German V-rockets (1943)
Desert Storm	US-led UN coalition offensive against Iraq (1991)
Downfall	Allied invasion of Japan (1945)
Eldorado Canyon	US air raid on Libya (1986)
Enduring Freedom	US invasion of Afghanistan (2001)
Frantic	US bombing of German-held Europe (1944)
Golden Pheasant	US deployment of forces in Honduras (1987)
Gymnast	Allied invasion of French northwest Africa (1941)
Husky	Allied invasion of Sicily (1943)

Name	*Campaign*
Iceberg	US capture of Okinawa (1945)
Iraqi Freedom	US invasion of Iraq (2003)
Just Cause	US invasion of Panama (1989)
Keystone	US withdrawal from Vietnam (1969)
Mailfist	Allied recapture of Singapore (1945)
Manhattan Project	US development of the atomic bomb (1942–45)
Market Garden	Allied airborne operation at Arnhem, in the Netherlands (1944)
Neptune	Allied landings in Normandy on D-Day (1944)
Overlord	Allied invasion of Normandy (1944)
Rolling Thunder	US bombing of North Vietnam (1965)
Roundup	Allied cross-Channel operations (1943)
Sea Lion (Seeloewe)	German invasion of the UK (1940)
Shingle	Allied amphibious landings at Anzio, Italy (1944)
Torch	Allied invasion of northwest Africa (1942)
Trebor	British recapture of embassy in Kuwait City (1991)
Urgent Fury	US invasion of Grenada (1983)
Watchtower	US invasion of Guadalcanal (1942)
Zipper	Allied recapture of Malaya (1945)

Blagging and twocking
Criminal slang

Criminals have always had their own special language, originally designed to communicate between themselves without the authorities understanding what was being said. Often, it may also function to create a sense of shared identity between criminal elements and to signal their rejection of establishment values. The following list includes some of the terms adopted by the criminal fraternity on the two sides of the Atlantic, among them slang words that circulate in British and US prisons:

Term	*Meaning*
UK	
blag	violent robbery or raid
brief	legal adviser
con	convict/confidence trick
cop [1]	police officer
datastreaming	hacking into a person's financial details to create fake credit cards
do time	serve a prison sentence
front	an apparently innocent person who helps conceal criminal activity
gate fever	emotional state of a convict nearing the end of a prison sentence
go down [2]	be sent to prison
grass [3]	informer
hobbit	convict who obeys the prison rules
ice cream	drugs
jumper	criminal who steals from offices
lag	an habitual criminal who has served several prison sentences
M.O.	*modus operandi* (a criminal's method of work)

Term	Meaning
nick	arrest/police station
nonce	sex offender
nut	a criminal's expenses
obbo	police observation of criminals
padding	the adding of drugs to a seized haul to increase the prisoner's likely sentence
pig	police officer
ramp	criminal swindle/police search
rozzer [4]	police officer
shoulder surf	to watch a cashpoint in order to steal a person's pin number and use it to defraud them
slammer	prison
snitch	informer
supergrass	a very significant police informer
twoc	take (a vehicle) without the owner's consent
zombie	an unpleasant police officer

US

badge	police officer or prison guard
big house	prison
big sleep	death
blade	knife
bracelets	handcuffs
bum rap	bad or false charge
caboose [5]	prison

1. possibly ultimately from the French *caper* (to seize)

2. because those who were convicted at the Old Bailey descended the stairs below the dock to the cells, while those who were acquitted went 'up the stairs'

3. from 'grasshopper', itself rhyming slang for 'shopper', signifying a person who sends others to the 'shop' (an old slang term for a prison)

4. possibly from Romany *roozlo* (strong) or *roast* (villain)

5. from the Dutch *kabuis* (cook's galley), a similarly confined space

Term	Meaning
cooler	prison
can [6]	prison
dick	detective
gumshoe [7]	detective
heat	close surveillance
hooker	prostitute
hoosegow [8]	prison
ice	diamonds
junkie	drug addict
kick off	die
mazuma [9]	money
mob	gang
nark	informer
pack	carry (a gun)
palooka [10]	fool
pen	penitentiary
rap	criminal charge
rat	informer
shank	homemade knife
shyster [11]	lawyer
stick	stab
stir	prison

6. being, like a prison, a container

7. from the notion that they wear rubber-soled shoes to creep about in

8. from the Spanish *juzgado* (court of justice)

9. via Yiddish from a Hebrew word meaning 'ready' or 'prepared'

10. after the comic strip 'Joe Palooka', first published in 1930

11. possibly after an eccentric New York lawyer called Scheuster

Headless body in topless bar
Memorable newspaper headlines

Good newspaper headlines are both concise and memorable. Some newspapers, especially tabloids such as *The Sun* in the UK, have become notorious for snappy, provocative headlines in which considerations such as spelling and grammar come second to impact. The following selection of headlines includes some of the most cherished examples composed over the last 100 years. All these actually appeared in real newspapers (no room, therefore, for J.B. Morton's suggestion for a sensational headline: 'Sixty horses wedged in a chimney', or for another suggestion for the most boring headline ever printed: 'Small earthquake in Peru. Not many hurt').

Headline	*Source and story*
Say it ain't so, Joe	*Chicago Daily News* (1920) 'Black Sox' baseball scandal
Wall Street lays an egg	*Variety* (1929) Wall Street Crash
It's that man again!	*Daily Express* (1929) story about Adolf Hitler
Hix nix pix in stix[1]	*Variety* (1935) failure of films about rural America with rural audience
No war this year	*Daily Express* (1939) ignoring impending outbreak of World War II
Dewey defeats Truman	*Chicago Tribune* (1948) US presidential election, won by Truman

1. in 2000 the *New York Daily News* paid tribute to this headline with a new version, 'Hicks nix knicks in six', referring to an NBA basketball game

Headline	Source and story
Whose finger do you want on the trigger when the world situation is so delicate?	*Daily Mirror* (1951) UK general election
Egghead weds hourglass	*Variety* (1956) wedding of Arthur Miller and Marilyn Monroe
All change	*Daily Mirror* (1971) introduction of decimal currency
Stick it up your Junta	*The Sun* (1982) Falklands War
Gotcha!	*The Sun* (1982) sinking of the *General Belgrano* in the Falklands War
Headless body in topless bar	*New York Post* (1983) New York murder story
Freddie Starr ate my hamster	*The Sun* (1986) story about comedian Freddie Starr
I found face of Jesus on my fish finger	*Sunday Sport* (1990) food story
Up yours, Delors	*The Sun* (1990) anti-European Community story (Jacques Delors being then the President of the European Commission)
If Kinnock wins tonight will the last person to leave Britain please turn out the lights	*The Sun* (1992) UK general election

Headline	*Source and story*
It was the Sun wot won it	*The Sun* (1992) UK general election (won against the odds by the Conservatives)
Killer bug ate my face	*Daily Star* (1994) flesh-eating superbug story
Super Caley go ballistic. Celtic are atrocious	*The Sun* (2000) Caledonian Thistle's upset in Scottish Cup against Celtic
Bloody Nasty People	*The Sun* (2004) criticism of the British National Party
Urs hole	*The Sun* (2004) reaction after World Cup referee Urs Meier disallowed a winning England goal
Tetbury man weds	*Bristol Evening Post* (2005) marriage of Prince Charles and Camilla Parker Bowles

---

I read the newspapers avidly.
It is my one form of continuous fiction.

Aneurin Bevan

Over the moon and sick as a parrot
Sporting idioms

Many idioms from the sporting world have entered the mainstream vocabulary. Some, such as 'early bath', 'on the ball' and 'keep one's eye on the ball', began as phrases common to a number of sports, while others, such as 'get to first base' and 'hit the bullseye', had their origins in individual sports.

Sport	Phrase	Meaning
baseball	ballpark figure [1]	an approximate figure
	get to first base	achieve the first of a series of aims
	off base	unprepared, mistaken
	whole new ball game	a change in events
boxing	out for the count	unconscious or in a deep sleep
	throw in the towel	admit defeat
darts	hit the bullseye	score a direct hit
cricket	catch someone out	outwit someone
	have a good innings	live a long life
	hit for six	strike forcefully
	it's not cricket	not fair play
fishing	hook, line and sinker	completely
football	a game of two halves	a change in fortune
	have the ball at one's feet	have an opportunity
	over the moon [2]	delighted
	sick as a parrot [3]	disappointed
	take each game as it comes	avoid planning ahead

Sport	Phrase	Meaning
ice hockey	sin bin [4]	place of isolation for offenders
pool	behind the eight ball [5]	in a difficult position
running	jump the gun	act over-hastily
tennis	the ball's in your court	it's up to you
wrestling	no holds barred	without restraint

1. originally referring to the estimates of crowd numbers attending baseball games

2. from the nursery rhyme line 'the cow jumped over the moon'

3. possibly a reference to the viral disease psittacosis (parrot fever)

4. originally the enclosure where players who commit fouls must sit for a stated time

5. describing the plight of a player who finds it impossible to strike one of the other balls directly because they are masked by the black ball, numbered eight

jump the gun

Yeah but no but – am I bothered?
Catchphrases

The entertainment industry has contributed numerous new words to the vocabulary, but it is perhaps in the catchphrase that the most impact has been made. Consider the following selection of the most famous catchphrases from films and radio and television shows:

Catchphrase	*Source*
a man's gotta do what a man's gotta do	John Wayne in the film *Stagecoach* (1939)
am I bothered?	Lauren in the TV series *The Catherine Tate Show* (2004)
and now for something completely different	the TV series *Monty Python's Flying Circus* (1969–74)
are you sitting comfortably?	the radio series *Listen with Mother* (1950–82)
bada bing [1]	the film *The Godfather* (1972)
can I do you now, sir?	Mrs Mopp in the radio series *ITMA* (1939–49)
doh!	Homer Simpson in the TV series *The Simpsons* (1987–present)
don't panic!	Corporal Jones in the TV series *Dad's Army* (1968–77)
eat my shorts	Bart Simpson in the TV series *The Simpsons* (1987–present)
elementary, my dear Watson [2]	Sherlock Holmes
evenin' all	Sergeant George Dixon in the TV series *Dixon of Dock Green* (1955–76)
exterminate, exterminate!	the Daleks in the TV series *Dr Who* (1963–present)

Catchphrase	Source
gissa job	Yosser Hughes in Alan Bleasdale's TV drama *Boys from the Black Stuff* (1982)
here's another nice mess you've gotten me into [3]	Oliver Hardy in the Laurel and Hardy films
here's Johnny	introduction to the TV series *The Johnny Carson Show* (1955–92)
here's looking at you, kid	Humphrey Bogart in the film *Casablanca* (1942)
hi-yo, Silver	the hero in the radio and TV series *The Lone Ranger* (1930s–60s)
I'm free	Mr Humphries in the TV series *Are You Being Served?* (1972–85)
it's a bird! it's a plane! it's Superman	the *Superman* comic strip (1938–present) and films (from 1978)
it's turned out nice again	George Formby in *Turned Out Nice Again* (1936) and other films
I've started, so I'll finish	*Mastermind* TV quiz show
I want to be alone	Greta Garbo in the film *Grand Hotel* (1932)
just like that	TV comedian and magician Tommy Cooper as he performed his tricks
may the Force be with you	*Star Wars* film series (1977–2005)
me Tarzan, you Jane [4]	Tarzan in the *Tarzan* films and TV series

1. further popularized 30 years later by the TV series *The Sopranos*

2. the catchphrase does not appear in precisely this form in the original Holmes stories, but comes instead from a 1929 film (*The Return of Sherlock Holmes*)

3. often misquoted as 'another fine mess', probably influenced by the release of a Laurel and Hardy film entitled *Another Fine Mess* in 1930

4. when the US swimmer Johnny Weissmuller was invited to play the role he is supposed to have replied with the words 'Me? Tarzan?'

Catchphrase	Source
my name's Bond, James Bond	James Bond in the *James Bond* film series (1962–present)
nice to see you, to see you, nice!	Bruce Forsyth in *The Generation Game* (1971–78) and other TV light entertainment shows
not a lot of people know that [5]	Michael Caine
nudge, nudge, wink, wink, say no more	*Monty Python's Flying Circus* TV series (1969–74)
phone home!	the alien in the film *E.T.* (1982)
shut that door!	Larry Grayson in various TV light entertainment shows of the 1970s and 1980s
suits you, sir!	Charlie Higson and Paul Whitehouse in *The Fast Show* TV series (1994)
the 64-thousand dollar question	*Double Your Money* radio and later TV quiz show (1950s–70s)
to infinity and beyond	Buzz Lightyear in the film *Toy Story* (1995)
very interesting, but stupid	*Rowan and Martin's Laugh-In* TV series (1968–71)
what's up, doc?	Bugs Bunny in the cartoon film series (from 1937)
who loves ya, baby	Telly Savalas in *Kojak* (1974–78)
yabbadabbadoo!	Fred Flintstone in *The Flintstones* cartoon series (1960–66)
yada yada yada	*Seinfeld* (from 1990)
yeah but no but yeah but	Vicky Pollard in the radio and TV series *Little Britain* (from 2000)

5. the line was not originally spoken by Caine but is said to have started life as an answering machine message recorded by comedian Peter Sellers imitating Caine with the words, 'My name is Michael Caine. Peter Sellers is not in at the moment. Not a lot of people know that'

Me, myself, I
Pseudonyms

One way to cope with success and the fame that comes with it is to disguise one's real identity behind a pseudonym. Alternatively, a pseudonym may be adopted where a person's real name is not thought to be appropriate in some way to their new status. Some people choose strong, straightforward names that suggest plain dealing, honest qualities, while others favour something much more flamboyant, implying a sense of creativity or fun. Consider the following selection of pseudonyms adopted by stars from a variety of professions:

Pseudonym	*Real name*
Alice Cooper (rock star)	Vincent Damon Furnier
Anthony Burgess (novelist)	John Wilson
Billie Holiday (singer)	Eleanora Fagan
Bob Dylan (singer-songwriter)	Robert Allen Zimmerman
Bono (rock musician)	Paul Hewson
Boris Karloff (film actor)	William Henry Pratt
Boz (novelist)	Charles Dickens
Brigitte Bardot (film actress)	Camille Javal
Burt Lancaster (film actor)	Stephen Burton
Cary Grant (film actor)	Archibald Leach
Charles Bronson [1] (film actor)	Charles Buchinsky
Cliff Richard (pop singer)	Harold Roger Webb
Currer, Ellis and Acton Bell (novelists)	Charlotte, Emily and Anne Brontë
Daniel Defoe (novelist)	Daniel Foe
Danny Kaye (actor, singer and dancer)	David Daniel Kaminski

1. a rare example of a pseudonym being used more than once, in this case by notorious British prison inmate Michael Peterson, who renamed himself Charles Bronson in homage to his favourite film star

Pseudonym	*Real name*
David Bowie (rock musician)	David Robert Hayward Stenton Jones
Dean Martin (singer and actor)	Dino Paul Crocetti
Doris Day (singer and actress)	Doris Mary Ann von Kapellhoff
Elton John (pop singer)	Reginald Kenneth Dwight
Eminem (rock musician)	Marshall Mathers
Enid Blyton (children's writer)	Mrs Daryl Walters
Fred Astaire (actor and dancer)	Frederick Austerlitz
Freddie Mercury (rock musician)	Farok Pluto Bulsara
George Eliot (novelist)	Mary Ann Evans
George Michael (pop singer)	Georgios Kyriacos Panayiotou
George Orwell (novelist)	Eric Arthur Blair
George Sand (novelist)	Amandine-Aurore Lucille Dupin
Ginger Rogers (actress and dancer)	Virginia Katherine McMath
Groucho Marx (actor and comedian)	Julius Henry Marx
Iggy Pop (rock musician)	James Newell Osterberg
Irving Berlin (composer)	Israel Isidore Baline
Isak Dinesen (novelist)	Baroness Karen Christentze Blixen
Jack London (novelist)	John Griffith
James Dean (film actor)	James Byron
James Herriot (novelist)	James Alfred Wight
Jennifer Aniston (television actress)	Jennifer Anastassakis
John Le Carré (novelist)	David Cornwell
John Wayne (film actor)	Marion Michael Morrison
Johnny Rotten (rock musician)	John Lydon
Judy Garland (singer and actress)	Frances Ethel Gumm
Katherine Mansfield (poet)	Katherine Beauchamp
Lauren Bacall (film actress)	Betty Joan Perske
Lenin (political leader)	Vladimir I. Ulyanov
Lewis Carroll (writer)	Charles Lutwidge Dodgson

Pseudonym	*Real name*
Marilyn Manson (rock musician)	Brian Warner
Marilyn Monroe (film actress)	Norma Jean Baker (or Mortenson)
Mark Twain (novelist)	Samuel Langhorn Clemens
Meat Loaf (rock musician)	Marvin Lee Aday
Michael Caine (film actor)	Maurice Micklewhite
Moby (rock musician)	Richard Hall
Molière (playwright)	Jean Baptiste Poquelin
Oscar Wilde (novelist)	Fingal O'Flahertie Wills
P.D. James (novelist)	Phyllis Dorothy James White
Pelé (footballer)	Edson Arantes do Nascimento
Ringo Starr (rock musician)	Richard Starkey
Roy Rogers (singer and actor)	Leonard Franklin Slye
Sid Vicious (rock musician)	John Simon Ritchie
Stan Laurel (film actor)	Arthur Stanley Jefferson
Stendhal (novelist)	Marie-Henri Beyle
Sting (rock musician)	Gordon Matthew Sumner
Tony Curtis (film actor)	Bernard Schwartz
Twiggy (model and actress)	Lesley Hornby
Vanilla Ice (rock musician)	Robert Van Winkle
Voltaire (writer)	François-Marie Arouet
Woody Allen (film actor and director)	Allen Stewart Konigsberg
Yul Brynner (film actor)	Taidje Kahn

No, Groucho is not my real name.

I'm breaking it in for a friend.

Groucho Marx

From Gazza to Bambi
Nicknames

Some nicknames are used generically of people with certain physical characteristics (thus, 'Ginger' for anyone with red hair, or 'Tubby' for anyone of large size). Other nicknames are traditional for people with given surnames (thus, 'Chalky' White, 'Nobby' Clark, 'Spider' Webb, 'Spud' Murphy). The following list comprises a random selection of well-known nicknames – and not just of people.

Nickname	Real name
Animated Meringue	Barbara Cartland
Attila the Hen	Margaret Thatcher
Auntie [1]	BBC
Bambi	Tony Blair
Big Apple	New York
Bloody Mary	Mary I
Blues	Chelsea football club
Bouncing Czech	Robert Maxwell
Butcher of Baghdad	Saddam Hussein
Capability Brown [2]	Lancelot Brown
Chemical Ali	General Ali Hassan al-Majid [3]
Comeback Kid	Bill Clinton
Cool Britannia	late 1990s UK
Dr Death	Dr Harold Shipman
Emerald Isle	Ireland
Gazza	Paul Gascoigne
Goldenballs	David Beckham/Sir James Goldsmith
The Greatest	Muhammad Ali
Gunners [4]	Arsenal football club
Hammers	West Ham United football club
Hanoi Jane	Jane Fonda
Iron Chancellor	Otto von Bismarck/Gordon Brown
Iron Duke	Duke of Wellington
Iron Lady	Margaret Thatcher

Nickname	Real name
Madge	Madonna
Magpies	Newcastle United football club
Merry Monarch	Charles II
Mr Dynamite	James Brown
Motown	Detroit
Old Hickory [5]	President Andrew Jackson
People's Princess	Diana, Princess of Wales
Posh [6]	Victoria Beckham
Red Devils	Manchester United football club
Red Planet	Mars
Smoke, The	London
Spurs	Tottenham Hotspur football club
The Thunderer	*The Times*
Tina [7]	Margaret Thatcher
Toffees	Everton football club
Two Jags [8]	John Prescott
Wacko	Michael Jackson

1. acquired in the 1950s

2. because he often said of landscapes that they had the 'capability' of being improved

3. the man who conducted chemical attacks under the Iraqi regime of Saddam Hussein

4. from the club's origins at Woolwich Arsenal in London

5. because he was 'tough as hickory'

6. the name she was given as one of the Spice Girls pop group

7. abbreviation for 'there is no alternative' (extract of a speech by Mrs Thatcher)

8. a reference to the fact that former British Labour deputy prime minister John Prescott, who wanted to reduce car ownership, himself used two Jaguar cars

---

A nickname is the heaviest stone the
Devil can throw at a man.

William Hazlitt

Tom, Dick and Harry
Popular first names

Certain names appear over and over again and seem never to go out of fashion. Others, however, come and go as the years pass and tastes change. Biblical names remain perennial favourites, especially for boys, but other choices vary under the influence of many factors, including names favoured by royalty and, nowadays, celebrities. It is interesting to note, for instance, that (for England and Wales) while the names John, William and Mary all featured consistently in the top three most popular first names for boys and girls in 1700, 1800 and 1900, none were in the top three most popular names in 2000. The following lists comprise the most popular names in various parts of the English-speaking world, as recorded for babies born in the year 2004:

Country	*Most popular boys' names*	*Most popular girls' names*
Australia	1 Jack	1 Emily
	2 Joshua	2 Chloe
	3 Lachlan	3 Olivia
	4 Thomas	4 Sophie
	5 William	5 Jessica
England and Wales	1 Jack	1 Emily
	2 Joshua	2 Ellie
	3 Thomas	3 Jessica
	4 James	4 Sophie
	5 Daniel	5 Chloe
Northern Ireland	1 Jack	1 Katie
	2 Matthew	2 Emma
	3 James	3 Ellie
	4 Adam	4 Sophie
	5 Daniel	5 Amy

Country	Most popular boys' names	Most popular girls' names
Scotland	1 Lewis	1 Emma
	2 Jack	2 Sophie
	3 James	3 Ellie
	4 Cameron	4 Amy
	5 Ryan	5 Chloe
USA		
	1 Jacob	1 Emily
	2 Michael	2 Emma
	3 Joshua	3 Madison
	4 Matthew	4 Olivia
	5 Ethan	5 Hannah

forename

A Boy named Sue
Unusual first names

Many new parents find that the stock of established first names does not provide them with sufficient opportunity to satisfy their creative impulses. New names are contributed to the central stock of names every year, and some of these become in time familiar favourites. There are risks, however, in such originality, as some names in the following list (all reported in surveys on the internet as having been registered around the English-speaking world in recent years) testify:

BOYS' NAMES

Abundie	Dearhart	Lucious
Ammo	Depressed	Macky
Beegie	Dweezil	Nimrod
Boo	Flipper	Oryan
Boof	Geronimo	Rawhide
Bossie	God	Rykeir
Busy	Goncalo	Siberio
Caraway	Ish	Split
Christmas	It	Tes
Dainis	Lawyer	Wattie
Dalis	Loser	Yippee

GIRLS' NAMES

Abcd	Bluebell	English
Aerophile	Bophary	Eternity
Affanita	Camy	Euthanasia
Antique	Cigarette	Fashion
Apple	Cynthanie	Female
Aquanetta	Deolanda	Fortina
Baby	Donisha	Heaven-Leigh
Barbie	Efghi	Jeehee

GIRLS' NAMES (*cont.*)

Jonola	Muffi-Jo	Somalia
Kaelyne	Nicey	Sosie
Katheron	Oceania	Spring
Kerripaula	Placenta	Sunday
Lasagna	Polly Esther	Syphillis
Latrina	Ralina	Tequila
Mahogany	Ramonda	Tuesday
Martini	Revolutionary	Ultraviolet
Maybe	Reyene	Vaselina
Merrian	Satin	Velveeta
Milynne	Shaunene	Vickigail
Mistymarie	Skylathornia	Wadine
Moon Unit	Snowy	Wednesday

'It's giving girls names like that,' said Buggins, 'that nine times out of ten makes 'em go wrong. It unsettles 'em. If ever I was to have a girl, if ever I was to have a dozen girls, I'd call 'em all Jane.'

H.G. Wells

The name game
Remarkable name combinations

When choosing names for children it is also important to consider how they will look in combination with the surname. Over the years many people have been blessed (or cursed) with eye-catching name combinations dreamt up by their parents, or (in the case of women) have similarly found themselves saddled with an unfortunate combination of names when changing their surname on getting married. All the following names are reported to have been registered somewhere in the English-speaking world in relatively recent times:

First name	*Surname*
Allison	Wunderland
Amber	Glass
April May	March
Blueberry	Hill
Campbell	Soup
Candy	Kane
Candy	Mountain
Christmas	Day
Chrystal	Ball
Clay	Potts
Dusty	Ball
Dwain	Pipe
Ella	Fant
Etta	Hamburger
Gene	Pool
Happy	Jack
Holly	Wood
Howdy	Neighbor
Ida	Down
Ivor	Million
Jack	Frost

First name	Surname
Justin	Case
Ko	Kaine
Margarita	Drinker
Mary-Chris	Smith
Misti	Glass
Olive	Green
Paige	Page
Penny	Lane
Pepperanne	Salt
Pepsi	Kohler
Polly	Filler
Precious	Stone
Rayne	Beau
Rick	O'Shea
Robin	Banks
Ruby	Diamond
Russell	Sprout
Rusty	Gunn
Safety	First
Sandy	Beaches
Sandi	Shaw
Satin	Sheets
Snow	White
Stormiee	Skye
Stormy	Gale
Strawberry	Fields
Sunni	Daye
Sunni Summer	Breeze
Sweet	Beauty
To	Morrow
Valen	Tine
Washington	Post
Woody	Forrest

Give a dog a bad name
Animal names

As if naming the children is not enough, there are also names to be found for family pets. If inspiration is lacking, consider the following selection of names bestowed upon animals of the great and good:

Name	Animal
Alley cat	Ernest Hemingway's cat
Apollinaris	Mark Twain's cat
Argos	Ulysses' dog
Arion	Hercules' horse
Bavieca	El Cid's horse
Beelzebub	Mark Twain's cat
Beppo	Lord Byron's cat
Bismarck	Florence Nightingale's cat
Black Bess	Dick Turpin's horse
Blackie	Chief Sitting Bull's horse
Boatswain	Lord Byron's dog
Bounce	Alexander Pope's dog
Boy	Prince Rupert's dog/Vivien Leigh's cat
Bucephalus	Alexander's horse
Bungey	Christopher Marlowe's dog
Cake	Warren Beatty's cat
Cavall	King Arthur's dog
Chopin	F. Scott Fitzgerald's cat
Cobby	Thomas Hardy's cat
Copenhagen	Wellington's horse
Dapple	Sancho Panza's donkey
Dash	Queen Victoria's dog
Diamond	Isaac Newton's dog

Name	*Animal*
Dinah	Alice in Wonderland's cat
Dolly	Tallulah Bankhead's cat
Eddie	Martin Crane's dog
Elvis	John Lennon's cat
Enzo	Jennifer Aniston's dog
Flush	Elizabeth Barrett Browning's dog
Foss	Edward Lear's cat
Gelert	Llewelyn's dog
General Butchkin	Iris Murdoch's cat
George Pushdragon	T.S. Eliot's cat
Gris Gris	General De Gaulle's cat
Hamlet	Sir Walter Scott's dog
Hippocampus	Neptune's horse
Hodge	Samuel Johnson's cat
Humphrey	10 Downing Street cat
Incitatus	Caligula's horse
Jeepers Creepers	Elizabeth Taylor's cat
Jock	Winston Churchill's cat
Kantaka	Buddha's horse
Keeper	Emily Brontë's dog
Lamri	King Arthur's horse
Lassie	Hollywood film star
Louisa	William Makepeace Thackeray's cat
Luath	Robert Burns' dog
Magnolia	George Washington's horse
Marcus	James Dean's cat
Marengo	Napoleon's horse
Margate	Winston Churchill's cat
Mitsou	Marilyn Monroe's cat

Name	Animal
Mr Famous	Audrey Hepburn's dog
Nana	the Darlings' dog in *Peter Pan*
Pegasus	Bellerophon's horse
Perruque	Cardinal Richelieu's cat
Punky	Doris Day's cat
Rosabelle	Mary, Queen of Scots' horse
Rosinante	Don Quixote's horse
Rufus	Winston Churchill's dog
Santa's Little Helper	the Simpson family's dog
Satellite	Jules Verne's dog
Shadowfax	Gandalf's horse
Silver	the Lone Ranger's horse
Sleipnir	Odin's horse
Sorrel	William III's horse
Strymon	Xerxes' horse
Susan	Elizabeth II's first corgi dog
Tiger	the Brontë family's cat
Toby	Punch's dog
Tom Kitten	the Kennedys' cat
Trigger	Roy Rogers' horse
Trump	Hogarth's dog
Vashka	Nicholas I's cat
Vic	General Custer's horse
Woof	Renée Zellweger's dog

5 Grumpy old men

The language of experience

As people get older they often develop firm opinions about language and vocabulary. They may stumble as much as the next person over niceties of grammar and pronunciation, but they also know what they do not like in the language of others, especially younger people. 'Bad' language, political correctness, split infinitives, slang, jargon – all provoke strong reactions.

The linguistic conservatism of older English speakers is a curious phenomenon. Beneath complaints about the lowering of linguistic standards and the social disintegration it implies may, indeed, lie a deep-seated fear of a familiar and comfortable world being replaced by something that is strange and even threatening.

Experience brings with it benefits, however. Although pressures on their time may limit opportunities, older people often have more money with which to indulge their leisure interests, for instance, and they may also travel the world on holiday and in the course of their business, thus coming into contact with regional variations of English that may surprise and perplex as well as entertain.

This chapter comprises an exploration of just some of the linguistic bugbears – and also delights – of the vocabulary that may divert the mind of the more experienced speaker of English.

Talking is often a torment for me and I need many days of silence to recover from the futility of words.

Carl Jung

U and non-U
Language and class

Class has always exerted a strong influence on the English vocabulary and even today, in what is allegedly a classless society, a person's choice of vocabulary may instantly (and possibly unwittingly) reveal their class status. Linguist Professor Alan Ross laid down the so-called 'U and non-U' ('U' standing for 'upper-class') guidelines in the 1950s and they were subsequently championed by such writers and society observers as British writer Nancy Mitford. Although some distinctions would appear to be redundant today, others still have their adherents. The list below comprises a selection of the more contentious 'U and non-U' usages that Ross identified in his study:

U	*Non-U*
bicycle	cycle
card	business/calling card
dinner	supper
dinner jacket	dress suit
have a bath	take a bath
house	home
jam	preserve
knave (cards)	jack
lavatory	toilet
looking-glass	mirror
lunch	dinner
mad	mental
pudding	sweet
rich	wealthy
riding	horse-riding
scent	perfume
ill	sick

U	Non-U
table-napkin	serviette
telegram	wire
vegetables	greens
what?	pardon?
wireless	radio
writing-paper	note-paper

As if plain words, useful and intelligible instructions,
were not as good for an esquire, or one that is in commission
from the King, as for him that holds the plough.

John Eachard

lavatory/toilet

Numpty sussuration
Favourite words

A poll conducted in association with The Word literary festival held in London in 2000 revealed the British nation's favourite word to be *serendipity* (an invention of the writer Horace Walpole in the 18th century, signifying the discovery of something through happy chance or accident). Runners-up included *quidditch, love, peace, why, onomatopoeia, hope, faith* and *football*. Favourite words that have appeared in similar lists elsewhere have included *melody, velvet, mellifluous, silken, mellow, dawn, dream, blossom, dusk, mist* and *laughter*. Other suggestions from the 2000 poll included the following:

Word	*Suggested by*
brownies	Richard Curtis (writer and producer)
comely	Mariella Frostrup (radio and television presenter)
compassion	Adrian Noble (theatre director)
darling	Barbara Windsor (actress)
eleemosynary [1]	Michael Palin (writer and actor)
energy	Jeffrey Archer (novelist and politician)
Everest	Brian Blessed (actor)
fish	Spike Milligan (comedian)
gnarled	Tony Robinson (writer and television presenter)
gonzo [2]	Ralph Steadman (cartoonist)
grace	Sir Trevor McDonald (television news presenter)
happiness	Ken Dodd (comedian)
harmony	Terry Waite (writer and broadcaster
holiday	Chris Tarrant (radio and television presenter)
laconic	Sting (rock musician)
little	Sue Townsend (writer)

Word	Suggested by
melancholy	Alain de Botton (writer)
nausea	Will Self (writer)
numpty	Andrew Neil (writer and broadcaster)
opsimath [3]	Magnus Magnusson (television presenter)
plinth	Stephen Fry (writer and actor)
prodigious	Louis de Bernières (writer)
sandwich	Willy Russell (playwright)
satisfactory	Patrick Moore (astronomer and broadcaster)
serenity	Ringo Starr (pop musician)
summer afternoon	Henry James (novelist)
susurration [4]	Terry Pratchett (novelist)
tomorrow	Tony Parsons (writer)
twelve	Carol Anne Duffy (poet)
you	Alan Ayckbourn (playwright)

1. meaning 'devoted to charitable purposes'

2. related to journalism in which the journalist is an integral part of the story being reported

3. meaning 'person who acquires education late in life'

4. meaning 'whispering' or 'rustling'

The two most beautiful words in the English language are 'check enclosed'.

Dorothy Parker

Cholmondeley of Beaulieu
Mispronunciations

Another particular source of irritation to the older user of English is any word that is mispronounced. Mispronunciation of foreign words is forgivable, but woe betide the person who blithely mispronounces a word from their own language – especially a personal name or place name. Some words, it should be said, may be accused of being deliberately deceitful in terms of their pronunciation, being pronounced in anything but the way one might expect from their spelling alone. The following list includes some of the most notorious examples:

Surname	*Pronunciation*
Beauchamp	beecham
Brome	broom
Cholmondeley	chumley
Cockburn	coburn
Colquhoun	carhoon
Dalziel	deeyell
Death	deeath
Farquhar	farkwa
Fiennes	fines
Featherstonehaugh	fanshaw
Ffoulkes	folks
Home	hume
Jekyll	jeekill
Keynes	kaynes
Mainwaring	mannering
Marjoribanks	marshbanks
Menzies	mingis
Pepys	peeps

Surname	Pronunciation
Powell	pole/powerl
Psmith	smith
Rhys	reece
Sandys	sands
St-Clair	sinclair
St-John	sinjun
Urquhart	erkut
Wemyss	weems
Wriothesley	roxlee

Place name	Pronunciation
Aldeburgh	orlbra
Althorp	olthrup
Auchinleck	aflek
Beaulieu	bewlee
Belvoir	beeva
Berkeley	barklee
Berkshire	barksha
Blyth	bly
Cherwell	charwell
Derby	darbee
Dereham	dareum
Dun Laoghaire	dun leeree
Eyke	ayeck
Frome	froom
Glamis	glarms
Gloucester	glosta
Horningsea	hornsee
Keighley	keethlee
Leicester	lesta
Leominster	lemsta

Place name	Pronunciation
Marlborough	maulbra
Norwich	norritch
Reading	redding
Ruthven	riven
Towcester	toasta
Walberswick	wobbleswick
Warwick	worrik
Worcester	wousta
Wymondham	windum

It is impossible for an Englishman to open his mouth without making some other Englishman despise him.

George Bernard Shaw

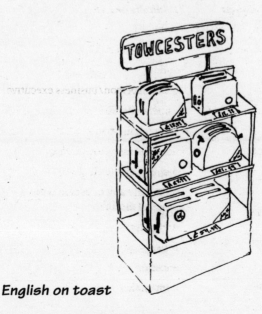

English on toast

Ugly or just aesthetically challenged?
Political correctness

Few things are guaranteed to provoke the older – and often the younger – speaker of English more than the notion of political correctness. The very idea that long-established and cherished linguistic formulations should suddenly be condemned, seemingly out of hand, as unsuitable for the modern ear will have many an English speaker frothing at the mouth. The battle between what is acceptable English in the modern world and what is not rages all around us, and the eventual fate of many of the terms listed below remains as yet undecided. Some politically-correct terms (like 'homemaker' or 'vertically challenged') seem set to retreat in the face of near-universal ridicule; others, however, would appear to have been (however reluctantly) accepted into the language by a majority of speakers. Consider the following:

Politically incorrect	Politically correct
actress	actor
Afro-American	African American
authoress	author
businessman	businessperson/business executive
cameraman	camera operator
chairman	chair/chairperson
cleaning lady	housecleaner/housekeeper
clergyman	member of the clergy
disabled	differently abled/person with physical disabilities
fireman	firefighter
fisherman	fisher
forefather	ancestor
housewife	homemaker

Politically incorrect	Politically correct
man	human/person
-man	-person/-operative
man in the street	average person/ordinary person
mankind	human beings/humankind/ humanity/men and women
man-made	artificial/synthetic
mentally handicapped	person with learning difficulties
negro[1]	black
poetess	poet
policeman	police officer
salesman	salesperson
short	vertically challenged
simple	mentally challenged
spokesman	spokesperson
stewardess	flight attendant
suffragette	suffragist
Third World	developing nations
ugly	aesthetically challenged
weatherman	weathercaster
workman	wage earner/worker

1. in the United States, 'African American' is used instead

Words, as is well known, are great foes of reality.

Joseph Conrad

To boldly go
Split infinitives

The split infinitive is probably the most contentious of all linguistic issues and the one over which any self-respecting English speaker of a certain age is most likely to have strong views.

The split infinitive (resulting from the insertion of an adverb or adverbial phrase between 'to' and the verb in a sentence) first became a focus of heated attention among linguists in the 19th century, on the grounds that as the infinitive form in Latin could not be split (consisting as it did of just one word) it was incorrect to do the same in English, even though the infinitive was now two words. On these shaky grounds writers and linguists divided into two camps and have ever since engaged in bitter debate over the issue. Today the prevailing opinion is that split infinitives are best avoided but are permissible where the alternative would be less elegant or might risk ambiguity.

Many writers managed to avoid the split infinitive throughout their written work, among them such luminaries as John Dryden, Alexander Pope, the compilers of the King James Bible and Kingsley Amis. Many others, however, have showed little compunction in splitting infinitives at whim.

Infinitive splitters [1]	*Example*
LAYAMON (*Brut*, early 13th century)	… for to countries seek.
WILLIAM SHAKESPEARE (Sonnet 142)	… thy pity may deserve to pitied be.
THOMAS MACAULAY (early 19th century)	… in order to fully appreciate …
LORD BYRON (early 19th century)	… to slowly trace the forest's shady scene.
MARIE CORELLI (late 19th century)	… to mentally acknowledge, albeit with wrath and shame, my own inferiority.

Infinitive splitters	*Example*
NEW YORK TIMES (20th century)	… failed to correctly diagnose …
THE TIMES (20th century)	… the time has come to once again voice the general discontent.
STAR TREK TV series (1960s)	… to boldly go where no man has gone before.
STATUS QUO the ('Break the rules', 1970s)	… everybody has to sometimes break rules.
BRITISH GOVERNMENT'S GOOD FRIDAY AGREEMENT (1998)	… the right to freely choose one's place of residence …

1. notable users of the split infinitive in literature have included the writers W.H. Auden, Jane Austen, Lewis Carroll, Willa Cather, Raymond Chandler, Geoffrey Chaucer (twice), Daniel Defoe, Charles Dickens, John Donne, Maria Edgeworth, George Eliot, Henry Fielding, F. Scott Fitzgerald, Ford Madox Ford, Benjamin Franklin, Mrs Gaskell, Oliver Goldsmith, Thomas Hardy, Henry James, Samuel Johnson, Rudyard Kipling, C.S. Lewis, Abraham Lincoln, Iris Murdoch, George Orwell, Samuel Pepys, John Ruskin, Sir Walter Scott, George Bernard Shaw, Percy Bysshe Shelley, Robert Louis Stevenson, Jonathan Swift, William Makepeace Thackeray, Anthony Trollope, H.G. Wells, Edith Wharton, Walt Whitman, Oscar Wilde, William Wordsworth

---

If you do not immediately suppress the person who takes it upon himself to lay down the law almost every day in your columns on the subject of literary composition, I will give up the *Chronicle*. The man is a pedant, an ignoramus, an idiot and a self-advertising duffer … Your fatuous specialist … is now beginning to rebuke 'second-rate' newspapers for using such phrases as 'to suddenly go' and 'to boldly say'. I ask you, Sir, to put this man out … set him adrift and try an intelligent Newfoundland dog in his place.

George Bernard Shaw

Doing the splits
Hyphenations

When hyphenating words, it is important to ensure that the letters on either side of the break will not mislead the reader, especially if resulting parts of the original word form a different word in their own right. In British English the convention is to split words between syllables. In US English (and increasingly in British English) the tendency is to be guided by pronunciation of the word. The following list comprises a few of the more notorious examples of what can result from careless word-splitting:

Incorrect break	*Correct break*
anal-ysis	ana-lysis
de-crease	*avoid breaking*
dog-ma	*avoid breaking*
ex-tractor	*avoid breaking*
fat-her	*avoid breaking*
homes-pun	home-spun
leg-end	le-gend
mace-rate	macer-ate
male-volence	mal-evolence
mans-laughter	man-slaughter
not-able	*avoid breaking*
rear-range	re-arrange
re-creation	recre-ation
the-rapist	therap-ist
un-ionized	union-ized

In two words: im-possible.

Sam Goldwyn (attributed)

Gaggle or skulk?
Collective nouns

What better way for a seasoned user of the English language to demonstrate his or her mastery of vocabulary than by knowing exactly the right collective noun for a particular group of animals? The stuff of pub quizzes and crosswords (cherished pastimes of those of a certain age), collective nouns are an endless source of argument and fascination, and there is considerable satisfaction in being able to identify the right word when virtually nobody else can. Pedantic maybe, but satisfying nonetheless. Learn the following and prepare to impress:

Animal	*Collective noun*
apes	shrewdness
asses	herd/pace
badgers	cete [1]
barracudas	battery
bears	sloth
beavers	colony
bees	swarm
bitterns	sedge/siege
boars	singular
camels	caravan
cats	clowder
cattle	drove
chickens	peep
choughs	chattering
coots	covert
cormorants	flight
cranes	herd/sedge/siege
crows	murder
curlews	herd
deer	herd
doves	dole

Animal	Collective noun
ducks	paddling [2]/team
eagles	convocation
elks	gang
ferrets	business
fish	shoal
foxes	skulk
geese	gaggle
goats	herd/tribe
goldfinches	charm
grasshoppers	cloud
grouse	covey/pack
guillemots	bazaar
hares	down/husk
hawks	cast
hedgehogs	array
hens	brood
heron	siege
herrings	glean/shoal
hounds	mute/pack
kangaroos	troop [3]
kittens	kindle
lapwing	deceit
larks	exaltation
leopards	leap
lions	pride
locusts	plague
magpies	tittering
mallards	flush
moles	mumble
monkeys	troop/wilderness
mules	barren

1. possibly derived from the Latin *coetus*, meaning 'assembly'

2. relating to ducks on water

3. 'court' is a humorous modern alternative

Animal	Collective noun
nightingales	watch
onions	rope
oxen	drove/herd/team/yoke
owls	parliament [4]
partridges	covey
peacocks	muster
pigs	litter
pheasants	nye [5]
plovers	congregation
polecats	chine
porpoises	school
ptarmigan	covey
quails	bevy
rabbits	nest
ravens	unkindness
rhinoceroses	crash
rooks	building/clamour
seals	herd/pod
sheep	flock
sheldrake	doping
snipe	walk
sparrows	host
squirrels	dray
starlings	murmuration
swans	bevy/herd
swine	drift/sounder
teals	spring
thrushes	mutation
toads	knot
whales	gam/pod/school
wolves	herd/pack/rout
woodcock	fall
woodpeckers	descent

4. best known from *Geoffrey Chaucer's* poem *The Parlement of Foules*

5. from the Latin *nidus*, meaning 'nest'

From aerophilatelist to vexillologist
Hobbyists and collectors

With middle age comes (for some) the opportunity to devote a little time to leisure interests of various kinds. The range of activities in which they may indulge is breathtakingly varied – but, of course, the English language has a name for them all …

Hobbyist	*Interest*
aerophilatelist	airmail stamps
ailurophile	cats
antiquary	antiquities
arachnologist	spiders
arctophile	teddy bears
argyrothecologist	money boxes
audiophile	sound reproduction, recordings and broadcasts
balletomane	ballet
bibliomane	collecting books
bibliopegist	bookbinding
bibliophile	books
cagophilist	keys
campanologist	bell-ringing
canophilist/cynophilist	dogs
cartophilist	cigarette and chewing-gum cards
coleopterist	beetles
conchologist	shells
copoclephilist	key-rings
cruciverbamorist	crossword puzzles
cumyxaphilist	matchboxes
deltiologist	picture postcards
ecclesiologist	churches
egger	birds' eggs

Hobbyist	*Interest*
entomologist	insects
ephemerist	diary or journal keeping
epicure	good food and drink
errinophilist	stamps (other than postage stamps)
ex-librist	bookplates
fusilatelist	phonecards
gastronome	good eating
gemmologist	gems
gourmet [1]	good food and drink
herpetologist	reptiles
hippophile	horses
hostelaphilist	pub signs
iconophilist	engravings, prints, pictures, etc.
incunabulist	early printed books
labeorphilist	beer bottle labels
lepidopterist	butterflies and moths
medallist	medals
monarchist	monarchy
myrmecologist	ants
notaphilist	banknotes
numismatist	coins and medals
oenophile	wine
omnibologist	buses
ophiophilist	snakes
orchidophilist	orchids
ornithologist	birds
paroemographer	proverbs
peridromophilist	transport tickets
philatelist	postage stamps
phillumenist	matchbox labels
philologist	learning and literature

1. not to be confused with *gourmand*, a person who is interested only in the quantity of food they eat, not its quality

Hobbyist	*Interest*
philometrist	envelopes with postmarks
phonophilist	gramophone records
plangonologist	dolls
pteridophilist	ferns
sericulturist	silkworms
speleologist	caves
steganographist	cryptography
stegophilist	climbing buildings
tegestologist	beer-mats
ufologist	UFOs
vexillologist	flags

entomologist

Buckle my shoe and bang on the drum
Bingo calls

Among the many leisure activities that appeal to people that of bingo has perhaps the richest linguistic heritage. The game itself is simple enough, but the language associated with the game can be bewildering to the uninitiated. The following list includes the more familiar bingo calls that traditionally accompany each number as it is announced, as well as some of the more obscure ones, with brief explanations of their origins.

The name 'bingo' itself, incidentally, is thought to have come about in imitation of the bell that used to be rung when a winner was announced.

	Call	*Explanation*
1	buttered bun	rhyming slang
	Kelly's eye	unknown [1]
2	baby's done it	after 'number two's'
	buckle my shoe	rhyming slang
	dirty old Jew	rhyming slang
	me and you	rhyming slang
3	up a tree	rhyming slang
	you and me	rhyming slang
4	being poor	rhyming slang for 'whore'
	door-to-door	rhyming slang
	knock at the door	rhyming slang
	Pompey whore	rhyming slang
5	man alive	rhyming slang
6	chopsticks	rhyming slang
	clickety-click	rhyming slang
	Joynson-Hicks [2]	rhyming slang
7	crutch	the shape

	Call	Explanation
7 (*cont.*)	God's in heaven	rhyming slang
8	Connaught Rangers	formerly the 88th Regiment
	garden gate	rhyming slang
	Harry Tate [3]	rhyming slang
	one fat lady	the shape
9	doctor	the number 9 pill prescribed by military doctors
	doctor's orders	doctor's instruction to say 'nine'
10	cock and hen	rhyming slang
	Downing Street	the address of the prime minister
	shiny ten	the 10th Royal Hussars, nicknamed the 'Shiny Tenth'
	Uncle Ben	rhyming slang
11	legs eleven	the shape
	snake eyes	the shape
12	monkey's cousin	rhyming slang for 'dozen'
13	unlucky for some	the superstitions surrounding the number
15	rugby team	the number of players
16	boy's favourite	the age of consent
17	never been kissed	the innocence of a 17-year-old girl
20	blind twenty	'0' representing a 'round' or 'blind' number
	horn of plenty	rhyming slang
21	key of the door	the age at which one is said to be entitled to a front door key
22	all the twos	twice two
	couple of ducks	the shape

1. possibly derived from a lost (maybe military) anecdote

2. British Conservative politician William Joynson-Hicks (1865–1932)

3. British music-hall comedian, famous in the 1930s

	Call	*Explanation*
22 (*cont.*)	dinky-doo	rhyming slang
	two little ducks	the shape
23	thee and me	rhyming slang
24	dad at the door	rhyming slang
26	bed and breakfast	2s 6d (the former cost of such lodging)
	chopsticks	rhyming slang
	half-a-crown	2 s 6d
30	blind thirty	'0' representing a 'round' or 'blind' number
	Burlington Bertie [4]	rhyming slang
	Dirty Gertie	rhyming slang
	speed limit	the urban speed limit
	all the threes	twice three
	Gerty Lee [5]	rhyming slang
34	dirty whore	rhyming slang
37	more than eleven	rhyming slang
39	all the steps	after the thriller *The 39 Steps*
40	blind forty	'0' representing a 'round' or 'blind' number
44	Aldershot ladies	punning rhyming slang on 'two whores'
	all the fours	twice four
	Diana Dors [6]	rhyming slang
	mouth is sore	rhyming slang
	open the door	rhyming slang
50	blind fifty	'0' representing a 'round' or 'blind' number
	half-way house	half the maximum number
51	tweak of the thumb	rhyming slang
52	Danny La Rue [7]	rhyming slang
55	all the fives	twice five
57	all the beans/Heinz	after Heinz 57 Varieties baked beans
	Brighton line	rhyming slang

	Call	*Explanation*
60	blind sixty	'0' representing a 'round' or 'blind' number
64	red raw	rhyming slang
65	old-age pension	the age of male retirement
	stop work	the age of male retirement
66	all the sixes	twice six
	clickety-click	rhyming slang
70	blind seventy	'0' representing a 'round' or 'blind' number
71	bang on the drum	rhyming slang
76	trombones	the song '76 trombones'
	was she worth it?	7s 6d [8]
77	all the crutches	the shape
	all the sevens	twice seven
	two little crutches	the shape
78	house in a state	rhyming slang
79	one more time	rhyming slang
80	blind eighty	'0' representing a 'round' or 'blind' number
81	stop and run	rhyming slang
82	hole in my shoe	rhyming slang
86	between the sticks	rhyming slang
88	all the eights	twice eight
	two fat ladies [9]	the shape
99	top of the shop	the maximum number

4. music-hall song character of the early twentieth century; the betting odds slang for 100/30 is also 'Burlington Bertie'

5. Victorian actress

6. British film actress, famous in the 1950s

7. British entertainer, born in 1917

8. formerly the price of a marriage licence

9. this is one of several bingo calls whose continued existence has been threatened in recent years on the grounds of political correctness

Wordplay
Word games

Word games of various kinds continue to provide new ways of appre-
ciating and enjoying the extraordinary richness of the English vocabulary and consequently appeal to a broad spectrum of English
speakers. The following list briefly details the rules of just a few:

acrostics
players are challenged to write sentences (often in the form of a short
poem) in which the first letter of each line can be read vertically to
spell out a particular word or name given to them at the start. A variation is the double acrostic, in which both the first letters and the last
letters make up a word when read vertically

anagrams
players rearrange the letters in a given word or phrase to make up other
words or phrases

clue words
one player selects a seven-letter word and challenges the others to
identify it from just three of the letters, given in order. If no one is
successful with their first guess the challenger gives a fourth letter, then
a fifth, and so on until the secret word is identified

doublets
players are given a word and challenged to transform it one letter at a
time into another word of the same length. The real challenge lies in
the fact that with each change of letter a valid word must be produced

ghosts
players take turns at building a word by adding to it one letter at a time,
making sure if possible that they avoid giving the final letter that com-
pletes a word. A player may be challenged to identify the word they had
in mind when adding their letter: if they had no word in mind, they lose

Guggenheim

players are given a word of five or six letters, which they write across the page. They are then given five categories (animals, colours, etc), which they write down the page. The challenge is to think of a word beginning with each of the letters written across the page relevant to each of the five categories, often within a given time limit

hangman

one player thinks of a word and then tells the other player how many letters it has, writing a dash on the page for each letter. The other player is then challenged to guess what the word is by choosing a letter at a time: if the letter occurs in the secret word it is written down over the appropriate dash. If it does not, then the challenger draws the base for a gibbet. The process continues, with letters being filled in or else (in order) the shaft, the crossbeam, the angled crossbeam, the rope, the head of the hanged man, the body, one leg, the other leg, one arm and the other arm (11 stages in all) being drawn. If the hanged man is completed before the word is guessed then the person who set the challenge is the winner

heads and tails

a player chooses a word from a particular category, following which the second player has to think of another word from the same category beginning with the letter with which the first word ended. The game continues until one of the players fails to think of a word that satisfies the rules

I love my love

each player has to think of a word beginning with the letter A, filling in the gaps in the sentence: 'I love my love with an A because she is a—. I hate her with an A because she is a—. Her name is A— and she comes from A—.' The game continues with the letter B and so on through the alphabet

last word

players are given a nine-letter word which they write in three lines of three letters. They then have to identify as many words of three or more letters as they can from adjoining letters by moving across, up, down or diagonally around the grid. The player who thinks of the most words wins

matching letters

two players each write down a six-letter word, which they keep hidden from each other. Each player has to guess the other's word by suggesting in turn a six-letter word of their own. Any letter that appears in exactly the same place in the hidden word is identified. Play continues until one of the players identifies the other's word

pangrams

players construct meaningful sentences that include all the letters in the alphabet

parson's cat

players take turns to describe the parson's cat, initially thinking of an adjective beginning with the letter 'a' and then progressing through the alphabet, following the formula 'The parson's cat is an a— cat'

pyramids

the first player writes down a letter of the alphabet. The second player repeats this letter on the line below and adds to it another letter, ensuring that the two letters together form a valid word. The first player then repeats the two existing letters on a new line below and adds a third letter, again ensuring the letters make a valid word. Play continues until no more new words can be formed: the player with the longest word wins

word squares

players write the same word both across and down the page then try to fill in the resulting square with words that all read the same across as down

Bren guns and Brussels sprouts
Toponyms

With increased disposable income and leisure time comes the oppor-tunity to travel, and travel not only broadens the mind – it broadens the vocabulary as well. It is of course a two-way process and many foreign languages today bear the impression of contact with English speakers. The French, above all, struggle to protect their vocabulary from Anglo-phone intruders such as 'le camping', 'le sandwich' and 'le weekend', with varying degrees of success. But English too has absorbed many foreign words and phrases – and this applies also to place names with which English speakers have become familiar through personal visits or through other cultural contact or business travel. The following list consists of a selection of place names that have contributed words to the English vocabulary:

Place	*Word*	*Origin*
Alsace	Alsatian	breed of dog bred in Alsace, France (formerly Germany)
Attica	attic	the ancient Greek style of pilaster added to big houses in the 18th century
Balaclava	balaclava	the woollen hoods worn by soldiers in the Crimean War battle fought near the village of Balaclava (1854)
Bayonne	bayonet	invented in Bayonne, France
Bengal	bungalow	the single-storey houses of Bengal, from the Hindi *bangla* ('house')
Bikini	bikini	the devastating impact of the atom-bomb tests between 1946 and 1958 on Bikini atoll in the Pacific
Bohemia	bohemian	the notion that the gypsies, with their un-conventional lifestyles, came originally

Place	Word	from Bohemia (modern Czech Republic) Origin
Bourbon County	bourbon	where bourbon was first made in the USA, named after the Bourbon royal family
Brno (and Enfield)	Bren gun	where the gun was first made (Brno, in the Czech Republic) and where production later continued (Enfield, in England)
Brussels	Brussels sprout	where sprouts were originally grown in large numbers
Calicut (Kozhikode)	calico	the town in India where such cloth was originally made
Cambrai	cambric	the town in northern France where the textile was made
Canary	canary bird	the islands where the birds flourish
Champagne	champagne	the champagne-growing region of France
Charleston	Charleston dance	the US city where the dance craze began
China	china	the manufacture of such wares in China
Congo	conga dance	its roots in African dance and music tradition
Corinth	currant	the grape-growing region of Corinth
Cyprus	copper	the early production of copper (called Cyprian metal by the Romans) in Cyprus
Damascus	damask	where the fabric was originally made
Demerara	demerara sugar	the region of Guyana noted for its sugar production
Duffel	duffle-coat	the Belgian town noted for its heavy woollen cloth
Dum-Dum	dumdum bullet	the town near Calcutta where such bullets were first made
Dungri	dungaree	the district of Mumbai (Bombay) where the cloth used for dungarees was first

made

Place	Word	Origin
Egypt	gypsy	the belief (in the 16th century) that gypsies originated in Egypt
Fez	fez	the city in Morocco where such hats were made
Florence	florin	Old Italian *fiorino* (a Florentine coin named after *fiore*, meaning 'flower')
Gaza	gauze	the place where such material was (supposedly) first made
Genoa	jeans	the Italian city where the fabric was made
Guinea	guinea	the manufacture of the first such coins with gold from Guinea
Hamburg	hamburger	the city where such food was invented
Jerez	sherry	the region of Spain where such fortified wine is produced
Jersey	jersey	the woollen sweaters worn by fishermen of Jersey in the Channel Islands
Jodhpur	jodhpurs	the town in Rajasthan, India, where men wore this style of clothing
Kaolin	kaolin china clay	the Chinese mountain that was the source of the clay
Kashmir	cashmere	the soft, fine wool from goats of the Kashmir region
Labrador	Labrador retriever	the area of Canada particularly associated with such dogs
Lesbos	lesbian	the love poetry of Sappho, who lived on the Greek island of Lesbos
Limerick	limerick	the refrain 'will you come up to Limerick?' sung between verses in nonsense songs

Place	*Word*	*Origin*
Macassar	antimacassar	Macassar oil was a hair preparation made with ingredients said to have come from Macassar, now Ujung Padang, Indonesia
Mahon	mayonnaise	the port in Minorca where it was first shipped from
Majorca	majolica	the island from which such pottery was first exported to Italy
Marathon	marathon	the place from which a Greek messenger ran more than 20 miles back to Athens with news of victory at the Battle of Marathon in 490 BC
Mazowia	mazurka	province of Poland where the mazurka was first danced
Milan	millinery	residents of Milan (Milaners) were noted for their production of fancy goods from the 16th century
Morocco	morocco leather	the country where this fine leather was first made in the 17th century
Mosul	muslin	the city in Iraq where such fabric was first made
Nîmes	denim	originally *serge de Nîmes*, Nîmes being the place where such twill-weave cotton fabric was first made
Oporto	port	the area in Portugal where port was first made
Palatine Hill	palace	the hill in Rome where the Roman emperors had their palaces
Panama	panama hat	the country where such hats were commonly made from the leaves of the jipijapa plant
Phrygia	frieze	the ancient region in the Anatolian

Highlands (in modern Turkey) noted for embroidery in gold

Place	Word	Origin
St Joachimstal	dollar	the original *Joachimsthaler* coin was made from metal mined in the Czech town of Joachimsthal Jachymov
Satsuma	satsuma orange	the province of Japan where such trees were originally grown
Siam	Siamese twin	the birth country (now Thailand) of the celebrated pair of conjoined twins Chai and Leng (1814–71)
Sweden	suede	from the French *gants de Suède*, gloves made in Sweden
Tangier	tangerine	the place from which such fruits came
Taranto	tarantula	the town in Italy particularly associated with a large hairy, venomous spider of southern Europe
Turkey	turquoise	from the Old French *turquoise*, meaning Turkish (stone), and a reference to the place where such green-blue rocks were mined
Tuxedo Park Country Club, New York	tux(edo)	country club in New York where diners wore such dinner suits
Ulster	ulster coat	the province where such coats were first made

The world is but a word.

William Shakespeare

From Accident to Zzyzx
Unusual place names

Hundreds of places throughout the English-speaking world boast unusual and often downright bizarre or unprintable names. Not that this phenomenon is restricted to English-language place names, of course: consider Cara Sucia ('dirty face') in El Salvador, or Strangolagalli ('strangle the roosters') in Italy. And then there are all those places in foreign countries that may well be unaware of how silly their name appears to English speakers – for instance, the French towns of Condom, Messy and Die, the Dutch towns of Hell and Monster, the Albanian town of Crap, the German town of Kissing, the Swiss town of Bad Egg, the Austrian town of Fucking and, last but not least, the Belgian town of Silly itself.

Place name	Location
Accident [1]	Maryland, USA
Bachelor's Bump	East Sussex, England
Bald Knob	Arkansas, USA
Bastard Township	Ontario, Canada
Blubberhouses [2]	Yorkshire, England
Boring [3]	Oregon, USA
Bottom	North Carolina, USA
Burrumbuttock	New South Wales, Australia
Chunky	Mississippi, USA
Cold Christmas	Hertfordshire, England
Cool	California, USA
Difficult	Tennessee, USA
Dildo [4]	Newfoundland, Canada
Ding Dong	Texas, USA
Dirt Pot	Northumberland, England
Dismal	Tennessee, USA
Eek	Alaska, USA
Eyebrow	Saskatchewan, Canada

Place name	*Location*
Foggy Bottom	Washington, USA
Frenchman's Butte	Saskatchewan, Canada
Gin Bottle	Arkansas, USA
Goosepimple Junction	Virginia, USA
Happy	Texas, USA
Head-Smashed-In Buffalo Jump [5]	Alberta, Canada
Helions Bumpstead	Essex, England
Hell Corner	Berkshire, England
Hell for Certain	Kentucky, USA
Hot Coffee	Mississippi, USA
Humptulips	Washington, USA
Indented Head	Victoria, Australia
Intercourse	Alabama/Pennsylvania, USA
Knickerbocker	Texas, USA
Knockemstiff	Ohio, USA
Learned	Mississippi, USA
Lick Skillet	Texas, USA
Little Snoring	Norfolk, England
Long Bottom	Ohio, USA
Looneyville	West Virginia, USA
Love	Illinois, USA
Lovely	Kentucky, USA
Lower Dicker	East Sussex, England
Matching Tye	Essex, England
Middle Wallop	Hampshire, England

1. so named after two surveyors hired to select the best plot for a new town coincidentally selected exactly the same spot, using the same tree as a starting point

2. possibly a reference to blueberries, the Blue Boar inn or a bubbling stream

3. named after an early resident W.H. Boring

4. possibly named after the round pegs of the name used in that region in the construction of traditional rowing boats

5. a reference to the buffalo hunts carried on in the area by native Americans

Place name	*Location*
Money	Mississippi, USA
Monkey's Eyebrow [6]	Kentucky, USA
Mousehole	Cornwall, England
Muck	Scotland
Nasty	Hertfordshire, England
Netherthong	Yorkshire, England
Nether Wallop	Hampshire, England
Noodle	Texas, USA
Normal	Illinois, USA
Nowhere	Arizona, USA
Odd	West Virginia, USA
Over Wallop	Hampshire, England
Oz	Kentucky, USA
Pity Me [7]	County Durham, England
Point Blank	Texas, USA
Popcorn	Indiana, USA
Pratt's Bottom	London, England
Punkeydoodles Corner	Ontario, Canada
Quaking Houses [8]	County Durham, England
Ramsbottom	Greater Manchester, England
Rest and be thankful	Argyll and Bute, Scotland
Satan's Kingdom	Vermont, USA
Six Mile Bottom	Cambridgeshire, England
Smiley	Saskatchewan, Canada
Splatt	Devon, England
Thong	Kent, England
Tiddleywink	Wiltshire, England
Tightsqueeze [9]	Virginia, USA
Tightwad [10]	Missouri, USA
Toad Suck Park	Arkansas, USA
Toast	North Carolina, USA
Truth or Consequences [11]	New Mexico, USA
Uncertain	Texas, USA
Upper Dicker	East Sussex, England

Place name	Location
Useless Loop	Western Australia
Wankers Corner	Oregon, USA
Waterproof [12]	Louisiana, USA
Wendy-cum-Jolly	Hertfordshire, England
Westward Ho! [13]	Devon, England
Wham	North Yorkshire, England
Whorehouse Meadows	Oregon, USA
Why	Arizona, USA
Whynot	Mississippi, USA
Wide Open	Tyne and Wear, England
Womenswold	Kent, England
World's End	Berkshire, England
Wyre Piddle	Worcestershire, England
Zap	North Dakota, USA
Zzyzx [14]	California, USA

6. inspired by its position within Ballard County, which resembles a monkey's head in shape

7. a humorous name for a barren piece of land

8. named after the original Quaker inhabitants

9. a reference to the narrowness of the road between the buildings

10. inspired by a local storekeeper who deliberately overcharged a customer by 50 cents

11. named after a popular US radio quiz programme

12. a reference to the fact that the site offered dry land for early wagon trains amid surrounding waters

13. named after an 1855 novel by Charles Kingsley

14. a name chosen in 1944 to make the last word in a dictionary

---

Some word with hidden meaning – like 'Basingstoke'

W.S. Gilbert

A French widow in every room
English for tourists

One of the delights of travel abroad is the chance to see what non-English speakers can do with (or, rather, to) the vocabulary. These are but a few of the gems from notices in hotels and restaurants around the world reported by gleeful English-speaking tourists on their return home:

Country	Notice
Austria	In case of fire, do your utmost to alarm the hotel porter.
	Not to perambulate the corridors in the hours of repose in the boots of ascension.
China	Come Broil Yourself at Your own Table.
	Invisible service is available for your rest not being disturbed.
	Mr Zheng and his fellowworkers like to meet you and entertain you with their hostility and unique cooking techniques.
	Special cocktails for women with nuts.
Czechoslovakia	Take one of our horse-driven city tours – we guarantee no miscarriages.
Denmark	We take your bags and send them in all directions.
Finland	To stop the drip, turn cock to right.
France	A sports jacket may be worn to dinner, but no trouser.
	Please leave your values at the front desk.
	Swimming is forbidden in absence of the Saviour.

Country	Notice
Germany	After the main course we suggest that you sample the tart of the house.
	It is strictly forbidden on our Black Forest camping site that people of different sex, for instance, men and women, live together in one tent unless they are married with each other for that purpose.
Greece	Spleen omelet, fisherman's crap soup, calf pluck, bowels.
	Visitors are expected to complain at the office between the hours of 9 and 11 am daily.
Italy	Fire! It is what can doing, we hope. No fear. Not ourselves. Say quickly to all people coming up down everywhere a prayer. Always is a clerk. He is assured of safety by expert men who are in the bar for telephone for the fighters of the fire to come out.
	Standing among savage scenery, the hotel offers stupendous revelations. There is a French widow in every room. We can offer you a commodious chamber, with balcony imminent to a romantic gorge. We hope you want to drop in. In the close village you can buy jolly memorials for when you pass away.
	Syrene Bellevue Hotel joins a modern functional equipment with a distinguished and smart style of the 18th century. It is located on the seas, far off the centre a few minutes afoot and owing to a number of gardens and sunny terraces, guarantee is given for an ideal stay in stillness and absolute rest. The restaurant salon with a large view of the Gulf of Naples, a restaurant service with a big choice, the private beach to be reached by a lift from inside directly, complete the undiscussable peculiarities of this unit.
	This hotel is renowned for its piece and solitude. In fact, crowds from all over the world flock here to enjoy its solitude.

Country	*Notice*
Japan	Is forbitten to steal hotel towels please. If you are not person to do such thing is please not to read notis.
	Please to bathe inside the tub.
	You are invited to take advantage of the chambermaid.
Mexico	Members and Non-Members Only.
	The manager has personally passed all the water served here.
Norway	Ladies are requested not to have children in the bar.
Poland	As for the tripes serves you at the Hotel Monopol, you will be singing its praise to your children as you lie on your deathbed.
	Salad a firm's own make; limpid red beet soup with cheesy dumplings in the form of a finger; roasted duck let loose; beef rashers beaten up in the country people's fashion.
Romania	The lift is being fixed for the next day. During that time we regret that you will be unbearable.
Russia	If this is your first visit to the USSR, you are welcome to it.
	You are welcome to visit the cemetery where famous Russian and Soviet composers, artists, and writers are buried daily except Thursday.
Spain	English well talking.
	Here speeching American.
	Peoples will left the room at midday of tomorrow in place of not which will be more money for hole day.

Country	Notice
Switzerland	Because of the impropriety of entertaining guests of the opposite sex in the bedroom, it is suggested that the lobby be used for this purpose.

Our wines leave you nothing to hope for.

Venezuela   In this Expedition you will know the highest water fall in the world. From Canaima, through the Sabana, the Jungles and the rivers Carrao and Churun, you'll enjoy one of the biggest emotions of this life. And the facilities Camp. Guides as natives, all experts, will bring you trough troubles waters, just where a few have made it. Be you one of them. Meals in open fire never taste so goo.

Yugoslavia   Guests should announce abandonment of their rooms before 12 o'clock, emptying the room at the latest until 14 o'clock for the use of the room before 5 at the arrival after the 16 o'clock at the departure will be billed as one more night.

The flattening of underwear with pleasure is the job of the chambermaid.

I don't hold with abroad and think that foreigners
speak English when our backs are turned.

Quentin Crisp

Criss budgie-smugglers, doudou!
World Englishes

Although English may be the dominant language in most popular holiday destinations around the world, this does not mean that even the seasoned traveller will be familiar with every word used there. Some coinages are unique to certain parts of the English-speaking world, and only time will tell if they will gain wider currency as part of global English. The following list includes just a few colourful additions to the vocabulary recorded around the English-speaking world in the early 21st century that have yet to escape their place of origin:

Regional English	Coinage	Meaning
Australian	arvo	afternoon
	budgie smugglers	tight-fitting swimming trunks
	plonko	winedrinker
	reffo	refugee
	roughie	trick
Canadian	courier parent	someone who obtains an immigration visa in order to get similar status for their children
Indian	desh	the place a person comes from
	history-sheeter	person with a criminal record
	maha	very large
	prepone	bring something forward (the opposite of postpone)
	rook	protest or demonstration
Caribbean	bad-minded	malicious
	criss	smart, fashionable
	doudou	darling

Regional English	Coinage	Meaning
Caribbean (*cont.*)	nyam	to eat
	upful	optimistic
South African	chalkdown	teachers' strike
	frail care	care for the elderly
	frothy	fit of temper
	pondok	shanty dwelling

budgie smugglers

Chips or French fries?
British/US equivalents

Nowhere is the English speaker from Britain liable to be more intrigued or perplexed by local variation in the English vocabulary than in the USA. Americans appear to speak the same language, but infuriatingly insist upon doing so in their own, very individual, way. The following list represents just a selection of the many pairs of equivalents that exist in the British and US vocabularies:

British English	US English	British English	US English
aerial	antenna	drawing-pin	thumbtack
aeroplane	airplane	dustbin	trashcan
anticlockwise	counterclockwise	eiderdown	comforter
anywhere	anyplace	estate agent	realtor
arse	ass	flat	apartment
autumn	fall	got	gotten
bill	check	ground floor	first floor
biscuit	cookie	hair grip	bobby pin
bonnet	hood	high street	main street
bookshop	bookstore	hoarding	billboard
boot	trunk	holdall	carryall
braces	suspenders	ice cream	ice
camp bed	cot	jug	pitcher
candy floss	cotton candy	jumble sale	rummage sale
car	auto	ketchup	catsup
caretaker	janitor	lemonade	lemon soda
chips	French fries	lift	elevator
crisps	chips	lodger	roomer
cupboard	closet	lorry	truck
curtains	drapes	luggage	baggage
draughts	checkers	marrow	squash

British English	US English	British English	US English
maths	math	somewhere	someplace
mince	ground meat	spanner	wrench
mudguard	fender	state school	public school
nappy	diaper	suspenders	garters
number plate	license plate	sweets	candy
paraffin	kerosene	tap	faucet
pavement	sidewalk	torch	flashlight
pelmet	valance	trade union	labor union
petrol	gasoline	trainers	sneakers
pharmacist	druggist	tramp	hobo
pillar box	mailbox	treacle	molasses
post	mail	trousers	pants
pram	baby carriage	underground	subway
railway	railroad	underpants	shorts
ring road	beltway	vest	undershirt
rubbish	garbage	waistcoat	vest
saloon	sedan	wallet	billfold
shop	store	windscreen	windshield
silencer	muffler	zip	zipper

**England and America are two countries
separated by the same language.**

George Bernard Shaw

Neighborly dialog
British/US spellings

There is much divergence in spelling between the versions of English employed on the two sides of the Atlantic. In a few cases the situation is further complicated by both alternatives (for instance, -ise and -ize endings) being encountered on both sides of the Atlantic. In the majority of cases, however, there is a clear distinction between the two alternatives and neither shows any sign of giving way to its equivalent.

British spelling	US spelling
aluminium	aluminum
anaemia	anemia
analyse	analyze
apologise	apologize
axe	ax
behaviour	behavior
carat	karat
catalogue	catalog
centre	center
cheque	check
colour	color
defence	defense
dialogue	dialog
distil	distill
draught	draft
faeces	feces
favourite	favorite
fibre	fiber
fulfil	fulfill

British spelling	US spelling
gaol/jail	jail
grey	gray
harbour	harbor
honour	honor
humour	humor
jeweller	jeweler
labour	labor
licence	license
metre	meter
mould	mold
moustache	mustache
neighbour	neighbor
odour	odor
offence	offense
plough	plow
pretence	pretense
pyjamas	pajamas
sceptic	skeptic
smoulder	smolder
storey	story
sulphur	sulfur
theatre	theater
travelling	traveling
tumour	tumor
tyre	tire
vigour	vigor
whisky	whiskey [1]
zed (letter z)	zee

1. it should be noted, however, that in Ireland *whiskey* is the usual spelling

If I were you...
Making language serve a purpose

With experience comes greater familiarity with the different nuances and varieties of expressions available to all English speakers. Skilled speakers of English become adept at choosing words that will serve their purposes to the best advantage. Consider, for instance, the range of expressions that can be chosen when offering advice or making a suggestion, each of which has its own subtle undercurrent of meaning reflecting the relationship between speaker and listener:

Ways of giving advice

A word of advice ...

Couldn't you ...

Have you thought of ...

How about ...

I advise you to ...

I advise you ...

I recommend you ...

I should ...

I strongly urge ...

I think we should ...

I think you should ...

I think you'd better ...

It might be a good idea ...

I wonder if ...

I would ...

I'd ...

If I were you ...

It would be best for you ...

It's a good idea ...

Let's ...

Make sure ...

My advice is ...

Shouldn't we ...

Suppose we ...

The best course seems to be ...

We could ...

We might as well ...

What about ...

Why don't you ...

Why not ...

You could ...

You could always try ...

You could do worse than ...

You may as well ...

You might as well ...

You might consider ...

You must ...

You should ...

You would do well to ...

You'd better ...

6 Lost for words

When words fail

Like the speakers who use them, words too can lose their vitality, totter and become confused. While some words continue to thrive, others become self-contradictory or lapse into proverb and cliché. Many is the word that escapes the memory altogether, leaving the speaker to fall back on 'whaddyacallems', 'oojamaflips' or 'thingamabobs'. It is all too easy for the unwary speaker to confuse words that look the same or share similar pronunciations or meanings. Through homophones, homographs and other linguistic quirks the door is opened into the shadowy kingdom of the malapropism, the spoonerism and the misquotation – and sometimes even the dictionary itself cannot be relied upon to make things much better.

All this does not mean that every word is necessarily doomed to fade and die: many words (like 'cool' or 'gay') drift along without much enthusiasm for decades and then suddenly enjoy an entirely new lease of life with a new meaning and spring phoenix-like back into the fashionable vernacular. Even if an early death does appear to loom, there is always comfort to be had in age-old sayings and euphemisms … so look on the bright side, worse things happen at sea.

Words are wise men's counters, they do but reckon with them, but they are the money of fools.

Thomas Hobbes

A Logophobic's nightmare
Phobias

Age brings with it much confusion and phobias. Language, inventive as always, has names for all such anxieties. The following list details a selection of some of the more common phobias as well as some of the more exotic complexes for which it has been found necessary to invent a name. There is even a word for a person who is afraid of fear.

Name	Fear of
acarophobia (or scabiophobia)	itching
acerophobia	sourness
achluophobia	darkness/night
acrophobia	heights
aerophobia	air/flying
agoraphobia	open spaces
ailourophobia (or gatophobia)	cats
alektorophobia	chickens
algophobia (or odynophobia)	pain
amathophobia	dust
androphobia	men
anemophobia	wind
anthropophobia	people
aperiophobia	infinity
apiphobia (or melissophobia)	bees
aphenphosmphobia	being touched
arachnophobia	spiders
astraphobia	lightning
ataxiophobia	disorder
atelophobia	imperfection
auroraphobia	the Northern Lights

Name	*Fear of*
bacillophobia	microbes
bacteriophobia (or microphobia)	bacteria
barophobia	gravity
batrachophobia	reptiles
belonephobia	needles
bibliophobia	books
brontophobia (or tonitrophobia)	thunder
cainophobia (or cainolophobia)	novelty
cancerophobia (or carcinophobia)	cancer
cardiophobia	heart conditions
carnophobia	meat
catagelophobia	being ridiculed
cheimophobia	cold
chionophobia	snow
chromatophobia	money
chromophobia	colour
chrystallophobia	crystals
claustrophobia	closed spaces
clinophobia	going to bed
cnidophobia	stings
coprophobia	faeces
coulrophobia	clowns
cremnophobia	precipices
cynophobia	dogs
demonophobia	demons
demophobia	crowds
dendrophobia	trees
dermatophobia	skin
doraphobia	fur
dromophobia	crossing streets
eisoptrophobia	mirrors
elektrophobia	electricity

Name	*Fear of*
emetophobia	vomiting
enetephobia	pins
enochlophobia	crowds
entomophobia	insects
eremophobia	solitude/stillness
ergasiophobia	surgical operations
ergophobia	work
erotophobia	physical love
erythrophobia	blushing
gamophobia	marriage
genophobia	sex
gephyrophobia	crossing bridges
gematophobia	blood
geumaphobia (or geumatophobia)	taste
graphophobia	writing
gymnophobia (or gymnotophobia)	nudity
gynophobia	women
hamartiophobia	sin
hedonophobia	pleasure
heliophobia	sun
helminthophobia	worms
hippophobia	horses
hodophobia	travel
homichlophobia	fog
hormephobia	shock
hydrophobia	water
hypegiophobia	responsibility
hypnophobia	sleep
iatrophobia	doctors
ichthyophobia	fish
ideophobia	ideas
iophobia	rust

Name	Fear of
kakorraphiaphobia	failure
kenophobia	voids
keraunothnetophobia	falling satellites
kinesophobia	motion
kleptophobia	stealing
kopophobia	fatigue
kristallophobia	ice
laliophobia	stuttering
leprophobia	leprosy
limnophobia	lakes
linonophobia	string
logophobia (or verbophobia)	words
lyssophobia (or maniaphobia)	insanity
maieusiophobia	pregnancy
mechanophobia	machinery
merinthophobia	being tied up
metallophobia	metals
misophobia (or mysophobia)	contamination
monophobia (or autophobia)	being alone
musicophobia	music
musophobia	mice
mysophobia	dirt/infection
necrophobia	corpses
nelophobia	glass
nephophobia (or nephelophobia)	clouds
nosemaphobia	illness
nosophobia (or pathophobia)	disease
ochophobia	vehicles
odontophobia	teeth
olfactophobia	smell
ombrophobia	rain
ommatophobia	eyes

Name	*Fear of*
oneirophobia	dreams
ophidiophobia	snakes
ophthalmophobia	being stared at
optophobia	opening one's eyes
orthinophobia	birds
paediphobia	children
panphobia (or pantophobia)	everything
parasitophobia	parasites
parthenophobia	girls
peniaphobia	poverty
phagophobia	eating
pharmacophobia	drugs
phasmophobia	ghosts
phengophobia	daylight
philematophobia	kissing
phobophobia	fear
phonophobia	noise
photophobia	light
phyllophobia	leaves
pnigerophobia	smothering
pogonophobia	beards
poinephobia	punishment
polyphobia	many things
potamophobia	rivers
potophobia	drinks
pteronophobia	feathers
pyrophobia	fire
ranidaphobia	frogs
rhytidophobia	getting wrinkles
satanophobia	Satan
scholionophobia	school
scorodophobia	garlic

Name	Fear of
selachophobia	sharks
siderophobia	stars
sitophobia	food
spermaphobia (or spermatophobia)	germs
spheksophobia	wasps
stasiphobia	standing
tachophobia	speed
taphophobia	being buried alive
teratophobia	deformity
thalassophobia	the sea
thanatophobia	death
thassophobia	sitting
theophobia	god
thermophobia	heat
tocophobia	childbirth
toxiphobia	poison
traumatophobia	wounds
trichopathophobia	hair
triskaidekaphobia	the number 13
trypanophobia	inoculations
xenoglossophobia	foreign languages
xenophobia	strangers
zoophobia	animals

Let me assert my firm belief that the only thing
we have to fear is fear itself.

Franklin D. Roosevelt

Buttered parsnips
Peculiar proverbs

Proverbs are sometimes interpreted as linguistic reflections of the wisdom of age, or, indeed, of the ages. There is considerable reassurance to be had from such time-worn gnomic utterances, even though the meaning may not be immediately obvious.

Proverb	*Probable meaning* [1]
all cats are grey in the dark	in some circumstances superficial differences cease to be important, or even detectable
a smart witch can also dance without a broomstick	a cunning person may still succeed without the necessary tools
cheap meat produces thin gravy	the quality of the finished product depends upon the quality of the ingredients
cold hands, warm heart	people who keep their feelings to themselves often turn out to be the most passionate
the big possum walks just before dawn	the best may happen when things are apparently at their worst
every man must skin his own skunk	a person should not expect someone else to do their own dirty work for them
fine words butter no parsnips	nothing can be achieved through talk alone
he that loves noise must buy a pig	pigs are the noisiest of animals
in the lake of lies there are many dead fish	lies may claim many casualties
matrimony is a school in which one learns too late	people realize the pitfalls of marriage only after they are married

Proverb	Probable meaning
money isn't found under a horse's hoof	wealth does not come without effort
never squat with your spurs on	do not hurt yourself with your own weapons
sleep faster – we need the pillows	it is selfish to overindulge oneself
sparrows that love to chirp won't put on weight	those who expend much energy in talk cannot expect to prosper
the roast duck can fly no more	you cannot have your cake and eat it [2]
too many Eskimos, too few seals	too many people in pursuit of scant opportunities
you can't shake hands with a clenched fist	you cannot make a good agreement without goodwill
you can't tell which way the train went by looking at the track	it is no use trying to work something out by looking in the wrong place
you can't pick up two melons with one hand	some tasks require more effort than others
you can't sip soup with a knife	some tasks are impossible to perform without appropriate equipment

1. it is one of the beauties of proverbs that the meaning of many of them can only be guessed at ...

2. a delightful example of a proverb being best explained by quoting another proverb

At the end of the day
Clichés

Some usages become so well worn with time they become clichés and their continued employment only grates on the listener. The following list comprises a selection of phrases that are virtually guaranteed to make more sensitive users of the English language wince. The word cliché, incidentally, comes from the French verb *clicher*, meaning 'to stereotype', and first appeared in English in the 19th century. The original French verb is thought to have been inspired by the repetitive sound of a die striking molten metal.

Cliché	*Meaning*
all good things must come to an end	time to stop
am I right or am I right?	I'm right
at the end of the day	in the end
at this moment in time	now
beat about the bush	prevaricate
don't call us, we'll call you	we don't want you
drive a nail into the coffin	deliver a final blow
every Tom, Dick and Harry	everyone
few and far between	infrequent
from time immemorial	for a long time
have a nice day	farewell
in a nutshell	to sum up
in point of fact	as a matter of fact
in this day and age	nowadays
it takes all sorts	other people are peculiar
last but not least	finally
leave no stone unturned	be thorough
lock, stock and barrel	everything
make a mountain out of a molehill	exaggerate something

Cliché	*Meaning*
not to mince words	to be frank
plus ça change	everything changes
so near and yet so far	not quite
stand head and shoulders above the rest	outperform
take the bull by the horns	address something
tell it like it is	tell the truth
the fact of the matter	the fact
the 64-thousand dollar question	the big question
upset the apple-cart	disrupt
variety is the spice of life	an unvaried routine is dull
when all is said and done	ultimately

Let's have some new clichés.

Sam Goldwyn (attributed)

last but not least

Pigments of the imagination
Malapropisms

Some people commonly mistake one word for another. Such idio-
syncrasy has been turned to comic effect in many literary works,
notably Richard Brinsley Sheridan's play *The Rivals*, in which Mrs
Malaprop (who gave her name to such linguistic errors) habitually
confuses the meanings of words. The following examples include
some of the most celebrated malapropisms of Shakespeare and Sheridan, as well as a few by a modern master of the form, US President
George W. Bush, originator of many so-called 'bushisms', and some
by unknown authors.

Dogberry [1] (in William Shakespeare's *Much Ado About Nothing*)
Comparisons are odorous [odious]

Our watch, sir, have indeed comprehended [apprehended] two auspi-
cious [suspicious] persons

You are thought here to be the most senseless [sensible] and fit man for
the constable of the watch

Mrs Malaprop (in Richard Brinsley Sheridan's *The Rivals*)
Illiterate [obliterate] him, I say, quite from your memory

O, he will dissolve [resolve] my mystery!

I have since laid Sir Anthony's preposition [proposition] before her

He is the very pine-apple [pinnacle] of politeness

I hope you will represent her to the captain as an object not altogether
illegible [eligible]

He can tell you the perpendiculars [particulars]

1. it could be argued that malapropisms should be more accurately called 'dog-
berryisms', as Shakespeare's Sergeant Dogberry made his contributions to the
genre some two centuries before Mrs Malaprop got to work

Mrs Malaprop (*cont.*)

A progeny [prodigy] of learning

It gives me the hydrostatics [hysterics] to such a degree

She's as headstrong as an allegory [alligator] on the banks of the Nile

I am sorry to say, Sir Anthony, that my affluence [influence] over my niece is very small

Sure, if I reprehend [apprehend] any thing in this world, it is the use of my oracular [vernacular] tongue, and a nice derangement [arrangement] of epitaphs [epithets]!

George W. Bush

They have miscalculated [underestimated] me as a leader

I am mindful not only of preserving executive powers for myself, but for predecessors [successors] as well

We need an energy bill that encourages consumption [conservation]

We cannot let terrorists and rogue nations hold this nation hostile [hostage] or hold our allies hostile [hostage]

Unattributed malapropisms

Under the affluence [influence] of incohol [alcohol]

He is a wolf in cheap [sheep's] clothing

He had to use a fire distinguisher [extinguisher]

Are you casting nasturtiums [aspersions]?

Dad says the monster is just a pigment [figment] of my imagination

'Don't' is a contraption [contraction]

Half-warmed fish
Spoonerisms

The tendency to muddle and mispronounce words created the spoonerism, in which words or parts of words are transposed, often with humorous results. The spoonerism was named after the celebrated Reverend William Archibald Spooner (1844–1930), who often fumbled with his words in such a way (to this day the Middle Common Room of New College, Oxford, where he went to university, is informally known as 'The Rooner Spoom' in his honour). The following list includes some of Dr Spooner's most famous utterances, as well as others by unknown originators:

REV. W.A. SPOONER

I remember your name [face] perfectly, but I just can't think of your face [name]

Is the bean dizzy? [dean busy?]

It is kisstomary to cuss [customary to kiss] the bride

Kinkering Kongs [Conquering Kings] Their Titles Take

Let us drink to the queer old Dean [dear old Queen]

Please sew me to another sheet [show me to another seat]

Sir, you have tasted two whole worms [wasted two whole terms]; you have hissed all my mystery lectures [missed all my history lectures] and have been caught fighting a liar [lighting a fire] in the quad; you will leave Oxford by the town drain [down train]

The cat popped on its drawers [dropped on its paws]

We'll have the hags flung out [flags hung out]

Yes, indeed, the Lord is a shoving leopard [loving shepherd]

REV. W.A. SPOONER (*cont.*)
You will find as you grow older the weight of rages [rate of wages] will press harder and harder on the employer

a blushing crow [crushing blow]

a half-warmed fish [half-formed wish]

a well-boiled icicle [well-oiled bicycle]

cattle ships and bruisers [battleships and cruisers]

in a dark, glassly [glass, darkly]

nosey little cook [cosy little nook]

tons of soil [sons of toil]

UNKNOWN
a lack of pies [pack of lies]

bedding wells [wedding bells]

flutterby [butterfly]

go help me sod [so help me God]

good consternoon, affable [good afternoon, constable]

hiss and lear [listen here]

know your blows [blow your nose]

mad bunny [bad money]

roaring with pain [pouring with rain]

soul of ballad [bowl of salad]

tease my ears [ease my tears]

Elicit the illicit
Confusable words

Some words resemble each other so closely that it is hardly surprising that they are sometimes confused. The following list includes pairs of words with different meanings that are often confused because of their superficial similarity:

First confusable	*Second confusable*
abuse (improper use)	misuse (incorrect use)
accede (agree)	exceed (go beyond)
accept (admit, receive)	except (exclude, leave out)
access (entry)	excess (surplus, unrestrained behaviour)
adverse (unfavourable)	averse (disinclined)
affect (influence)	effect (bring about)
afflict (distress)	inflict (impose)
agnostic (doubting the existence of God)	atheist (denying the existence of God)
allusion (indirect reference)	illusion (misleading impression)
ambiguous (obscure)	ambivalent (indecisive)
amoral (not concerned with morality)	immoral (against accepted moral standards)
bathos (anti-climax)	pathos (evoking pity)
broach (mention, open)	brooch (piece of jewellery)
capital (seat of government)	capitol (government building)
censure (criticize)	censor (ban from publication)
ceremonial (marked by ceremony)	ceremonious (pompous, ceremony-loving)

First confusable	*Second confusable*
coherent (logically consistent)	cohesive (clinging together)
complement (something added)	compliment (expression of admiration)
council (body of representatives etc.)	counsel (advice)
decry (criticize)	descry (notice)
derisive (expressing derision)	derisory (deserving derision)
dinghy (small boat)	dingy (gloomy, shabby)
disinterested (impartial)	uninterested (indifferent)
dispel (drive away)	disperse (break up)
elicit (draw out)	illicit (unlawful)
eminent (outstanding, distinguished)	imminent (impending)
exalt (elevate)	exult (rejoice)
exhausting (tiring)	exhaustive (thorough)
explicit (unambiguous)	implicit (implied)
flaunt (show off)	flout (disregard)
immunity (freedom from obligation)	impunity (freedom from punishment)
intolerable (unbearable)	intolerant (lacking in tolerance)
judicial (of a court of law)	judicious (prudent)
literary (relating to literature)	literate (able to read and write)
luxuriant (lush)	luxurious (sumptuous)
meretricious (insincere)	meritorious (praiseworthy)
naturalist (student of nature)	naturist (nudist)
nutritional (relating to nutrition)	nutritious (nourishing)

First confusable	Second confusable
official (authorized)	officious (interfering, self-important)
ordinance (decree, regulation)	ordnance (military supplies)
peaceable (disposed to peace)	peaceful (characterized by peace)
peremptory (dogmatic, decisive)	perfunctory (quick, careless)
sensual (appealing to the body)	sensuous (appealing to the senses)
stalactite (rock formation from the ceiling)	stalagmite (rock formation from the ground)
tortuous (twisting, winding)	torturous (agonizing, painful)
unexceptionable (inoffensive)	unexceptional (usual, ordinary)

He said true things, but called them by the wrong names.

Robert Browning

naturist naturalists

Write rite, right?

Homophones

Some words share the same pronunciation, but are spelt differently. The following list comprises examples of words that are the source (or sauce?) of much confusion:

First homophone	*Second homophone*
air (atmosphere)	heir (one who succeeds/offspring)
allowed (permitted)	aloud (audibly)
band (group)	banned (forbidden)
bare (unornamented/naked)	bear (omnivorous mammal)
cannon (large gun)	canon (church ruling, cleric)
caught (captured)	court (legal body)
cereal (foodstuff)	serial (belonging to a series)
cite (quote as authority)	sight (vision/view)/site (location)
cue (signal)	queue (line of people)
discreet (prudent)	discrete (distinct)
fair (attractive/satisfactory)	fare (price/goods)
father (male parent)	farther (further)
foreword (introduction to a book)	forward (in a forwards direction)
foul (illegal act in sport)	fowl (chicken/bird)
gilt (gilded)	guilt (culpability)
gorilla (great ape)	guerrilla (irregular soldier)
grate (fireplace)	great (wonderful/large)
hear (detect sound)	here (at this point)
key (means of entry)	quay (landing place)

First homophone	*Second homophone*
knead (work into shape)	need (lack/necessity)
knows (is aware of)	nose (facial feature)
lightening (getting lighter)	lightning (as in thunder and lightning)
muscle (fibrous tissue)	mussel (shellfish)
one (single in number)	won (gained victory)
peak (high point)	peek (brief glimpse)
plum (fruit)	plumb (provide with plumbing)
principal (of the first importance/ head of a school etc.)	principle (fundamental standard)
rain (precipitation from clouds)	reign (rule)
rapt (absorbed)	wrapped (enveloped)
right (just/true)	rite (ritual)/write (inscribe)
rye (crop)	wry (sardonic)
sauce (liquid foodstuff)	source (fount)
sew (thread together)	so (therefore)
stationary (unmoving)	stationery (writing materials)
straight (uncurved, direct)	strait (narrow channel, difficult situation)
suite (set of something)	sweet (pleasant/not sour)
their (belonging to them)	there (in or to that place)
thyme (herb)	time (duration/occasion)
to (towards)	too (as well)/two (number)
wails (laments/cries)	whales (sea mammals)
which (defining a person or thing)	witch (practitioner of witchcraft)
yoke (crossbar for animals)	yolk (yellow part of an egg)

Intolerable wrestling
Homographs

To compound the confusion, numerous words are spelt identically but have different meanings and may even operate as different parts of speech. Some, helpfully, are pronounced differently, but others cannot be distinguished in this way at all. Below are just a few examples of such traps for the unwary:

Word	First meaning	Alternative meaning
better	partly recovered	completely recovered
bolt	secure	run away
bow	lowering of the head	weapon for firing arrows/front of a ship
compact	agreement	container for make-up
content	satisfaction	what is contained
contract	agree formally	become smaller
hold up	support	hinder
light	illuminate	ignite
model	archetype	copy
object	purpose	thing
peer	equal	nobleman
present	now	attending
project	stick out	envisage, plan
quite	fairly	totally
scan	check superficially	check minutely
second-guess	evaluate with hindsight	predict
see	observe	understand
tear	rip	moisture from the eye
transport	conveyance	rapture
wax	coat with wax	become larger

Janus words
Words with contradictory meanings

Many words have alternative meanings that contradict one another, with the result that any confusion between them might lead to the opposite of what was intended being understood. These eccentrics are known by various names, including antilogies, auto-antonyms, contronymns, and Janus words (after the Greek god of doorways who was conventionally depicted with two faces looking in opposite directions).

Word	First meaning	Contradictory meaning
belie	misrepresent	show to be false
cleave	stick together	split apart
clip	cut	fasten together
crop	plant	harvest
cull	select	reject
dust	remove dust	sprinkle with dust
fast	fixed	moving quickly
fight with	fight against	fight alongside
go off	start	stop
left	gone	remaining
put out	generate	put an end to
rent	lend	borrow
sanction	approve	ban
screen	show	conceal
seed	remove seeds from	add seeds to
splice	join together	cut in two
temper	soften	strengthen
trim	pare down	ornament
weather	withstand	wear away
wind up	start	finish

Harmless drudgery
Dubious dictionary definitions

When words threaten to become confused, the obvious solution is to consult a dictionary. Some dictionary definitions, however, are more reliable than others. At least two lexicographers, Samuel Johnson (compiler of the first great dictionary, 1755) and Ambrose Bierce (author of the wittily cynical *Devil's Dictionary*, 1911), seized the opportunity to share not only their wisdom but also their mischievous sense of humour. Chambers dictionaries continue the tradition of mischievous definitions to this day.

SAMUEL JOHNSON

dull	to make dictionaries is dull work
excise	a hateful tax levied upon commodities
lexicographer	a harmless drudge
net	anything reticulated or decussated at equal distances, with interstices between the intersections
oats	a grain, which in England is generally given to horses, but in Scotland supports the people
patron	commonly a wretch who supports with insolence, and is paid with flattery

AMBROSE BIERCE

bore	a person who talks when you wish him to listen
brain	an apparatus with which we think that we think
debauchee	one who has so earnestly pursued pleasure that he has had the misfortune to overtake it
egotist	a person of low taste, more interested in himself than in me
future	that period of time in which our affairs prosper, our friends are true and our happiness is assured

AMBROSE BIERCE (*cont.*)

grammar
: a system of pitfalls thoughtfully prepared for the feet of the self-made man, along the path by which he advances to distinction

marriage
: the state or condition of a community consisting of a master, a mistress and two slaves, making in all two

patience
: a minor form of despair, disguised as a virtue

peace
: in international affairs, a period of cheating between two periods of fighting

proof-reader
: a malefactor who atones for making your writing nonsense by permitting the compositor to make it unintelligible

CHAMBERS DICTIONARY

bachelor's wife
: an ideal woman with none of the shortcomings of married men's wives

back-seat driver
: someone free of responsibility but full of advice

fish
: to catch or try to catch or obtain fish, or anything that may be likened to a fish (such as seals, sponges, coral, compliments, information or husbands)

flag-day
: a day on which collectors solicit contributions to a charity in exchange for small flags as badges to secure immunity for the rest of the day

jaywalker
: a careless pedestrian whom motorists are expected to avoid running down

middle-aged
: between youth and old age, variously reckoned to suit the reckoner

perpetrate
: to commit or execute (especially an offence, a poem, or a pun)

picture restorer
: a person who cleans and tries to restore old pictures

Santa Claus
: an improbable source of improbable benefits

Beam me up, punk

Misquotations

One consequence of a failing memory is that one tends to forget things one has heard said, or confuses exactly how they were said. The following list includes just a few of the more celebrated misquotations that continue to circulate despite the evident fact that they have been communicated in garbled form, or are, indeed, entirely fictitious:

Misquotation	*Original quotation / Comment*
a cloud no bigger than a man's hand	behold, there ariseth a little cloud out of the sea, like a man's hand (*Bible*, 1 Kings 18:44)
alas, poor Yorick, I knew him well	alas, poor Yorick. I knew him, Horatio … (William Shakespeare, *Hamlet*)
beam me up, Scotty	never said (*Star Trek* TV series)
blood, sweat and tears	I have nothing to offer but blood, toil, tears and sweat (Sir Winston Churchill)
bubble, bubble, toil and trouble	double, double, toil and trouble (William Shakespeare, *Macbeth*)
do you feel lucky, punk?	… you've got to ask yourself a question. Do I feel lucky? Well, do you, punk? (Clint Eastwood, *Dirty Harry*)
elementary, my dear Watson	never said (*Sherlock Holmes*)
et tu, Brute?	kai su, teknon? [you too, my child?] (Julius Caesar)
fresh fields and pastures new	to-morrow to fresh woods, and pastures new (John Milton, *Lycidas*)
go the way of all flesh	go the way of all the earth (*Bible*, Joshua 23:14 and 1 Kings 2:2)

Misquotation	*Original quotation / Comment*
let them eat cake [*qu'ils mangent de la brioche*]	probably never said (by Marie Antoinette)
me Tarzan, you Jane	never said (by Tarzan)
methinks the lady doth protest too much	the lady doth protest too much, methinks (William Shakespeare, *Hamlet*)
money is the root of all evil	the love of money is the root of all evil (*Bible*, 1 Timothy 6:10)
music has charms to soothe the savage beast	music has charms to soothe a savage breast (William Congreve, *The Mourning Bride*)
not tonight, Josephine	never said (by Napoleon)
ours not to reason why	theirs not to reason why (Alfred, Lord Tennyson, *The Charge of the Light Brigade*)
peace in our time	peace for our time (Neville Chamberlain)
play it again, Sam	play it, Sam, for old times' sake. Play 'As Time Goes By' (Ingrid Bergman, *Casablanca*)
pride goes before a fall	pride goeth before destruction, and an haughty spirit before a fall (*Bible*, Proverbs 16:18)
religion is the opiate of the masses	religion is the sigh of the oppressed creature … it is the opium of the people (Karl Marx)
the lion shall lie down with the lamb	the wolf also shall dwell with the lamb, and the leopard shall lie down with the kid; and the calf and the young lion and the fatling together; and a little child shall lead them (*Bible*, Isaiah 11:6)
to gild the lily	to gild refined gold, to paint the lily (William Shakespeare, *King John*)

Misquotation	*Original quotation / Comment*
we are not amused	probably never said (by Queen Victoria)
why don't you come up and see me sometime?	why don't you come up some time and see me? (Mae West, *She Done Him Wrong*)
you dirty rat!	never said (by James Cagney)
your need is greater than mine	thy necessity is yet greater than mine (Sir Philip Sidney)

music has charms to soothe the savage beast

Whaddyacallems

Replacements for forgotten words

When words vanish from the memory altogether there is no option
but to replace the sought-for term with something else, a nonsense
word that will serve to fill the resulting vacuum. The process even
has its own formal name: lethologica. The following list includes just
some of the many nonsense words that may be resorted to when
particular words go walkabout. Note that several of these words may
be spelled in a variety of ways.

deeleebob	thingamajig
deeleebobber	thingummy
diddleebob	thingummybob
diddleydo	thingy
diddleythingy	thingybob
dingus	whaddyacallem
dingdong	whaddyamacallit
dingy	whatchacallem
dohickey	whatchacallit
doobrie	whatchamacallit
doodad	what-d'you-call-it
doodah	whatnot
geega	whatsisname
gewgaw	whatsit
gizmo	whosis
hootenanny	whosit
howsyerfather	widget
jiminycricket	wotsit
oojamaflip	thingamabob
oojamaflop	thingamabobbit

Once a word has been allowed to escape, it cannot be recalled.

Horace

Golden oldies
Euphemisms of old age

The discussion of advancing age and its accompanying disadvantages is often a cause of much unease and this is reflected in the language people use in relation to such topics. The horrors of failing physical and mental health that are frequently associated with the latter stages of life are rarely discussed without recourse to a rich fund of euphemisms and circumlocutions.

The following list suggests a few alternatives for some of the blunter, less palatable terms connected with the ageing process. Some are relatively uncontentious, while others many would consider outlandish examples of political correctness.

Word	Euphemism
false teeth	alternative dentation; dentures
to grow old	to get along/on; to make old bones; to wear down
old	ageful; chronologically gifted; distinguished; elderly; experientially enhanced; forward at the knees; gerontologically advanced; grey; in the departure lounge of life; in the evening of one's days; longer-living; long in the tooth; mature; not as young as one was; not in one's first youth; of mature years; on borrowed time; seasoned; senior
old age	certain age; golden years; maturity; sunset/twilight years; third age
old people's home	convalescent home; eventide home; God's waiting-room; home; rest home; twilight home
old person	advanced adult; blue hair/rinse; Darby and Joan[1]; golden ager; golden oldie; no spring chicken; old-timer; senior citizen; white top

1. a reference to a placid and content elderly couple who first appeared in a ballad published in 1735

7 Words without end

The death and rebirth of words

It is a sad fact that words, like their human users, are not guaranteed to last forever. As Samuel Johnson remarked in his *Dictionary of the English Language*, 'I am not yet so lost in lexicography, as to forget that words are the daughters of earth.'

Words emerge and disappear as fashions change. Some words linger for decades or even centuries after their fellows have fallen by the wayside. Others perish prematurely after they are found no longer to suit contemporary tastes. Their decease may be celebrated or regretted: more often than not no one attends the funeral, for the world has forgotten them and may possess no record of the fact that they existed in the first place. But it is inevitable that these casualties of neglect will soon be replaced by fresh upstarts and changelings and that the life of language as a whole will go on.

In rare cases words that would appear to have died and been buried deep in the clay of universal neglect spring from the grave and are reincarnated in new forms or with new meanings. The language lover may shudder at the thought of a word dying, forsaken and rotten with age, and seek shelter from this awful reality in comforting euphemisms, but such deaths (lamentable though they may be) are essential to the survival of any language and might even be interpreted as a sign of inward health and vigour.

Bethumped with words.

William Shakespeare

Gone for a Burton
Euphemisms of illness and death

English speakers can be very squeamish when referring to serious illness or death. Some euphemisms are more familiar than others, while others are derided as examples of politically correct over-sensitivity or are only used in jocular contexts. Still more have proved contentious in different ways: the now-dated euphemistic 'join the great majority', for instance, might reasonably be rejected nowadays as no longer strictly accurate, on the grounds that the number of people living today is greater than the sum of those who lived before. This might be true as far back as the building of the Pyramids over 4000 years ago (since when some six billion people – equivalent to the population of the earth today – have lived and died), but certainly not if taking into account all the humans who have lived since the species emerged around 45,000 years ago (estimated to be around 60 billion in number).

ill   fading away; feeling funny; in a condition non-conducive to life; indisposed; looking like death warmed up; off colour; on one's last legs; physically inconvenienced; under the weather; with one foot in the grave

to die   to answer the last call; to baste the formaldehyde turkey; to be called to higher service; to bite the biscuit/dust; to breathe one's last; to buy it/the farm [1]; to cash in one's chips; to cease to be; to check out; to climb the golden stair; to come to a sticky end; to come to the end of the road; to cop it; to croak; to cross the bar/River Jordan; to dance at the end of a rope; to depart this life; to donate the liver paté; to drop off the perch; to enter the next world; to fall asleep; to feed the fishes; to flatline; to get

1. arose from the fact that when aircraft of the US Air Force crashed on farmland the farmer could sue the government for any damage caused (often enough to buy the farm outright)

to die (*cont.*)   one's halo; to give up the ghost; to go for a Burton [2]; to go
the way of all flesh; to go to a better place; to go to a
dance party with God; to go to one's reward; to go to the
big glass house in the sky; to go west; to hand in one's
dinner pail; to hang up one's boots; to join one's ancestors/
the great majority; to keel over; to kick the bucket [3], to
kick the oxygen habit; to lay down one's burden; to leave
the building; to make the ultimate sacrifice; to meet one's
Maker; to meet with an accident; to pass away; to peg
out; to pop off; to pop one's clogs; to push up the daisies;
to shuffle off this mortal coil; to snuff it; to strike out; to
take a long walk off a short pier; to turn up one's toes; to
turn one's face to the wall; to turn up one's toes

to kill   to blow away; to bump off; to burn; to deconflict; to
degrade; to despatch; to eliminate; to ice; to knock off; to
liquidate; to neutralize; to nobble; to put to sleep; to rub
out; to sanction; to service a target; to snuff out; to take
out; to terminate with extreme prejudice; to top; to waste

death   auction of kit; awfully big adventure [4]; big D; big jump;
big sleep; diagnostic misadventure of high magnitude;
end of the line; eternal yawn; final curtain; great leveller;
health alteration; journey's end; last debt; last round-up;
little gentleman in black velvet [5]; negative patient care
outcome; one-way ride; terminal episode; therapeutic
misadventure; undiscovered country

dead   at peace; at rest; beyond salvage; combat ineffective;
cooking for the Kennedys; deanimated; departed;
immortally challenged; living-impaired; metabolically
different; no longer a factor; no longer with us; nonviable;
passed away; reformatted by God; six feet under; termi-
nally inconvenienced; toasted; worm food

corpse   non-living person; remains; stiff

coffin   pine/wooden overcoat; tree suit

undertaker dismal trader; sanitarian

grave   long home; narrow bed

2. possibly a reference to Burton ale, or alternatively short for 'Burton-on-Trent' (rhyming slang for 'went' as in 'went west') or a reference to tailors Montague Burton

3. some authorities point out that when freshly slaughtered pigs were hung on a beam or frame (known as a *bucket*) at a market, they writhed around and would *kick the bucket*. Other authorities suggest that the bucket is the pail on which someone who intends to commit suicide stands on. The noose is then tied around the neck, the bucket is kicked away, and death inevitably follows

4. a quotation from J.M. Barrie's *Peter Pan*: 'To die will be an awfully big adventure', and perhaps what US theatre producer Charles Frohman, who staged *Peter Pan*, had in mind when he stepped into the water from the torpedoed *Lusitania* in 1915 with the words 'Why fear death? It is the most beautiful adventure in life.' He drowned

5. the original 'little gentleman in black velvet' was a mole whose molehill caused William III's horse to stumble, the king later dying from his injuries

---

It's not that I'm afraid to die.

I just don't want to be there when it happens.

Woody Allen

Either that wallpaper goes, or I do
Famous last words

Some people reserve their most memorable words for their dying breath. This list includes some of the most notable (sometimes apocryphal) deathbed observations of the great and good. Note that in some cases the deceased managed to linger on long enough to be credited with more than one last utterance.

Last words	*Author and date of death*
All my possessions for a moment of time	Elizabeth I (English monarch) 1603
All right, then, I'll say it: Dante makes me sick	Lope Félix de Vega Carpio (Spanish playwright and poet) 1635
Bugger Bognor [1]	George V (British monarch) 1936
Die, my dear Doctor, that's the last thing I shall do!	Lord Palmerston (British statesman) 1865
Does nobody understand?	James Joyce (Irish novelist) 1941
Don't give up the ship	James Lawrence (American naval captain, as he lay dying in battle) 1813
Dying is a very dull, dreary affair. And my advice to you is to have nothing whatever to do with it	W. Somerset Maugham (British writer) 1965
Either that wallpaper goes, or I do	Oscar Wilde (Irish writer and wit) 1900
Everything has gone wrong, my girl [2]	Arnold Bennett (British novelist) 1931
God bless ... God damn	James Thurber (US humorist) 1961

Last words	Author and date of death
Good night, my darlings, I'll see you in the morning	Noël Coward (British playwright and actor) 1973
Go on, get out! Last words are for fools who haven't said enough	Karl Marx (German social, political and economic theorist) 1883
I am dying as I have lived – beyond my means	Oscar Wilde (Irish writer and wit) 1900
I am going in search of a great perhaps. Bring down the curtain, the farce is over	François Rabelais (French satirist) 1553
I am just going outside and may be some time [3]	Captain Lawrence Oates (British explorer) 1912
I am not afraid to die	Benjamin Disraeli (British statesman) 1881
If this is dying, I don't think much of it	Lytton Strachey (British writer) 1932
I realize that patriotism is not enough. I must have no hatred or bitterness towards anyone [4]	Edith Cavell (British nurse) 1915
I shall hear in heaven	Ludwig van Beethoven (German composer) 1827
Is it my birthday or am I dying?	Nancy Astor (British politician) 1964
It has all been very interesting	Mary Wortley Montagu (British writer) 1762

1. his response to a suggestion that he would soon be well enough to visit Bognor Regis. Other sources insist his last words were the more stately, but far less memorable 'How is the empire?'

2. said as he lay dying after drinking Parisian tap water to demonstrate how safe it was

3. said as he left his tent, frostbitten and very weak, and walked into an Antarctic blizzard with the intention of dying so as not to slow down his companions; it was his 32nd birthday

4. said as she faced a German firing squad in World War I

Last words	*Author and date of death*
I think I am becoming a god	Vespasian (Roman emperor) AD 79
I think I could eat one of Bellamy's veal pies	William Pitt the Younger (British statesman) 1806
I've had eighteen straight whiskies, I think that's the record … After 39 years, this is all I've done	Dylan Thomas (Welsh poet) 1953
I've never felt better	Douglas Fairbanks Snr (US film actor) 1939
Kiss me, Hardy [5]	Horatio Nelson (British admiral) 1805
Let not poor Nelly starve [6]	Charles II (English monarch) 1685
More light!	Johann Wolfgang von Goethe (German writer) 1832
Mozart!	Gustav Mahler (Austrian composer) 1911
Nonsense, they couldn't hit an elephant at this distance [7]	General John Sedgwick (US general) 1864
Nothing but death	Jane Austen (British novelist) 1817
Now I'll have eine kleine pause	Kathleen Ferrier (British contralto) 1953
Oh, I am so bored with it all	Winston Churchill (British statesman) 1965
On the whole, I'd rather be in Philadelphia	W.C. Fields (US comedian) 1946
See in what peace a Christian can die	Joseph Addison (English essayist) 1719
So it has come at last, the distinguished thing	Henry James (US novelist) 1916

Last words	*Author and date of death*
So little done, so much to do	Cecil Rhodes (South African statesman) 1902
So the heart be right, it is no matter which way the head lieth	Sir Walter Raleigh (English explorer and writer) 1618
Such is life	Ned Kelly (Australian outlaw) 1880
The rest is silence	Hamlet (in William Shakespeare's *Hamlet*) *c*.1601
We are all going to Heaven, and Vandyke is of the company	Thomas Gainsborough (English artist) 1788
Well, if it must be so	Edvard Grieg (Norwegian composer) 1907
What an artist dies in me!	Nero (Roman emperor) AD68
What is the answer? … in that case, what is the question?	Gertrude Stein (US writer) 1946
Why are you weeping? Did you imagine that I was immortal?	Louis XIV (French monarch) 1715

5. said to Captain Hardy, as Nelson lay dying at the Battle of Trafalgar (1805), although it has been suggested he actually said 'Kismet, Hardy' in the sense of 'Kismet' meaning 'Fate'

6. referring to his mistress Nell Gwynne

7. said when he was advised to stay concealed from enemy fire during the Battle of Spotsylvania (1864) in the American Civil War: he was then shot and killed by a Confederate sharpshooter

---

The tongues of dying men enforce attention like deep harmony.

William Shakespeare

A nice derangement of epitaphs
Memorable epitaphs

The language of death is at its most succinct in the case of memorial inscriptions, which have to be laboriously carved letter by letter. This does not mean that all the following epitaphs actually made it to immortality on a gravestone – this is particularly true of the self-mocking suggestions made by the famous for their own tombs. Even when carved in stone, the accuracy of such sentiments cannot necessarily be relied upon, for, as Samuel Johnson observed, 'In lapidary inscriptions a man is not upon oath.'

Ezekiel Aikle (*inhabitant of Nova Scotia*)
Here lies Ezekiel Aikle age 102
The good die young.
gravestone in East Dalhousie, Nova Scotia

Anonymous
Here lie I and my four daughters,
Killed by drinking Cheltenham waters.
Had we but stuck to Epsom salts,
We wouldn't have been in these here vaults.
gravestone in Cheltenham, Gloucestershire, 18th century

Anonymous
Here lie I by the chancel door;
They put me here because I was poor.
The further in, the more you pay,
But here lie I as snug as they.
gravestone in a Devon church

Anonymous
Here lies my wife,
Here lies she;
Hallelujah!
Hallelujee!
gravestone in a Leeds churchyard

Mel Blanc (*US cartoon voice artist*)
That's all, folks!
a reference to his work as a voice artist on
Warner Brothers cartoons, 1989

George Burns (*US comedian*)
I wish I were reading this.
his own suggestion

Johnny Carson (*US television presenter*)
I'll be right back.
his own suggestion

Charles II (*English monarch*)
Here lies our sovereign lord the king,
Whose word no man relies on,
Who never said a foolish thing
Nor ever did a wise one.
anonymous, after the king's death in 1685

Emily Dickinson (*US poet*)
Called Back.
her gravestone in Amherst, Massachusetts,
as chosen by her sister Lavinia, 1886

Lydia Eason (*Englishwoman*)
All who come my grave to see
Avoid damp beds and think of me.
gravestone in St Michael's, Stoke

Benjamin Franklin (*US statesman, printer and scientist*)
The body of
Benjamin Franklin, printer,
(Like the cover of an old book,
Its contents worn out,
And stript of its lettering and gilding)
Lies here, food for worms!
Yet the work itself shall not be lost,
For it will, as he believed, appear once more
In a new
And more beautiful edition,
Corrected and amended
By its Author!
his own suggestion

Frederick Louis, Prince of Wales [1]
Here lies Fred,
Who was alive and is dead:
Had it been his father,
I had much rather;
Had it been his brother,
Still better than another;
Had it been his sister,
No one would have missed her;
Had it been a whole generation,
Still better for the nation:
But since 'tis only Fred,
Who was alive and is dead, –
There's no more to be said.
anonymous

Clark Gable (*US film actor*)
Back to the silents.
his own suggestion

1. the eldest son of George II, who predeceased him

George S. Kaufman (*US playwright*)
Over my dead body!
his own suggestion

John Keats (*British poet*)
Here lies one whose name was writ in water.
his own suggestion, after Beaumont and Fletcher,
and after his death in 1821 inscribed on his gravestone in Rome

Mary Ann Lowder (*US invalid*)
Here lies the body of Mary Ann Lowder,
She burst while drinking a seidlitz powder.
Called from the world to her heavenly rest,
She should have waited till it effervesced.
gravestone in New Jersey

Lester Moore (*US railway agent*)
Here lies Lester Moore
Four slugs from a .44
No Les no More.
gravestone in Tombstone, Arizona, 19th century

Captain Lawrence Edward Grace Oates (*Antarctic explorer*)
Hereabouts died a very gallant gentleman, Captain L.E.G. Oates
of the Inniskilling Dragoons. In March 1912, returning from the Pole,
he walked willingly to his death in a blizzard, to try and save his
comrades, beset by hardships.
memorial in the Antarctic (composed by his comrade,
British naval physician E.L. Atkinson)

John Round (*US seafarer*)
Underneath this stone
Lies poor John Round:
Lost at sea
And never found.
gravestone in Marblehead, Massachusetts

George Routledge (*English watchmaker*)
Here lies in horizontal position
The outside case of
George Routledge, watchmaker,
In the hope of being taken in hand
By his maker.
And of being thoroughly cleaned, repaired
And set going
In the world to come.
gravestone in Lydford, Devon

William Shakespeare
Good frend for Jesus sake forbeare,
To dig the dust encloased heare!
Blest be the man that spares thes stones,
And curst be he that moves my bones!
his gravestone in Stratford-upon-Avon

He was not of an age but for all time.
Ben Jonson

Skugg (*a pet squirrel*)
Here Skugg
Lies snug
As a bug
In a rug.
*Benjamin Franklin (written to commemorate
the death of his daughter's pet squirrel)*

Edsel Smith (*US accident victim*)
Here lies Henry Edsel Smith. Born 1903. Died 1942. Looked up the
elevator shaft to see if the car was on the way down. It was.
gravestone in Albany, New York

Robert Louis Stevenson
Here lies one who meant well, tried a little and failed much.
his own suggestion

Captain Anthony Wedgwood
Sacred to the memory of
Captain Anthony Wedgwood
Accidentally shot by his gamekeeper
Whilst out shooting
'Well done thou good and faithful servant'
anonymous

Sir Christopher Wren (*English architect*)
If you seek his monument, look around you.
in St Paul's Cathedral, London, which he designed, 1723

W.B. Yeats (*Irish poet and playwright*)
Cast a cold eye
On life, on death
Horseman, pass by!
*from his own poetry, on his gravestone in the churchyard
of the village of Drumcliff, County Sligo* [2]

2. though buried in Ireland, Yeats actually died (in 1957) on the French Riviera

Nowhere probably is there more true feeling and nowhere
worse taste, than in a churchyard – both as regards
the monuments and the inscriptions. Scarcely a word
of true poetry anywhere.

Benjamin Jowett

Galvanizing sandwiches
Eponyms

Another class of words offers the deceased a unique chance of immortality, at least linguistically, through the absorption of their names into the general vocabulary. In some cases such eponyms may arise in salute to a particular person's fame, achievements or ingenuity; in others they emerge as signals of contempt for that person's shortcomings or misdeeds.

Eponym	*Origin*
bowdlerize	Thomas Bowdler (1754–1825), English editor of a notoriously expurgated edition of Shakespeare
boycott	Captain Charles Cunningham Boycott (1832–97), British land agent who was ostracized by his Irish tenants as a means of coercing him to reduce rents
bunsen burner	R.W. Bunsen (1811–99), German chemist who actually refined an earlier burner invented by Michael Faraday
cardigan	James Thomas Brudenell, 7th Earl of Cardigan (1797–1868), British soldier who wore a knitted woollen jacket against the cold of the Crimea
clerihew	Edmund Clerihew Bentley (1875–1956), British writer who devised the humorous verse form that now bears his name
Dickensian	Charles Dickens (1812–70), British novelist whose works were characterized by depictions of urban deprivation
earl grey tea	Earl Grey (1764–1845), British statesman who passed the recipe to Jacksons of Piccadilly in 1830
galvanize	Luigi Galvani (1737–98), Italian physiologist who discovered the phenomenon of animal electricity
Kafkaesque	Franz Kafka (1883–1924), Austrian novelist known for his portrayal of the world as bizarre and irrational
leotard	Jules Léotard (1842–70), French acrobat who wore such an outfit

Eponym	*Origin*
magnolia	Pierre Magnol (1638–1715), French botanist who first described the plant
mansard roof	François Mansart (1598–1666), French architect who designed such double-angled high-pitched roofs
masochism	Leopold von Sacher-Masoch (1836–95), Austrian writer whose works depicted sexual pleasure derived from receiving pain
maverick	Samuel Maverick (1837–70), Texan cattle-rancher who refused to brand his stock
mesmerism	Franz Mesmer (1734–1815), Austrian physician who conducted early experiments in hypnotism
nicotine	Jean Nicot (1530–1600), French diplomat and scholar who introduced the tobacco plant to France
pavlova	Anna Pavlova (1881–1931), Russian ballerina to whom the dessert dish was dedicated while touring Australia and New Zealand
peach melba	Dame Nellie Melba (1861–1931), Australian soprano to whom the dish was dedicated by the French chef Escoffier at the Savoy Hotel in 1892
quisling	Vidkun Quisling (1887–1945), Norwegian politician considered a traitor after he collaborated with the country's Nazi invaders
sadism	Marquis de Sade (1740–1814), French writer long imprisoned for his works depicting sexual fantasy and perversion
Sam Browne belt	Sir Sam Browne (1824–1901), British general who won a VC during the Indian Mutiny [1] of 1857
sandwich	4th Earl of Sandwich (1718–92), English aristocrat who devised the sandwich as a handy snack to be eaten while watching horse-racing

1. many in India find 'mutiny' offensive and prefer the term 'First War of Independence'

Eponym	*Origin*
silhouette	Étienne de Silhouette (1709–67), French politician whose name came to signify anything cheap
tarmac	John McAdam (1756–1836), British surveyor who invented it
teddy bear	Theodore Roosevelt (1858–1919), US president fabled to have spared a young bear tied up for him to shoot
volt	Alessando Volta (1745–1827), Italian physicist who invented the electrochemical battery in 1800
wellington boot	Arthur Wellesley, 1st Duke of Wellington (1769–1852), British general who wore a boot reaching to the mid-calf or knee

'Tis pleasant, sure, to see one's name in print.

Lord Byron

Wellington boot

Humboldt's parrot
Lost languages

It has been estimated that there are some 6800 languages in the world today, but also that on average one language dies every month. At this rate of mortality some 90 per cent of the world's languages will have perished by the year 2100. One famous extinction was that of the language of the Atures Indians of Venezuela: 200 years ago German explorer Alexander von Humboldt is said to have encountered a parrot speaking in a tongue he did not recognize. When he asked where the parrot had come from he was informed, to his dismay, that the parrot had learned to talk among the long-vanished Atures people and that it was the last surviving speaker of their language. Examples of languages that have been lost in recent times include Catawba (Massachusetts), the last fluent speaker of which died in 1996, Eyak (Alaska) and Livonian (Latvia). Below are some facts and figures recently published by UNESCO about the world's vanishing languages.

Figure Fact

96%   of all languages are spoken by just 4% of the world's population

90%   of languages are not found on the internet

90%   of Australia's languages (250) have died since 1800

80%   of African languages have no formal written form

80%   of the world's languages have died since languages diversified several thousand years ago (possibly more)

75%   of Brazil's languages (540) have died since 1530

50%   of the world's languages are found in just eight countries [1]

1. namely, Papua New Guinea, Indonesia, Nigeria, India, Mexico, Cameroon, Australia and Brazil

Endangered species
Threatened languages

In order to survive in the long term, linguists generally agree that a language needs to have at least 100,000 speakers. The dominance of a small number of so-called 'predator' languages (Chinese, English, Spanish, Hindi, Swahili, etc.) threatens to swamp the world. Little hope can realistically be entertained for the minority tongues of places like Papua New Guinea, which can currently boast some 800 indigenous languages. Even less exists for a language like the aboriginal Mati Ke, which has just three speakers left (of which one speaks a different dialect, while the other two are forbidden to communicate as they are brother and sister). Some threatened languages have drawn back somewhat from the brink of extinction through energetic campaigns aimed at their revival. These include Icelandic (with currently 275,000 speakers), Faroese (lately promoted by the Danish government, which went to the extent of putting phrases in Faroese on the sides of milk cartons), Maori, Hawaiian and the native American languages Mohawk and Navajo.

This list includes a selection of languages that have, according to recent surveys, been reduced to fewer than half-a-dozen speakers.

Language	Where spoken	Number of speakers
Abaga	Papua New Guinea	5 (1994)
Amis	Taiwan	5 (2000)
Arutani	Venezuela	2 (2002)
Ata	Philippines	2–5 (2000)
Atsugewi	USA	3 (1991)
Babuza	Taiwan	3–4 (2000)
Baldemu	Cameroon	3–6 (2003)
Berakou	Chad	2 (1995)
Berbice Creole Dutch	Guyana	4–5 (1993)
Bonerif	Indonesia	4 (1994)

Language	Where spoken	Number of speakers
Bung	Cameroon	3 (1995)
Chamicuro	Peru	2 (2000)
Coeur d'Alene	USA	5 (1999)
Dumi	Nepal	3 (2000)
Gamilaraay	Australia	3 (1997)
Garig-Ilgar	Australia	4 (2003)
Iñapari	Peru	4 (1999)
Jabutí	Brazil	5 (1990)
Júma	Brazil	4 (1998)
Karaim	Lithuania	3 (2000)
Kayeli	Indonesia	3 (1995)
Kerek	Russia	2 (1997)
Klamath-Modoc	USA	1 (1998)
Kulon-Pazeh	Taiwan	1 (2000)
Lardil	Australia	2 (2000)
Lengilu	Indonesia	3–4 (2000)
Lingkhim	Nepal	1 (1991)
Lom	Indonesia	2–10 (2000)
Luo	Cameroon	1 (1995)
Mabire	Chad	3 (2001)
Maidu	USA	4–8 (1994)
Mapoyo	Venezuela	3 (2000)
Margu	Australia	1 (2000)
Mati ke	Australia	3 (2005)
Nisenan	USA	1 (1994)
Nyulnyul	Australia	1 (2001)
Ona	Argentina	1–3 (1991)
Oro Win	Brazil	5 (1996)
Osage	USA	5 (1991)
Pémono	Venezuela	1 (2000)
Puruborá	Brazil	2 (2002)
Ratagnon	Philippines	2–3 (2000)

Language	Where spoken	Number of speakers
Saaroa	Taiwan	5–6 (2000)
San Miguel Creole French	Panama	3 (1999)
Saponi	Indonesia	4–5 (2000)
Serrano	USA	1 (1994)
Tagish	Canada	2 (1995)
Tandia	Indonesia	2 (1991)
Tanema	Solomon Islands	3 (1999)
Taushiro	Peru	1 (2002)
Tehuelche	Argentina	4 (2000)
Thao	Taiwan	5–6 (2000)
Tinigua	Colombia	2 (2000)
Tolowa	USA	4–5 (1994)
Totoro	Colombia	4 (1998)
Turumsa	Papua New Guinea	5 (2002)
Uru	Bolivia	2 (2000)
Warrwa	Australia	2 (2001)
Wichita	USA	3 (2000)
Wintu	USA	5–6 (1997)
Woria	Indonesia	5–6 (2000)
Xetá	Brazil	3 (1990)
Xipaya	Brazil	2 (2000)
Yámana	Chile	1 (2003)
Yugh	Russia	2–3 (1991)
Záparo	Ecuador	1 (2000)
Zire	New Caledonia	4 (1996)

I am always sorry when any language is lost,
because languages are the pedigree of nations.

Samuel Johnson

So unenglish
Extraordinary words from threatened languages

The English vocabulary is remarkably flexible and covers most eventualities. There are, however, words in other languages for which English has no exact equivalent. This fact makes their loss particularly poignant, as these often express concepts far beyond the scope of the English vocabulary. The following list gives details of just 10 examples from endangered languages:

Word	Language	Meaning
blart	Ullans (Northern Ireland)	to fall flat in mud
coghal	Manx (UK)	big lump of dead flesh after a wound is opened
egthu	Boro (NE India)	to create a pinching sensation in the armpit
merripen	Romany	life and death
nwik-ga	Wagiman (Australia)	to have a tickle in the throat
onsra	Boro (NE India)	to love for the last time
puijilittatuq	Inuktit (Canada)	he does not know which way to turn because of the many seals he has seen come to the ice surface
th'alatel	Halkomelem (Canada)	a device for the heart
tkhetsikhe'ten-hawihtennihs	Mohawk (USA)	I am bringing sugar to somebody
tl'imshya'isita'itlma	Nootka (Canada)	he invites people to a feast

Spiffing wights
Defunct English words

The English language is not immune to the process of death and decay. Hundreds of words listed in dictionaries are no longer in regular current use or, though still generally understood, are only used in a self-consciously ironic manner or survive only as historical curiosities. Words do not generally vanish from use overnight but over many years, gradually falling into disuse (and typically being labelled 'dated' in dictionaries) before falling out of use altogether (and being labelled 'obsolete' and dropped from all but the largest dictionaries).

The following list comprises a selection of words that were once well known, but are unlikely to have cropped up in conversation for many decades and would be considered by most people to be functionally 'dead'. Certainly they are unlikely to be found in most modern dictionaries.

Word	Meaning	Date of birth
affictitious	feigned	17th century
cloakatively	superficially	17th century
crassulent	very fat	17th century
diffibulate	unbutton	17th century
drollic	of or pertaining to a puppet show	18th century
fabrefaction	making a work of art	17th century
gelicide	frost	17th century
gleimous	slimy	14th century
impigrity	speed	17th century
incabinate	confine	17th century
kexy	dry, brittle	17th century
lubency	willingness	17th century

Word	Meaning	Date of birth
magistricide	the killing of a teacher	17th century
murklins	in the dark	16th century
noscible	knowable	17th century
oporopolist	fruitseller	17th century
pamphagous	all-consuming	18th century
pessundate	cast down, ruin	17th century
pigritude	slothfulness	17th century
prandicle	small meal	17th century
redamanacy	loving in return	17th century
roomthily	spatially	17th century
sacricolist	devout worshipper	18th century
scathefire	conflagration	17th century
senticous	prickly	17th century
slimikin	slim, slender	18th century
snobographer	one who writes about snobs	19th century
tortiloquy	crooked speech	17th century
tremefy	cause to tremble	19th century
vanmost	foremost	19th century
varlet	villain	15th century
venundate	to buy and sell	17th century
welmish	pale or sickly in colour	17th century
wight	person	Old English
wot	know	Old English

Phoenix words
Reborn words

Some words fall from fashion only to reappear years later, typically with a new meaning. More still acquire new meanings without ever losing their original ones. In fact the vast majority of new words introduced each year are no more than reinventions of already-existing words, combined in new ways or altered in meaning or context. The following list provides some examples of words that have changed their meanings over the centuries:

Word	Original meaning	Modern meaning
deer	animal	reindeer, roe deer, etc.
glamour	enchantment	allure
lewd	of the laity	improper
lush	soft, tender	luxuriant, sexually alluring
meat	food	animal flesh
naughty	wicked	cheeky, ill-behaved
nice	foolish	pleasant
silly	deserving compassion	foolish
sly	wise	cunning
treacle	antidote for poison	sugary syrup
villain	serf	criminal, rogue

What follows is a list of words that have acquired new meanings in addition to their original ones.

Word	Original meaning	Additional modern meaning
bad	not good	(slang) excellent
edgy	on the edge	(slang) cutting-edge
fascia	flat architectural surface	mobile phone covering
gay	bright, jolly	homosexual/unfashionable
marinate	steep in liquid	(slang) take it easy, hang out

Word	Original meaning	Additional modern meaning
out	opposite of in	openly homosexual
portal	gateway	internet site with links to other sites
radical	extreme	(slang) excellent
random	haphazard	(slang) bizarre, wonderful
rude	ill-mannered	(slang) excellent
sticky	adhesive, glutinous	a website that attracts repeated visits
virtual	having the essence of	computer-simulated
wicked	evil	(slang) excellent

Our language, or any civilized language, is like the phoenix:
it springs anew from its own ashes.

T.S. Eliot

sticky

8 Quizzes

Chapter 1 Baby talk

Test your knowledge of the topics covered in Chapter 1 with these questions. Answers can be found on page 267.

1 Which language of the world has the most speakers?
2 Which word appears most frequently in both written and spoken English?
3 What is the letter V called in the Nato alphabet?
4 What is T for in the Cockney alphabet?
5 Which is the oldest letter in the alphabet?
6 Which letter in English appears more frequently than any other?
7 Which is the only word in English that ends in the letters -mt?
8 How many letters are there in Rotokas, which has the least number of letters in the alphabet?
9 Which is the only word in English to have five consecutive vowels?
10 What is the last letter of the Greek alphabet?

Chapter 2 Child's play

Test your knowledge of the topics covered in Chapter 2 with these questions. Answers can be found on page 267.

1 What does the prefix 'proto-' mean?
2 Who invented the word 'quark'?
3 What does the dialect word 'brock' refer to?
4 What was the original meaning of the word 'treacle'?
5 What does the word 'coin' mean in French?
6 From which language did the word 'cravat' come?
7 Which two words were blended to produced the word 'infomercial'?
8 What was the original meaning of the word 'sardonic'?
9 From which language comes the word 'ombudsman'?
10 In which book did the word 'yahoo' first appear?

Chapter 3 Yoof rap

Test your knowledge of the topics covered in Chapter 3 with these questions. Answers can be found on page 267.

1 In which decade were the slang terms 'gimmick', 'hijack' and 'kitsch' first heard?

2 What do the letters 'ILYA' on the back of an envelope stand for?

3 What does the polari word 'oglefakes' mean?

4 What does the text message 'ROTFL' stand for?

5 What is the Cockney rhyming slang term for a wife?

6 In computer jargon what is a 'screenager'?

7 What do Australians call an outside lavatory?

8 What does a 'trev' wear?

9 What does the text message 'GAL' stand for?

10 In rap slang what two words were combined to create 'bodacious'?

Chapter 4 All growed up

Test your knowledge of the topics covered in Chapter 4 with these questions. Answers can be found on page 268.

1 What is the slang name for £500?

2 What does the business acronym 'glam' stand for?

3 Who owned a horse called Copenhagen?

4 What was the most popular girls' name in Australia, England and Wales and the USA in 2004?

5 By what name is Jennifer Anastassakis better known?

6 Whose catchphrase is 'am I bothered?'

7 What does the acronym 'twoc' stand for?

8 What was the codename for the D-Day invasion of Normandy in 1944?

9 What was Cary Grant's real name?

10 In which war was the term 'friendly fire' first used?

Chapter 5 Grumpy old men

Test your knowledge of the topics covered in Chapter 5 with these questions. Answers can be found on page 268.

1 What does the politically correct term 'vertically challenged' mean?

2 Which term is non-U, 'lavatory' or 'toilet'?

3 In cars, what is the English equivalent for what Americans call the 'hood'?

4 What word did the Indian town of Dungri contribute to the English language?

5 In bingo, which number is called 'trombones'?

6 What is the American equivalent of the English noun 'tap'?

7 What place name does the word 'sherry' refer to?

8 What is a fusilatelist interested in?

9 What is the American spelling of 'carat'?

10 What is the collective noun for a group of ravens?

Chapter 6 Lost for words

Test your knowledge of the topics covered in Chapter 6 with these questions. Answers can be found on page 268.

1 Which Shakespearean character observed that 'comparisons are odorous'?

2 In which direction do stalactites grow?

3 What is the fear of open spaces called?

4 Can you complete the proverb 'fine words butter … '?

5 What is the difference between 'homograph' and 'homophone'?

6 Who is reputed to have said (but probably never did) 'Let them eat cake'?

7 Can you decipher the spoonerism 'the queer old dean'?

8 Can you complete the proverb 'cold hands … '?

9 What is ophidiophobia the fear of?

10 What are the meanings of 'complement' and 'compliment'?

Chapter 7 Words without end

Test your knowledge of the topics covered in Chapter 7 with these questions. Answers can be found on page 268.

1 What word was inspired by Austrian physician and hypnotist Franz Mesmer?

2 Whose last words were 'What an artist dies in me!'?

3 What does the defunct English word 'welmish' mean?

4 To whom was the epitaph beginning 'Hereabouts died a very gallant gentleman ... ' dedicated?

5 What does the euphemistic 'reformatted by God' mean?

6 After whom was the road surface tarmac named?

7 Who died with the words 'the rest is silence'?

8 Whose last words were 'So the heart be right, it is no matter which way the head lieth'?

9 What does the Ullans word 'blart' mean?

10 Who was the author of the epitaph to William Shakespeare 'He was not of an age but for all time'?

Answers

Chapter 1 Baby talk

1 Mandarin Chinese. 2 the. 3 Victor. 4 tea for two. 5 O. 6 E. 7 dreamt. 8 12. 9 queueing. 10 omega.

Chapter 2 Child's play

1 first, primitive. 2 James Joyce. 3 a badger. 4 'antidote against the bite of a wild beast'. 5 corner. 6 Serbo-Croat. 7 'information' and 'commercial'. 8 'of Sardinia'. 9 Swedish. 10 *Gulliver's Travels*.

Chapter 3 Yoof rap

1 1920s. 2 I love you always. 3 glasses. 4 rolling on the floor laughing. 5 trouble and strife. 6 young internet user. 7 dunny. 8 designer clothes. 9 get a life. 10 'bold' and 'audacious'.

Chapter 4 All growed up

1 monkey. 2 greying, leisured, affluent and married. 3 The Duke of Wellington. 4 Emily. 5 Jennifer Aniston. 6 Catherine Tate's Lauren. 7 take (a vehicle) without the owner's consent. 8 Overlord. 9 Archibald Leach. 10 Vietnam War.

Chapter 5 Grumpy old men

1 short. 2 toilet. 3 bonnet. 4 dungaree. 5 76. 6 faucet. 7 Jerez. 8 phonecards. 9 karat. 10 unkindness.

Chapter 6 Lost for words

1 Dogberry. 2 downwards. 3 agoraphobia. 4 'fine words butter … no parsnips.' 5 'homograph' describes words that are spelt the same but have different meanings; 'homophone' describes words that are pronounced the same but are spelt differently. 6 Marie Antoinette. 7 'the dear old queen'. 8 'cold hands, warm heart'. 9 snakes. 10 'complement' means 'something added'; 'compliment' means 'expression of admiration'.

Chapter 7 Words without end

1 mesmerism. 2 Nero. 3 pale or sickly in colour. 4 Captain Oates. 5 dead. 6 John McAdam. 7 William Shakespeare's *Hamlet*. 8 Sir Walter Raleigh. 9 fall flat in mud. 10 Ben Jonson.

Index

Words strain,
Crack and sometimes break, under the burden,
Under the tension, slip, slide, perish,
Decay with imprecision, will not stay in place,
Will not stay still.

T.S. Eliot